# Learning Progressive Web Apps

---

## Building Modern Web Apps
## Using Service Workers

John M. Wargo

✦ Addison-Wesley

Boston • Columbus • New York • San Francisco • Amsterdam • Cape Town
Dubai • London • Madrid • Milan • Munich • Paris • Montreal • Toronto • Delhi • Mexico City
São Paulo • Sydney • Hong Kong • Seoul • Singapore • Taipei • Tokyo

Visit us on the Web: informit.com/aw

Library of Congress Control Number: 2019954833

Copyright © 2020 Pearson Education, Inc.

Cover: welcomia/Shutterstock

ISBN-13: 978-0-13-648422-6
ISBN-10: 0-13-648422-0

1 2020

# Learning Progressive Web Apps

# The Pearson Addison-Wesley
# Learning Series

Visit **informit.com/learningseries** for a complete list of available publications.

The **Pearson Addison-Wesley Learning Series** is a collection of hands-on programming guides that help you quickly learn a new technology or language so you can apply what you've learned right away.

Each title comes with sample code for the application or applications built in the text. This code is fully annotated and can be reused in your own projects with no strings attached. Many chapters end with a series of exercises to encourage you to reexamine what you have just learned and to tweak or adjust the code as a way of learning.

Titles in this series take a simple approach: they get you going right away and leave you with the ability to walk off and build your own application and apply the language or technology to whatever you are working on.

Make sure to connect with us!
informit.com/socialconnect

❖

*I normally dedicate my books to my wife Anna, but for this one,*
*she suggested I do something different. With that in mind,*
*I hereby dedicate this book to the number 42.*

❖

# Contents

# Foreword

I remember how I first became acquainted with John Wargo. I was speaking at a PhoneGap Day conference in Portland, Oregon, and I looked over to see Brian LeRoux speaking with someone I didn't recognize. I leaned over and asked a friend, "Hey, who's the guy in the suit?," to which the friend responded, "Oh, that's John Wargo. He's an analyst." The suit set John apart at this nerd gathering, as most of the attendees were wearing t-shirts with funny slogans. This was before the time when Mark Zuckerberg popularized the "coder wearing a hoodie" look.

If I remember correctly, my t-shirt had a pig on it with a speech bubble that said, "Mmmm . . . bacon," and as I reflect back on that time, it wasn't even a suit John was wearing—it was just a blazer. However, it's not an exaggeration to say he was the best-dressed man at the conference, but I digress.

"Oh boy!" I thought, "An analyst." You see, I had just recently transitioned from the telecom industry to full-on software development. In telecom, analysts do not have the greatest of reputations. Then I talked to John. He proceeded to ask me insightful questions about my work on PhoneGap and in the Apache Cordova community.

Folks, at this point, I'm resisting the urge to insert a don't judge a book by its cover joke, and I've never been good at not making a bad joke.

John went on to become an important member and educator of the Apache Cordova community and to write not one, but four authoritative books on the subject, not unlike the one you hold in your hands now on Progressive Web Apps.

One of the oft-cited tenets of the PhoneGap/Cordova project was to ultimately "cease to exist," but the other less-mentioned tenet was to "make the web a first-class development platform." Now that promise of being a first-class platform has been fulfilled by Progressive Web Apps. Being a major part of the Apache Cordova community for so long puts John in a great position, as he has been there every step of the way to see the evolution of the mobile web.

Should you happen to bump into John at a conference or at a book-signing someday, come prepared with a recommendation on where to get a fresh, delicious doughnut. This is one of the two traits we share in common. The other being a dry, sardonic wit.

You have made an excellent decision in picking up this book. If I were just starting on my learning path to mastery of Progressive Web Apps, there are not many folks I would trust more than John to get me there. I only wish that you could hear John's voice while you are reading this book like I did.

—*Simon MacDonald, Developer Advocate, Adobe*
*November 2019*

# Preface

When building apps targeting desktops, laptops, smartphones, and tablets, developers have generally two options to use: native apps built specifically for the target platform or web apps that ultimately can run on most any system due to the abstraction layer provided by web browsers. Building native apps for any target platform is a time-consuming and expensive proposition, especially when your app targets multiple types of systems (desktop computers, smartphones, televisions, etc.).

Web apps were challenging because a user's experience could vary dramatically depending on which type of system the user accessed the app from. Desktop browsers are fully capable, but mobile device browsers have limitations due to reduced screen real estate, processor speed, network bandwidth, and more. Many of these limitations have disappeared, but there's still considerable disparity between native app and web app capabilities.

Web developers have a lot of tools and technologies at their disposal to help them build rich, engaging apps. Over the years, different technologies such as Sun Microsystems' Java[1] and Adobe Flash[2] appeared with the expectation that they'd change the world for web apps—delivering a more engaging experiences for users. Both did that but ultimately disappeared from the browser for good reason.

What developers and users need is a way to enable web apps to work more like native apps. If we had that, our web apps would soar and enable us to more easily deliver cross-platform apps through the browser rather than handcrafting native apps for each supported platform.

Over the years, web browsers, especially those running on mobile devices such as smartphones and tablets, started exposing more native capabilities to web apps. For example, modern web apps can access the device's file system and let a browser-based app know the device's geolocation. This enables web apps to work more like native apps, but there were still limitations. Service workers are a relatively new technology that makes it easier for web apps to bridge the gap between native and web capabilities, removing many limitations from web apps.

This is a book about service workers.

Yes, I know, the title says the book is about Progressive Web Apps (PWAs), and it is, but the book focuses on how to use service workers to enhance the capabilities of a web app and create PWAs.

There are several books out there that focus on the engagement impact of PWAs; how to build PWAs that delight and inspire users to do more in the app. This isn't that kind of book.

This book is focused as much as possible on the technologies enabling PWAs and how to use them to enhance your web apps to deliver a more native-like experience in your web apps.

I come to you with 15 years of experience with mobile development (I wrote the first book on BlackBerry development so many years ago), and, as Simon said in the Foreword, PWAs are the

---

1. https://en.wikipedia.org/wiki/Java_(software_platform)
2. https://en.wikipedia.org/wiki/Adobe_Flash

next step in making the web a first-class development platform—especially for mobile apps. My interest in writing this book focuses on PWAs' impact on mobile developers, but everything here applies to web apps running on a desktop browser as well.

If you've read any of my books, you already know that this manuscript contains no phrases or content in any language but English (I refuse to make you put down the book to go look up some obscure phrase in Latin or French to understand a point). This book also contains no pop culture references (well, except for one that I describe completely so you won't feel left out if you don't already know it).

Unlike my previous technical books, which were focused on the technologies and how to use them (with lots of code examples), this book is project- based. As you work through the chapters, at different points you'll start with one of three complete, standalone web apps, then convert them into PWAs using service workers and other technologies.

The sample apps for this book were written specifically to be simple and easy to understand, so they're not fancy. I could have built them as amazing, reactive, modern web apps, leveraging JavaScript frameworks such as VueJS[3] or React,[4] but instead I built them using plain, vanilla HTML, CSS, and JavaScript. This approach removes a lot of extraneous code from the apps and leaves just what you need to understand the topic at hand.

You can find all of the source code for the sample apps on GitHub at https://github.com/johnwargo/learning-pwa-code. To make it easier for readers consuming the printed version of this book, I added a `resources.md`[5] file to the source code folder for each chapter; it lists all of the links used in the chapter. Rather than typing in long URLs from the chapter content, you can simply open the resources file in a browser and quickly access any link from the chapter.

Unlike the source code repositories for other books, the book's source code doesn't contain only before and after versions of the apps. Instead, as you complete a chapter section, you'll find the source code modifications for just that section in a separate file. This enables you to more easily build the app along with the chapter content while having just that section's code available in case you have an issue and want to compare the completed code with yours. This approach should streamline your following along, especially if you create typos or bugs as you work.

If you have any questions or comments about the book or if you find an error in the text or code, please submit them through the issues area in the book's GitHub repository at https://github.com/johnwargo/learning-pwa-code/issues. The code there is open source, so feel free to use it in your applications (it would be especially nice if you referenced the source for the code so others can learn about this book).

If you find a bug in the code and want to fix it yourself, do so, then submit a pull request against the repository, and I'll take a look. I'm usually very good about responding, so you should hear back from me in a day or so. Please be nice—GitHub is a very public forum, and we should all treat people there as we expect to be treated by others.

---

3. https://vuejs.org/
4. https://reactjs.org/
5. https://github.com/johnwargo/learning-pwa-code/blob/master/chapter-01/resources.md

I created a public web site for the book at https://learningpwa.com. I'll publish errata and, hopefully, related content there over time. Forestalling any complaints, as I write this, the site isn't a PWA. It isn't a PWA because it doesn't need to be a PWA. It's just a marketing landing page for the book, and there are no browser notifications I want to send to visitors, nor is there a need to cache the site's content for increased performance or offline use. Just because I *can* make the site into a PWA doesn't mean that I should. Use the power of PWAs only for those sites that really need them.

Two of the three sample apps from the book are published online as well. The first is the Tip Calculator from Chapter 2, which you can access at https://learningpwa.com/tipcalc/. The other is the PWA News site from Chapters 3, 4, and 5—you can find that app at https://pwa-news.com. The Learning Progressive Web Apps site is a static site hosted at Netlify,[6] so that one will probably stay active as long as the book is publicly available. The PWA News site requires computing resources (its server-side is a node.js[7] application), so I'll leave the site up as long as there is interest in the book. Eventually, I'll shut it down, but the full source for the server is included with the book's source code, so you'll always be able to run a local copy of the server or host the site somewhere else yourself.

That's it! This preface contains everything I wanted to tell you about the book. I believe in PWAs and think they are the future of mobile app development, so that's why I worked to put this book into your hands. I really enjoyed writing it, and I hope you enjoy reading it as much or more.

---

Register your copy of *Learning Progressive Web Apps* on the InformIT site for convenient access to updates and/or corrections as they become available. To start the registration process, go to informit.com/register and log in or create an account. Enter the product ISBN (9780136484226) and click Submit. Look on the Registered Products tab for an Access Bonus Content link next to this product, and follow that link to access any available bonus materials. If you would like to be notified of exclusive offers on new editions and updates, please check the box to receive email from us.

---

6. https://www.netlify.com/
7. https://nodejs.org/

# Acknowledgments

This book wouldn't exist except for the work of several people. Thank you, Greg Doench at Pearson, for having the faith in me to publish this book (this is our sixth book together). I'm an experienced software developer, but I suck at making apps beautiful, so the only reason you have cool-looking sample apps to work with herein is due to the styling magic of my friend Scott Good.

Thank you, Simon MacDonald, for your kind words in the Foreword and for sharing the same love for doughnuts that I have. It's so cool to know that when I speak at a developer conference somewhere, Simon will be there to lead me to another cool doughnut shop.

Thank you, Maxim Salnikov, for providing feedback on the first draft of the manuscript and connecting me to the PWA community.

Thanks to Jeff Burtoft, David Rousset, and Justin Willis from the PWABuilder team for bringing me up to speed on PWABuilder and helping me with the content for Chapter 8.

This book absolutely wouldn't exist except for the hard work from the Pearson production team to bring it to print. Thanks to Julie Nahil, Carol Lallier, Vaishnavi Venkatesan, and others at Pearson working diligently behind the scenes to finish the manuscript and take it to print.

Finally, I would never be able to even write a sentence of this book without the full support of my wife Anna. I spend a lot of time in my office tinkering, writing apps, and learning new technologies for fun, profit, and career growth. Whenever I start a book project (this is my seventh, the eighth if you count the collection of magazine articles I wrote that ultimately became a book), I make sure she understands how the effort is going to consume a lot of my time. She always laughs and reminds me that a book project isn't any different in her eyes, as it's just a bunch of time I spend toiling away in my office while she hangs out with the kids and the dogs. I do get away without doing many dishes while working on a book, but I try to make up for that later.

# About the Author

**John M. Wargo** is a product manager, software developer, writer, presenter, father, husband, and geek. He spent more than 30 years working as a professional software developer first as a hobbyist, then in enterprise software, and finally, for the last 15 years, in mobile development. He authored six books on mobile development, and was a long-time contributor to the open source Apache Cordova project.

By day, he's a Principal Program Manager on the App + Cloud Experiences team at Microsoft.

He loves tinkering with IoT, building and writing about projects for Arduino, Particle Photon, Raspberry Pi, Tessel 2, and more. His latest project was a remote-controlled, flame-throwing pumpkin.

He lives in Charlotte, North Carolina, with his wife Anna, 16-year-old twins, and two dogs.

# Introducing Progressive Web Apps

A Progressive Web App (PWA) is a web app that leverages special browser capabilities that enable the app to act more like a native or mobile app when running on capable browsers. That's it, that's all that needs to be said—the rest of this book is all about showing you how to build them (with lots of code examples, of course).

Developers build PWAs primarily using two technologies available in most modern browsers: web app manifest files and service workers. Chapter 2, "Web App Manifest Files," tells you pretty much everything you need to know about web app manifest files. The remaining chapters cover service workers and what you can do with them.

There's no standard or standards body for PWAs; a PWA is just a web app built to act a certain way. Use as much or as little PWA functionality as you want in your web apps. You can have web apps that use some PWA capabilities but aren't PWAs and PWAs that use only some PWA capabilities.

PWA has its own community-driven logo, shown in Figure 1.1. You can even create your own version of the logo, specifying any color for the *W* portion using the tool at https://diekus.net/logo-pwinter.

Figure 1.1   The Community-Driven PWA Logo

Unfortunately, there are different views of what PWAs are; let me fill you in on my view. . .

## First, a Little Bit of History

Google and other browser vendors add special features to their browsers all the time, striving to provide more tools developers can use to enhance the web. In 2015, a designer named Frances Berriman and a Google Chrome engineer named Alex Russell coined the term *Progressive Web Apps* to describe, according to Wikipedia, "apps taking advantage of new features supported by modern browsers, including service workers and web app manifests, that let users upgrade web apps to progressive web apps in their native operating system (OS)."

Google Chrome was the leading browser at the time that supported the required technologies, so Google started heavily promoting this new approach to building web apps.

## PWAs Are . . .

Google's Progressive Web Apps landing page[1] says that PWAs are

- Reliable

- Fast

- Engaging

These terms describe a user's perception of an app, not anything about how the app is built, what technologies it uses, or what it can do. The technologies used to build PWAs enable developers to build web apps that are reliable, fast, and engaging, but only if web developers have the skills and take the time to do it. I think Google's description is off base, since there are a lot of inexperienced web developers out there who can build PWAs that aren't reliable, fast, or engaging, but the apps are still PWAs.

So, with that in mind, in this book, PWAs are about the technologies used and how to make them. There are a lot of online articles and books available about how PWAs are more engaging and the impact they've had on businesses' success or revenue; the best place to start for that information is on PWA Stats.[2]

I align with Jeremy Keith's definition from *What Is a Progressive Web App?*[3] Here's my take: PWAs are web apps with a little bit of special magic that enable them to act more like mobile apps. It's the concept of web apps working more like mobile apps that makes PWAs so interesting.

If you think about most native mobile apps you use on your phone, they

- Are installable from the phone platform's public app store (and enterprise stores for employee apps), putting an app icon on the device's home screen.

- Will load and operate (although in a potentially limited fashion) regardless of whether the device has network connectivity. The app's UI is embedded in the application binary and loads locally when you open the app (pulling data from the network when it can).

---

1. https://developers.google.com/web/progressive-web-apps/

2. https://www.pwastats.com/

3. https://adactio.com/journal/13098

- Can run in the background, even doing things or processing data while you're doing something else on the device.

- Can receive push notifications (messages sent to the device or an app from an external system).

- With some extra work, can even deliver a rich and robust offline experience, caching new records for upload later and synchronizing data with a server-based app.

Does that describe many of the mobile apps you use today? Does your email (or fill in another app name here) app work regardless of whether the device has network connectivity? If you turn off the radio and open the app, does the app's UI open and display much of the data that was there earlier? When you send a message while offline, does the app queue the data for transmission later? Does the app receive notifications (like when new mail is available)? Yeah, I thought so; those are core capabilities of modern mobile apps.

Turning to PWAs:

- PWAs are installable: mobile and desktop users can quickly install them on their phone's home screen or desktop using an installation UI provided in the app. Mobile phones have pretty much always had the ability to copy a web site's URL to the device's home screen, but installing the app is better. I explain more about it in Chapter 2.

- PWAs cache the app's core UI on the local device, so when the user opens the app, the UI loads quickly before the app tries to go out and get updated data from the network. Consequently, PWAs feel snappier than traditional web apps.

- PWAs run background tasks, enabling resource caching and background processing. Traditional web apps can't do this (well, they can, but it takes a lot of handcrafted code or a third-party library).

- PWAs can receive push notifications from a backend server regardless of whether the app is running.

When Apple announced the iPhone, they famously failed when they assumed developers would be happy having the ability to build web apps only for the platform. Steve Jobs and company arrogantly assumed the browser was enough and could accommodate most app needs. The developer community quickly rebelled, forced Apple's hand, and that's how we got the ability to code native apps on iOS.

They rebelled because even though the Safari was quite capable on iOS, and Apple provided some great developer tools (no, not Xcode, anyone remember Dashcode?[4]), there were things that app developers just couldn't do in the browser. These limitations were also the motivation for the PhoneGap project (which later became Apache Cordova); the project started specifically to enable cross-platform mobile development and give browser developers access to device capabilities that weren't, at the time, available in the native browser.

Over the years, many of those capabilities made it into the browser through open standards covering things like the device accelerometer, camera, compass, microphone, and much more. Browser apps became more capable, but the few final requirements giving the browser equal footing

---

4. https://en.wikipedia.org/wiki/Dashcode

with native mobile apps were—and this should sound familiar—the capabilities to install a web app on a device, cache code and content locally, run background tasks (even when the app isn't running), and receive push notifications. The technologies enabling PWAs deliver those final required capabilities to the browser; and, with these capabilities in place, a web app can now act more like a native app.

# Making a Progressive Web App

Several technologies enable PWAs; without them, a web app simply can't be a PWA. Those technologies are web app manifest files, service workers, and Hypertext Transfer Protocol Secure (HTTPS) or, more accurately, HTTP over Transport Layer Security (TLS). HTTPS enables secure communication between a client and server and isn't a topic I cover in this book except to describe later that it's required for most PWA capabilities and I explain why. The following chapters describe in detail how to use web app manifest files and service workers to build a PWA. For now, it's good to know that web app manifest files enable installation of a web app on the local system running the app, and service workers make everything else PWAs do possible.

Table 1.1 lists the app capabilities from the previous section mapped against the PWA technologies that enable them.

Table 1.1  **PWA Capabilities by Implementation Technology**

| Capability | Web Manifest | Service Workers | TLS (HTTPS) |
| --- | --- | --- | --- |
| Install shortcut | Yes | Required, but not involved | Yes |
| Cache content | No | Yes | Yes |
| Background processing | No | Yes | No |
| Push notifications | No | Yes | Yes |

A developer must do a lot of work to make a web site interesting, engaging, and useful. This means crafting the site's pages so they look good and work well on screens or browser windows of varying dimensions (width and height). Web developers must take the client-side browser's capabilities into account when building these sites, and many developers deliver different capabilities in their sites based on what does or doesn't work in the browser used at runtime. Some mobile browsers (like the ones on feature phones) can't process a lot of client-side code, so JavaScript may be disabled or have limited capabilities on that device.

The process developers use to build web pages for these scenarios is called *progressive enhancement*, where the developer focuses on the content first, then layers on additional functionality for more capable browsers. This means that the app simply works, displaying the required content, regardless of whether the browser supports the extra bells and whistles (like fancy CSS transforms) the developer added for more robust browsers. If those capabilities are there, then the user gets the full experience. If they're not, the user can at least view the content.

Web apps are more interactive, like Wikipedia (web site) vs. Gmail (web app). Web apps use client-side scripting languages such as JavaScript (or its sister language TypeScript) to deliver a more dynamic and exciting client-side experience. With a web app, when you first hit the app's URL, the app's shell downloads and renders before the app goes out to the server for the app's data.

You can see an example of this in Figure 1.2. The app shell consists of the side navigation and the top button bar, while the content in the content area (bound within the orange border) changes dynamically based on the choices the user makes in the app.

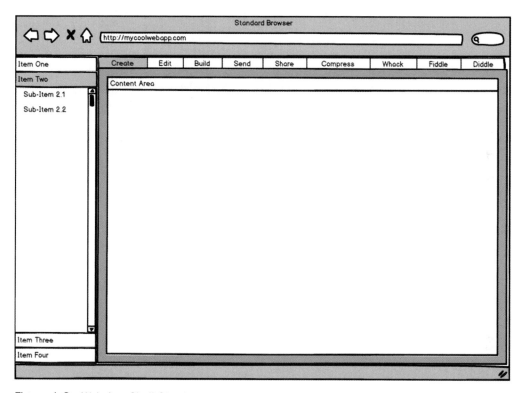

Figure 1.2   Web App Shell Structure

PWAs progressively enhance web apps—that's, um, why they're called Progressive Web Apps.

So, let's assume we have a dynamic web app that's all about user interaction and dynamic data. The app requires a more capable browser and certainly means that there's JavaScript involved (to deliver the dynamic nature of the app). The app runs in the browser and uses the system's network connection to download the shell, then, or perhaps in parallel, it retrieves the app's data from a server. When the browser running the app doesn't have network connectivity, the browser displays a spinner or an error message, and the user simply can't use the app.

True to PWA's progressive moniker, you'll enhance the app when you add a web manifest file to enable client-side installation and add a service worker to enable caching, background processing, and support for push notifications. On browsers that support those capabilities, the PWA becomes installable and lets the user run the app when there's no network connection (service worker caching), holds new or updated records for upload later when there's a network connection (service worker caching coupled with background processing), and notifies users when new push messages arrive (service worker background processing).

On systems that don't support web manifest files and/or service workers? The app works the same way it did before you added the web manifest file or service worker to the app. When you access the app, the app content and data are requested in real time from one or more servers.

# PWA Market Impact

So, what impacts are PWAs having in the market? Development organizations quickly adopted the technology because the progressive enhancement nature of the approach enables development teams to dramatically affect performance (for any user running a browser that supports it) for their users with just a few small, simple changes. When users run the app on a browser that doesn't support PWA technologies, they won't notice anything different—the app simply continues to work as it always had.

Web app performance, especially on mobile devices, suddenly seems better for some apps. That's because many app developers implement web manifest files and service workers, and these apps now actively manage their client-side behavior (using background processing and caching) to the user's benefit.

Users engage more with PWA-enabled apps. That's just because the apps are snappier (load faster) and work even when the mobile device its running on doesn't have a network connection. The app might not have all its features when offline, but it still works, and that's likely all that it takes to make users happy.

Modern web application frameworks and cross-platform development tools adopted PWAs in a big way. For example, React, a very popular JavaScript library for building user interfaces (UIs) (their words, not mine), preloads its default sample project with a service worker automatically. It disables it by default, but all you must do to turn a React app into a PWA is change one line of code, as described in Listing 1.1.

Listing 1.1  **Sample React app index.js**

```
import React from 'react';
import ReactDOM from 'react-dom';
import './index.css';
import App from './App';
import * as serviceWorker from './serviceWorker';

ReactDOM.render(<App />, document.getElementById('root'));

// if you want your app to work offline and load faster, you
// can change unregister() to register() below. Note this comes
// with some pitfalls. Learn more about service workers:
// https://bit.ly/CRA-PWA
serviceWorker.unregister();
```

I've been doing a lot of work lately using the Ionic Framework. Ionic is a cross-platform UI and component framework for building mobile and desktop apps. Until a short time ago, Ionic apps were typically built using Angular, but the Ionic team recently switched to web components and Stencil (their open web component compiler) and published a PWA Toolkit that delivers a PWA-first approach to web apps.

Most important, PWAs are easier (much, much easier) to create than native mobile apps. That means these apps cost less to make and maintain. When you package a PWA in an Apache Cordova, Ionic Capacitor, or GitHub Electron app, you address the needs of users who want a native version for mobile devices or desktop computers.

The technology is so popular that research firm Gartner predicts that by 2020, 50% of consumer mobile apps will be PWAs (I would give you an online reference for this, but that statement is everywhere online). But you knew that, right? You already purchased, borrowed, or stole this book to learn how to create PWAs.

## PWAs and App Stores

Developers build native mobile apps for many reasons, but one of them is so that they can distribute their apps through the mobile device platform's public app store. While you can install a PWA by just opening a web app in the mobile browser (you'll learn all about this in the next chapter), the mobile platform vendors trained their users to look for apps in the app stores. This means that users looking for your app are going to look for it in their phone's app store first.

Some interesting things are happening in this space. In early 2019, Google announced Trusted Web Activity[5] (TWA) for Android. TWA enables developers to bundle a PWA into a native mobile app for Android. A TWA is essentially a chromeless (no browser UI), full-screen Chrome browser inside an Android app. With it, you get a PWA packaged with a browser in a native app—fresh and ready for deployment through the Google Play Store.

Microsoft took a different approach, announcing in mid-2018 that developers can publish their PWAs to the Microsoft Store. If they don't publish their app to the store, Microsoft will do it for them anyway (if the PWA meets specific criteria). You'll learn more about this in Chapter 8, "Assessment, Automation, and Deployment."

## Wrap-Up

In this chapter, I gave you a quick introduction to Progressive Web Apps. You'll find a lot more material online and many authors who dig deeper into the marketing and engagement side of PWAs. Since this is really a book about service workers, I want to get to coding as quickly as possible.

In the next chapter, I show you all about how to make your PWA installable using service workers and web manifest files. After that, the remainder of the book is all about service workers and everything you can do with them.

---

5. https://developers.google.com/web/updates/2019/02/using-twa

# 2

# Web App Manifest Files

One of the features of Progressive Web Apps (PWAs) is the ability to configure a web app so users can install the app on the device running the app. Mobile users have been able to do this sort of thing for a long time, through the *Save to Home Screen* option available in mobile browsers, but PWAs deliver a better user experience.

The component that delivers this capability to PWAs is an app's web app manifest file. In this chapter, I introduce web app manifests and show you how you can use them to make your web app installable.

> **Note**
>
> Throughout the remainder of the book, I refer to a web app manifest by its full name but may also refer to it as a *manifest* or *manifest file*.

For those who already know a bit about manifests and PWAs, the placement of this chapter may seem odd because it takes more than just a manifest file to make a web app installable. We talk in more depth later about the requirements for installability, but an app must meet specific criteria and have a manifest file and a service worker installed to be installable. The rest of the book covers service workers in detail, so rather than stick a chapter that isn't about service workers in the middle of the book, I decided to cover this topic now and leave the remainder of the book all about service workers.

For the purpose of the examples in this chapter, I've added a simple service worker, just to make installation possible, but I provide only cursory coverage of the topic. You'll get more than enough coverage in the following chapters, so I ask you to just ignore the service worker for now with the promise that you'll learn all you need to know later in the book.

If you're not happy with this approach, please skip this chapter and come back to it after you've completed Chapter 3, "Service Workers."

In this chapter, we use the first of several apps I created for this book, the Tip Calculator shown in Figure 2.1. It is a simple single page app (SPA) that renders a rudimentary tip calculator. When users open the app, they enter a meal cost in the input field, and the app automatically calculates several tip options based on the overall quality of the meal (food, service, environment, etc.).

You can access the app today at https://learningpwa.com/tipcalc, and the full source for the app is in the book's GitHub repository at https://github.com/johnwargo/learning-pwa-code in the chapter-02 folder. I'd like to give a special shout out to my friend Scott Good who took my horrible-looking app and converted it (through the application of some masterful styling) into the beautiful page you see in the figure (Scott suggested his version is "less horrible" but I decided to stick with "beautiful page").

We start with a rudimentary version of the app (Tip Calc 1.0), then enhance it throughout this chapter by adding a web app manifest to give users a better installed app experience.

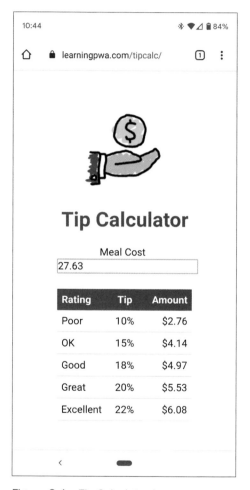

Figure 2.1   Tip Calculator App

Another great learning example of an installable web app is Google's Air Horner app (https://airhorner.com/ with source at https://github.com/GoogleChromeLabs/airhorn).

# Save to Home Screen

Browser users can install web apps on the system desktop and device home screens today. For example, in Chrome (and most Chrome-based browsers) running on a desktop PC, just open the Chrome menu (the three vertical dots on the upper-right corner of the browser window) and select More Tools, then Create Shortcut. Chrome will prompt you for a title for the shortcut, grabbing the app's favicon to use in the shortcut icon, and save it to the desktop.

On Android devices, you open the browser menu and select Add to Home screen, as shown in Figure 2.2. For iOS devices, the process is similar: in the browser, tap the Share button in the bottom of the browser window and select the Add to Home Screen button, highlighted in Figure 2.3.

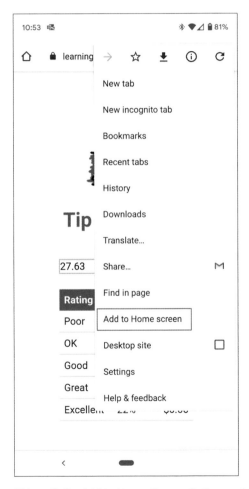

Figure 2.2    Add to Home Screen Option on Android (Chrome Browser)

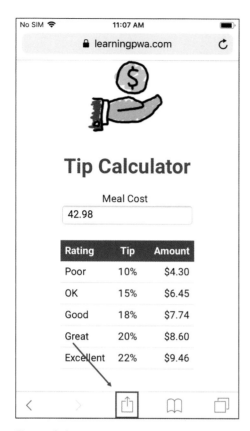

Figure 2.3    iPhone Share Button (Safari Browser)

Next, the browser gives you a chance to name the shortcut, as shown in Figure 2.4.

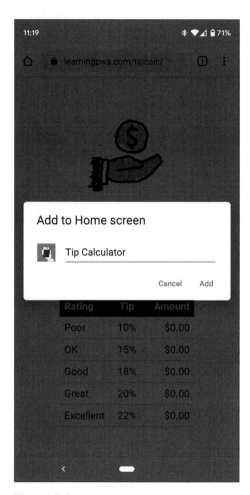

Figure 2.4   Setting the Home Screen Icon Title

The browser then gives you a chance to decide where you want the shortcut placed, or you can let the browser do it for you, as shown in Figure 2.5. Note that on iOS, Safari doesn't give you a choice—it just throws the icon wherever the device wants to put it.

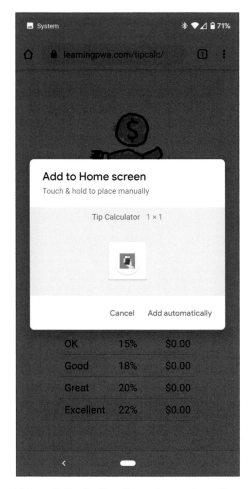

Figure 2.5    Setting Home Screen Icon Placement

Finally, the Figure 2.6 shows the shortcut where I placed it in the top-left corner of the device home screen.

When you tap the icon, the device opens the browser and renders the same page you see in Figure 2.1. This is not too horrible a user experience, but it could be better, right? The user probably doesn't want that huge Chrome logo covering a portion of the shortcut, and opening the browser with all its chrome doesn't make this app feel like an app. Also, you probably want the app shortcut in the applications list as well, since not all users want a lot of icons on their home screen.

Figure 2.6    Home Screen Icon Added

> **Note**
>
> The word *chrome* with a lowercase *c* is used to describe the browser's UI elements outside of the web page rendered in the browser (e.g., menu, address input, borders, toolbar, and so on) and should not be confused with Chrome, Google's browser.

Another problem with this approach is that the act of "installing" the app is an out-of-app experience. Users must interact with the browser's menu system to save the app for later access. PWAs, through the web app manifest file, solve this problem and a few more.

# Making a Web App Installable

OK, so I told you that adding a web app manifest file to your web app enables you to make the app installable; throughout the remainder of this chapter, I'll show you how.

*Web App Manifest*[1] is an evolving specification published by the World Wide Web Consortium (W3C). The specification "defines a JSON-based manifest file that provides developers with a centralized place to put metadata associated with a web application." It describes how user agents (browsers) should act when a manifest file is linked to a web application. As Google has done the most to support web manifests on Chrome, it has a lot of good information available on its Web App Manifest page in an article written by Matt Gaunt and Paul Kinlan.[2]

> ### Note
>
> Web app manifests aren't supported in all modern browsers; in fact, as I type this, support is rather dismal. For example, as popular as the Safari browser is for iOS and macOS users, Apple still hasn't added full support for PWAs; its Safari browser supports manifest files but not the events you need to install the PWA on the device.
>
> The good news is that browser developers frequently update their products, so your favorite browser should have support soon. The best way to tell if browsers your app targets support the technology is to check the Can I Use site.[3] Normally, I'd include a screenshot of the results here, but things change so quickly that it would be a waste of time to do so.

For PWAs, the metadata we're talking about are properties in the manifest file that define what the app looks like when it's installed (basically just the app icon and title) and runs (splash screen, browser chrome options, etc.) and how the browser launches and runs the app when the user clicks or taps the app icon.

We'll get to the specific format of this file in a bit, but first let's talk about how a browser decides that an app's installable. The criteria browsers use to determine if a web app is installable varies depending on the browser. Using Google's Chrome browser as an example, it looks like this:

- Is not already installed on the local system.

- Meets a user engagement heuristic; basically, users must look like they're interested in the app.

- Includes a web app manifest that defines a minimum set of properties (a `short_name` and/or `name`, the `icons` array must reference icons at 192 and 512 pixels, a `start_url`, and `display` property of `fullscreen`, `standalone`, or `minimal-ui`). You'll learn more about these properties later.

- Served over HTTPS (or localhost for testing).

- Has registered a service worker with a `fetch` event handler.

---

1. https://www.w3.org/TR/appmanifest/
2. https://developers.google.com/web/fundamentals/web-app-manifest/
3. https://caniuse.com/#feat=web-app-manifest

To make a web app manifest available to your web app, you must add a link reference to it in the <head> section of the web app's index.html file:

```
<link rel="manifest" href="app.webmanifest">
```

In this example, the link reference points to a file called app.webmanifest located in the root folder of the web app. For the chapter's sample project, the <head> section looks a little like this:

```
<head>
  <meta charset="utf-8">
  <title>Tip Calculator</title>
  <meta name="description" content="A simple tip calculator app">
  <meta name="viewport" content="width=device-width, initial-scale=1">
  <link rel="manifest" href="app.webmanifest">
</head>
```

Now that I've shown how a browser uses a manifest and how to link the manifest into the app, let's talk about what goes in the manifest file.

## Anatomy of a Web App Manifest

A web app manifest is a simple JavaScript Object Notation (JSON) file. The file doesn't have to have a specific file name or file extension; all that matters is that it contains a JSON object with specific properties as shown in Listing 2.1. In the early days, developers usually called it something like manifest.json, but nowadays the convention is to use a file name with the .webmanifest extension. We're going to use the file shown in Listing 2.2 later, but for now let's use it as an example of a simple .manifest file.

Listing 2.1    **A Sample Web App Manifest File**

```
{
  "short_name": "TipCalc",
  "name": "Tip Calculator",
  "icons": [
    {
      "src": "icons/android-icon-192x192.png",
      "sizes": "192x192",
      "type": "image/png"
    },
    {
      "src": "icons/android-icon-512x512.png",
      "sizes": "512x512",
      "type": "image/png"
    }
  ],
  "start_url": "/index.html?source=pwa",
  "display": "standalone",
  "background_color": "#FFFFFF",
  "theme_color": "#3653B3"
}
```

> **Note**
>
> If an app's index.html file has multiple link elements referencing manifest files, the browser will use the first one (in tree order) and ignore all others, even if the first reference is invalid.

In the sections that follow, I highlight the manifest properties used in this chapter's sample app, then cover some of the other options as well before showing you the app in action.

## Setting the App Name

A web app's manifest file uses one of two JSON string values to define the name or title for the app: short_name and name. According to the specification, it's up to the browser to decide which one to use when displaying the app icon or information about the app on the device where the app is installed.

```
"short_name": "TipCalc",
"name": "Tip Calculator",
```

Both properties are string values, and your manifest can have either or both values specified. In my testing in the Chrome browser on the desktop and on an Android device, Chrome uses the name property value in the installation prompt and the applications list. On Android, it uses the short_name property value for the app title on the screen.

For installable apps, you must provide a value for either the name or short_name property.

## Setting App Icons

A web app's manifest file uses the icons property to define the array of icon objects for the app. The browser uses one of these icons, depending on the screen resolution of the device, for the shortcut icon for the app on the desktop or mobile device home screen. Populate the array with the list of icon files you have defined for the app, as shown in the following example:

```
"icons": [
  {
    "src": " icons/app_icon_192x192.png",
    "sizes": "192x192",
    "type": "image/png"
  }, {
    "src": " icons/app_icon_512x512.png",
    "sizes": "512x512",
    "type": "image/png"
  }
],
```

> **Note**
>
> Requirements will differ based on the browser running the app, but according to Google's documentation, at a minimum you'll need icons 192 × 192 and 512 × 512 pixels. The browser scales one of the available icons to fit the target device's requirements. The app source includes some extra icons at different resolutions if you want to add them to the manifest.

When you create the icon files for your app, pay special attention to how the icons render on the target device. They must render properly against any possible home screen or desktop background, so you may want to skip transparency unless your app icon can render cleanly against any background.

For installable apps, you must provide an `icons` property containing icons at 192 and 512 pixels.

## Configuring Display Mode

The web app manifest specification enables developers to set how the browser renders an installed app's UI using the `display` property. The available options control how much of the browser's UI (its chrome) displays around the app window. The supported options are

- `fullscreen`
- `standalone`
- `minimal-ui`
- `browser`

Each option is described in the following sections.

Remember, one of the criteria for a browser to consider an app installable is a `display` property set to `fullscreen`, `standalone`, or `minimal-ui`. The `browser` property value does not affect PWA app installation through the web app manifest.

The specification allows developers to use `display-mode` in Cascading Style Sheets (CSS) media selectors in their web apps to adjust the UI styling depending on which display mode is in play when the app launches, as shown in the following CSS example:

```
@media all and (display-mode: fullscreen) {
  /* some styling stuff for the `fullscreen` version*/

}
```

Using this approach, you can add a toolbar or status bar to the top of the screen to mimic the look of a native mobile app when the app is installed as a full screen app.

### `fullscreen` Display Mode

With `display` set to `fullscreen`, the installed web app opens without any browser UI and consumes the entire screen, as shown in Figure 2.7.

If the browser doesn't support `fullscreen` mode, it falls back to `standalone` mode.

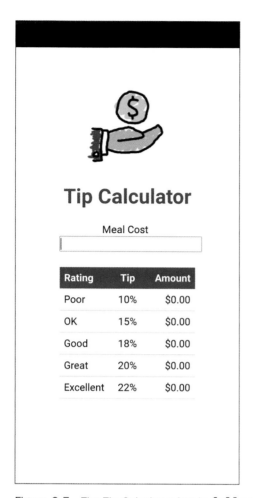

Figure 2.7    The Tip Calculator App in `fullscreen` Display Mode

## standalone Display Mode

With `display` set to `standalone`, the installed web app opens without any browser UI (chrome) but does not consume the entire screen. Instead, the device displays the app as it would display other native apps. On Android, it doesn't hide the device status bar, as shown in Figure 2.8, but may show other UI elements depending on the browser.

If the browser doesn't support `standalone` mode, it falls back to `minimal-ui` mode.

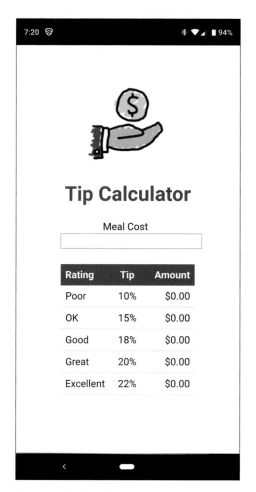

Figure 2.8   The Tip Calculator App in `standalone` Display Mode

## `minimal-ui` Display Mode

With `display` set to `minimal-ui`, the installed web app opens with a subset of the browser window's default UI, as shown in Figure 2.9. In this example, the Android Chrome browser shows the address bar but none of the other navigational elements (for example, the next and previous buttons). Don't forget, it's the browser developer, not the W3C, who decides what UI to display in this mode.

If the browser doesn't support `minimal-ui` mode, it falls back to `browser` mode.

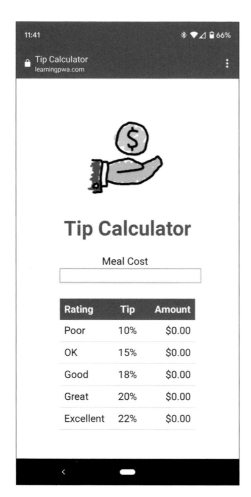

Figure 2.9   The Tip Calculator App in `minimal-ui` Display Mode

### browser Display Mode

With `display` set to `browser`, the installed web app opens using the standard way the device opens hyperlinks (URLs), which basically means opening a new window (or tab) using the default browser app, as shown in Figure 2.10.

Remember, `browser` display mode isn't supported for installable PWAs, so the figure shows the results after saving the app to the home screen, not installed using an in-app installation process.

There is no fallback mode for the `browser` display mode; all browsers conforming to the specification must support `browser`.

Figure 2.10    The Tip Calculator App in `browser` Display Mode

## Setting the Installed App's Start URL

A browser uses the `start_url` property to define the URL used to launch the app. Using it is just a recommendation in the specification, so it's possible that the browser will just ignore it. There's a lot of flexibility in how you use this property for your PWAs; how you configure it depends on how your app is coded and served.

Some examples show setting `start_url` like this:

```
"start_url": ".",
```

In this case, it instructs the browser to open the root folder for the web app. Other examples suggest using the following:

```
"start_url": "./",
```

This is essentially doing the same thing but applying a Unix convention for specifying the current folder.

Other examples show doing something like this:

```
"start_url": "/?utm_source=homescreen",
```

or this:

```
"start_url": "/?source=pwa",
```

These examples tack a query parameter on to the URL, enabling the app to distinguish whether the app was loaded directly from the hosted site via the browser or launched as an installed PWA. For example, when loading an app from the server using `https://myapp.com`, if the query string doesn't include the parameter, the app knows the request comes directly from a URL typed or clicked in the browser. When the user launches the PWA version, the extra query string parameter tells the app it's a PWA, and based on that knowledge, the app can then do things differently if it wants to.

The query string parameter doesn't have to be anything special; you could use `/?pwa=1` or `/?pwa=99` if you wanted. How you use this is up to you; you could change the page content to somehow show it's a PWA (like changing the background color or adding "(PWA)" to the first heading.

Later, when we're adding a web manifest to the Tip Calculator app, I'll have you install a local web server to use for testing. The server doesn't enable you to set the startup page for the server, so I changed the `start_url` property value to

```
"start_url": "/index.html?source=pwa",
```

This forces the browser to open the folder's `index.html` file and enables my PWA to install correctly in a variety of environments.

On the book's web site, I have the Tip Calculator app serving from a subfolder in the site, `https://learningpwa.com/tipcalc/`, so I had to do things a little differently. For my hosting environment, I had to configure my manifest file with the following:

```
"start_url": "/tipcalc/index.html?source=pwa",
"scope": "/tipcalc/",
```

In this example, I had to specify the target folder for my app plus add the `scope` parameter pointing to the same folder. If I didn't have the `scope` parameter defined, the app would install, but when I launched it, the hosted site's 404 (not found) error page displayed instead of the Tip Calculator.

As Gaunt and Kinlan describe it:

> The `scope` defines the set of URLs that the browser considers to be within your app, and is used to decide when the user has left the app. The `scope` controls the URL structure that encompasses all the entry and exit points in your web app. Your `start_url` must reside within the scope.

In this case, I'm using the `scope` property to tell the installed app that the root of all its code begins at the `tipcalc` folder.

> **Warning**
>
> If the web app contains links that point to resources outside the `scope` defined in the manifest file, the browser will load the links in the current browser window. If the target page doesn't provide navigation help to get the user back to the launching PWA, the user will be stuck in the new location.
>
> To avoid this, include the `target="_blank"` attribute in any HTML anchor (`<a>`) tags on the page; with this in place, clicking those links will open them in a new browser window and leave the PWA window intact:
>
> ```
> <a href="https://learningpwa.com" target="_blank">Learning PWA</a>
> ```

## Setting App Options

All I've shown so far are manifest options required to make an app installable. In this section, I cover other options that are useful but not required to install your PWA.

When launching an installed PWA, the browser builds a simple splash screen using the app icon and title (defined by the `name` or `short_name` properties in the manifest) and displays that screen while it loads your app's start page and other content. The background for the splash screen defaults to white, but if your app's main page uses a different color, the transition from the splash screen's stark white to your app's background color may be jarring for users. To improve the user experience, use the manifest file's `background_color` property to set the background color for the splash screen to match the background color of your app's main page. With this in place, the UI transitions more smoothly from the splash screen to the app.

In the manifest file for the Tip Calculator app, I've set the background color to white to match the background color in the icon file, as shown here:

```
"background_color": "#FFFFFF",
```

If I was better at making app icons, I'd put a fancy border around the app icon, leaving the icon background white, then use a contrasting, but cool, color for the background so the icon pops off the page as it loads. I'll leave this work to you.

## Additional Options

The complete list of supported properties is provided in the specification at https://www.w3.org/TR/appmanifest. There are just a couple more I want to bring to your attention here. Look to the specification for other interesting things you can do with manifest files.

On compatible browsers such as Google Chrome, the manifest's `theme_color` property is a hint that tells the browser what color to use for styling around the installed app (for example, the styling of the address bar). For the Tip Calculator app, I set the theme color to match the blue in the app icon's jacket sleeve:

```
"theme_color": "#3653B3",
```

You can also force an orientation for your installed app using

```
"orientation": "landscape",
```

Available options are defined in the `OrientationLockType` defined at https://www.w3.org/TR/screen-orientation/#screenorientation-interface and include any, `landscape`, `portrait`, and many others. One example of this property in action is a game app that must operate in landscape mode for the best user experience.

## Controlling the Installation Experience

All right, we've spent a lot of time in this chapter talking about the manifest file and how you can use it to describe how you want the app to look and work when installed as a PWA. In this section, I cover the capabilities exposed through the browser that give developers control over the installation process.

If you add the manifest file to the Tip Calculator's `index.html` file and the app meets the other criteria for installation described earlier in "Making a Web App Installable," when you load the app in the Chrome browser, the browser displays the installation prompt shown in Figure 2.11.

Figure 2.11   Chrome App Installation Banner

This is the browser's helper, showing users that they can add this app to the device's home screen. Firefox does it a little differently, showing a badge in the address bar, as shown in Figure 2.12.

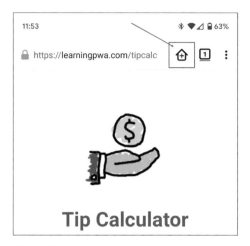

Figure 2.12    Firefox App Installation Badge

> **Note**
>
> You may be wondering why you're not seeing a lot of iOS screenshots in the chapter so far. That's because at the time I wrote the app, Apple's Safari browser didn't support installing a PWA using the mechanisms discussed in this part of the chapter. Safari may support installing PWAs by the time you read this; if it does, installing PWAs should work the same way it does on Android.
>
> I'm not showing any iOS examples because iOS doesn't support installing PWAs either (no matter which browser you use). You can't even add an icon to the home page using Chrome on iOS. It's a dismal state of affairs that I hope will get better over time.

What if you want more control over this process? What if you want to display the installation prompt inside your app or want to offer installation only after the user logs into your app or completes some initial configuration? Well, the browser exposes capabilities enabling you to do so.

Right before the browser displays the installation banner, it fires the `beforeinstallprompt` event. A web app listening for that event can manage the process any way it wants to. I'll show how to do this later when we make the Tip Calculator app installable.

# Preparing to Code

Before we start modifying code to make the Tip Calculator installable, you must install some software prerequisites you'll use as you follow along. Who knows, you may already have them installed (you should).

## Node.JS

To test the PWA capabilities of the Tip Calculator app, you must run the app through a web server, so shortly, I'm going to have you install a node-based web server. If your development workstation already has Node.js installed, then skip ahead to the next paragraph. If not, hop over to https:// nodejs.org/en/ and follow the instructions to install the client on your development workstation.

To confirm that you have Node.js installed, open a new terminal window and execute the following command:

```
node -v
```

If the terminal returns a version number (mine reports v10.16.0), then Node.js is properly installed. If you see an error message, then you have some work to do resolving the error before continuing.

To test the web app locally, we'll use the HTTP Server app from https://github.com/http-party/ http-server. The server is node based, so to install it, just open a terminal window and execute the following command:

```
npm install http-server -g
```

When the installation completes, execute the http-server command, and the system should respond with something like the following:

```
Starting up http-server, serving ./
Available on:
  http://172.20.154.161:8080
  http://172.28.224.1:8080
  http://192.168.86.247:8080
  http://192.168.60.1:8080
  http://192.168.19.1:8080
  http://127.0.0.1:8080
Hit CTRL-C to stop the server
```

If that's what you see, then you're good. Hit Ctrl-C to kill the process. If not, look for any error messages and troubleshoot the installation until you get it right.

## Git Client

I published the source code for the book in a GitHub repository at https://github.com/johnwargo/ learning-pwa-code. The easiest way to get the code, and to update it when I publish changes, is through Git. If your development workstation already has Git installed, then you're good. If not, hop over to https://git-scm.com/ and follow the instructions to install the client on your development workstation.

To confirm that you have Git installed, open a new terminal window and execute the following command:

```
git --version
```

If the terminal returns a version number (mine reports `git version 2.22.0.windows.1`) then Git is properly installed. If you see an error message, then you have some work to do resolving the error before continuing.

With Git installed, open a terminal window or command prompt, navigate to the folder where you want the book's code stored, then execute the following command:

```
git clone https://github.com/johnwargo/learning-pwa-code
```

Once the cloning process completes, navigate the terminal into the cloned project's `\learning-pwa-code\chapter-02\tip-calculator-start` folder. This folder contains the non-PWA version of the Tip Calculator web app, and that's where we'll work.

> **Note**
>
> If you want to leave this version of the app in a pristine state, then copy the project's `tip-calculator-start` folder to a different location and work there.

## Visual Studio Code

I use Visual Studio Code as my primary code editor for most projects; this isn't because I work for Microsoft (I do), but because it's a very capable editor and the large catalog of available extensions enables me to configure the editor environment with some really cool capabilities to make coding easier. If you haven't tried it out yet, hop over to https://code.visualstudio.com/ and give it a try.

As you'll learn later, there's a feature in Visual Studio Code I use in the project's JavaScript files to automatically catch errors in my code as I write them. This alone is the best reason to give Visual Studio Code a try.

# App Installation in Action

OK, so we've spent a lot of time so far learning all about manifest files and how you use them to make a PWA installable. In this section, we take an initial version of the Tip Calculator app and add stuff to it to turn it into a PWA and make it installable. At the end of this section, you'll have the Tip Calculator app running against a local web server and be able to test app installation in the desktop browser.

> **Note**
>
> We're going to test the app modifications only on desktop browsers because accessing the app on a mobile device is more complicated. One of the requirements to make an app installable is to access it over a TLS (HTTPS) connection. To do this in your local development environment requires that you generate a TLS certificate for the local web server or host the app on a web server somewhere. Hosting the app on a web server requires a web server, a custom domain, and a TLS certificate—setting up all of that is beyond the scope of this book.

## Adding a Service Worker

As explained earlier, installable apps must have a service worker registered, and the service worker must offer specific capabilities. The remaining chapters deal with service workers in detail, so for now we're just going to use a simple one I included in the project and dig into how they work in later chapters. I'll explain a little about what's going on here, but I promise you'll get all the details you need on service workers starting with the next chapter.

Open the project's index.html file, and add the following code to the end of the file's <head> section:

```
<script>
  // does the browser support service workers?
  if ('serviceWorker' in navigator) {
    // then register our service worker
    navigator.serviceWorker.register('./sw.js')
      .then(function (reg) {
        // display a success message
        console.log(`Service Worker Registration (Scope: ${reg.scope})`);
      })
      .catch(function (error) {
        // display an error message
        console.log(`Service Worker Error (${error})`);
      });
  } else {
    // happens when the app isn't served over a TLS connection (HTTPS)
    console.warn('Service Worker not available');
  }
</script>
```

> **Tip**
>
> In this sample code and much of the code in the remainder of the book, I use JavaScript's template literals[4] to format console output with values from the running app. Pay special attention to the quote marks used: templates use the back tick (`` ` ``) character, whereas nontemplate code uses the single-quote mark (').

This code checks whether the browser supports service workers, then installs the service worker if it does or writes a warning to the console if it doesn't. The service worker is in a file called sw.js; it doesn't do much of anything—it's there just to help make the app installable (fill one of the installable requirements).

Could you put this code in an external JavaScript file? Yes. There's no reason it's here instead of in a JavaScript file. I use that approach in the remaining chapters of this book.

---

4. https://developer.mozilla.org/en-US/docs/Web/JavaScript/Reference/Template_literals

Next, add the following line to the <head> section of the project's index.html file:

```
<link rel="manifest" href="app.webmanifest">
```

This code links the manifest file (we haven't created yet) to the web app. Listing 2.2 shows the complete source code for the project's index.htm file.

Listing 2.2  **Tip Calculator index.html File**

```
<!doctype html>
<html>
<head>
  <meta charset="utf-8">
  <title>Tip Calculator</title>
  <meta name="description" content="A simple tip calculator app">
  <meta name="viewport" content="width=device-width, initial-scale=1">
  <link rel="manifest" href="app.webmanifest">
  <!-- FavIcon generated by: https://www.favicon-generator.org/ -->
  <!-- Icon image: https://thenounproject.com/search/?q=34839&i=34839 -->
  <link rel="apple-touch-icon" sizes="57x57" href="icons/apple-icon-57x57.png">
  <link rel="apple-touch-icon" sizes="60x60" href="icons/apple-icon-60x60.png">
  <link rel="apple-touch-icon" sizes="72x72" href="icons/apple-icon-72x72.png">
  <link rel="apple-touch-icon" sizes="76x76" href="icons/apple-icon-76x76.png">
  <link rel="apple-touch-icon" sizes="114x114" href="icons/apple-icon-114x114.png">
  <link rel="apple-touch-icon" sizes="120x120" href="icons/apple-icon-120x120.png">
  <link rel="apple-touch-icon" sizes="144x144" href="icons/apple-icon-144x144.png">
  <link rel="apple-touch-icon" sizes="152x152" href="icons/apple-icon-152x152.png">
  <link rel="apple-touch-icon" sizes="180x180" href="icons/apple-icon-180x180.png">
  <link rel="icon" type="image/png" sizes="192x192"
    href="icons/android-chrome-192x192.png">
  <link rel="icon" type="image/png" sizes="32x32" href="favicon-32x32.png">
  <link rel="icon" type="image/png" sizes="96x96" href="favicon-96x96.png">
  <link rel="icon" type="image/png" sizes="16x16" href="favicon-16x16.png">
  <meta name="msapplication-TileColor" content="#ffffff">
  <meta name="msapplication-TileImage" content="icons/ms-icon-144x144.png">
  <meta name="theme-color" content="#ffffff">
  <link rel="stylesheet" href="css/normalize.css">
  <link rel="stylesheet" href="css/main.css">

  <script>
    // does the browser support service workers?
    if ('serviceWorker' in navigator) {
      // then register our service worker
      navigator.serviceWorker.register('./sw.js')
        .then(function (reg) {
          // display a success message
          console.log(`Service Worker Registration (Scope: ${reg.scope})`);
        })
        .catch(function (error) {
```

```
            // display an error message
            console.log(`Service Worker Error (${error})`);
          });
      } else {
        // happens when the app isn't served over a TLS connection (HTTPS)
        console.warn('Service Worker not available');
      }
    </script>
  </head>

  <body>
    <div id='pageLogo'></div>
    <h1 id="title">Tip Calculator</h1>
    <div class='costArea'>
      <label for="mealCost">Meal Cost</label>
      <input type="number" id="mealCost" min="0" value="" autofocus>
    </div>
    <table style="width:100%" cellspacing="0">
      <tr>
        <th class='rating'>Rating</th>
        <th class='tip'>Tip</th>
        <th class='amount'>Amount</th>
      </tr>
      <tr>
        <td class='rating'>Poor</td>
        <td class='tip'>10%</td>
        <td class='amount' id="tip10">$0.00</td>
      </tr>
      <tr>
        <td class='rating'>OK</td>
        <td class='tip'>15%</td>
        <td class='amount' id="tip15">$0.00</td>
      </tr>
      <tr>
        <td class='rating'>Good</td>
        <td class='tip'>18%</td>
        <td class='amount' id="tip18">$0.00</td>
      </tr>
      <tr>
        <td class='rating'>Great</td>
        <td class='tip'>20%</td>
        <td class='amount' id="tip20">$0.00</td>
      </tr>
      <tr>
        <td class='rating'>Excellent</td>
        <td class='tip'>22%</td>
        <td class='amount' id="tip22">$0.00</td>
      </tr>
```

```
  </table>
  <script src="js/main.js"></script>
</body>
</html>
```

## Adding a Web Manifest File

The app's web app manifest file tells the browser how to install and run the app. We don't have one yet, so create a file called app.webmanifest in the same folder as the project's index.html file. Populate the new file with the JSON code from Listing 2.1.

## Running the App

Before we make the app fancy, lets test it in the browser to make sure the manifest file is configured correctly. Open a terminal window, navigate to the folder where you modified the code, and execute the following command:

```
http-server
```

The server task should report something like the following:

```
Starting up http-server, serving ./
Available on:
  http://172.20.154.161:8080
  http://172.28.224.1:8080
  http://192.168.86.247:8080
  http://192.168.60.1:8080
  http://192.168.19.1:8080
  http://127.0.0.1:8080
Hit CTRL-C to stop the server
```

Due to security concerns I'll explain in Chapter 3, "Service Workers," a PWA will work correctly only over an HTTPS connection or when accessed via the localhost hostname. Even though the HTTP Server task tells you it's listening on all those IP addresses, the browser won't treat the app like a PWA unless you access it through localhost. You won't even be able to access the local web server from an Android emulator running on the device, since localhost on the Android device is on the actual device. To access the web server from the Android emulator, you must use the IP address 10.0.2.2, and since that's not localhost, Chrome won't allow you to install the app from that host.

Jot down the port number listed after the colon in each IP address line (for example, the 8080 in http://172.20.154.161:8080). Open a PWA-compatible browser (for help selecting the right browser, see Can I Use[5]—in my testing on Windows, it worked only in Chrome and the Chrome-based Edge browsers) and navigate to the following URL:

```
http://localhost:8080/index.html
```

---

5. https://caniuse.com/#feat=web-app-manifest

substituting your actual port number for the 8080 in the example. Chances are, it will be 8080 on most systems, but if your development workstation already has a task listening on that port, the HTTP Server will select a different port from a range of available ports.

The Tip Calculator app should open and display the page shown in Figure 2.1. Most desktop browsers don't display the installation banner (see Figure 2.11), so we won't be able to install the app yet. At this point, we're just checking to make sure the browser sees the manifest correctly. Open the browser's developer tools and look for an **Application** or **Service Workers** tab and select it. The browser should display manifest information, as shown in Figure 2.13. If the pane doesn't list any errors, you're good and the browser should eventually allow you to install the app.

Figure 2.13  Chrome Dev Tools App Manifest Page

If Chrome has any issues with the manifest file, it will list them here. Some of the issues aren't easily understood, so see the troubleshooting section at the end of the chapter for more details.

### Creating an Environment to Test the App on a Physical Device or Device Emulator/Simulator

If you point a mobile device browser to https://learningpwa.com/tipcalc, you can test installing the app on the device. This is because that version of the app fulfills many of the requirements for the app to be installable:

- Includes a web app manifest that defines a minimum set of properties (a `short_name` and/or name, `icons` must reference icons at 192 and 512 pixels, a `start_url`, and `display` property of `fullscreen`, `standalone`, or `minimal-ui`).
- Has a registered service worker with a `fetch` event handler.
- Is served over HTTPS (or `localhost` when testing).

The first two are covered by the manifest and service worker files, but the last requirement in that list can be done only if you have an SSL/TLS certificate installed in the local web server running on your development workstation or you're hosting the app via a service provider that provides the certificate.

There's an easy and relatively inexpensive way to set this up yourself. All you need is a domain (I get mine from Google Domains[6] at US$12 each) and a hosting provider. For the Learning Progressive Web Apps site, I'm hosting the app at Netlify,[7] which offers a free hosting package that's perfect for your testing. All you must do is point Netlify at your web project's GitHub repository and it will build and host the app for free. Once you configure your domain to point to the Netlify DNS servers and set up an SSL/TLS certificate for the domain, you're all set. When you hit the domain from the browser on an Android device (iOS doesn't support installing PWAs yet) the Install button will appear, and you can install the app.

The reason I'm not proposing you install a self-signed certificate in your local web server is that you must generate your own SSL certificate, which creates all sorts of trust issues in the browser. I don't want to get into all that in this book (it's about PWAs, not configuring SSL/TLS certificates).

## Enhancing the Installation Process

All right, remember that we want to be able to control the process, so we're going to make some changes to the app. Open the project's index.html file and add the following code to the top of the <body> section, right above the pagelogo div:

```
<div id='installButtonDiv'>
  <button id='installButton'>Install</button>
</div>
```

---

6. https://domains.google/#/

7. https://www.netlify.com/

> **Note**
> The styling for this button is already in the app's `main.css` file. The button is hidden by default, so it won't appear until we want it to.

This adds the install button the user taps or clicks to install the app.

Open the project's `/js/main.js` file. At the bottom of the file, add the following code:

```
// get a handle to the install button
let installButton = document.getElementById('installButton');
// now set the click handler for the install button
installButton.onclick = doInstall;
```

This creates an `installbutton` variable that points to the install button page element (we'll need this later to hide the button after installation) and adds a click event handler for the button.

Now, let's start working on the installation process, which all centers around the `beforeinstallprompt` event described earlier. At the bottom of the file, add the following code:

```
// create an object we'll use to hold the reference to the PWA
// install event
let deferredPrompt;

// now add an event listener to respond to the event. Right
// before the browser installs the PWA, it fires the
// beforeinstallprompt event. Here, we'll manage the
// installation ourselves
window.addEventListener('beforeinstallprompt', (event) => {
    // don't allow the browser to do its install now, we want to
    // do it when the user taps our install button
    event.preventDefault();
    // stash the event object so we can use it later (when the
    // user taps the install button)
    deferredPrompt = event;
    // now unhide the Install button so the user can tap it!
    installButton.style.display = 'block';
});
```

The code creates the `deferredPrompt` object, which we'll use later to capture the event object created with the `beforeinstallprompt` event. You'll see why this is important in a little bit.

Next, it creates the `beforeinstallprompt` event listener. The first thing the listener does is make a call to `event.preventDefault()`, which tells the browser not to worry about installing the app and should suppress the installation banner shown in Figure 2.11. The suppression feature is in the desktop version of Chrome today and hasn't made it into the Android version of Chrome yet, but it should be there by the time you read this book.

Next, the code stores the event object passed to the listener in the `deferredPrompt` object created earlier. We'll use methods on this object later to actually install the app.

Finally, the code sets the button's display style to `block`, unhiding the button on the page so the user can now see it. With that in place, we now need the code that does the installation. Above the `beforeinstallprompt` event listener we just added to the project's `js/main.js` file, add the following function:

```
function doInstall() {
  // we've tapped the install button, so hide it
  installButton.style.display = 'none';
  // execute the deferred installation prompt
  deferredPrompt.prompt();
  // wait for the response from the deferred prompt
  deferredPrompt.userChoice.then((res) => {
    // did the user approve installation?
    if (res.outcome === 'accepted') {
      console.log('doInstall: accepted');
    } else {
      console.log('doInstall: declined');
    }
    // clear the deferred prompt object so we
    // can only do this once
    deferredPrompt = null;
  });
}
```

As described in the comments, this code

- Hides the Install button (no need to install the app twice).

- Calls the `prompt` method on the `deferredPrompt` object; we captured that object specifically for this reason, so we could call its `prompt` method later to prompt the user to install the app.

- Waits for the user to decide whether or not to install the app.

- Once the user decides what to do, logs the results to the console and clears the `deferredPrompt` object so it's not used again.

When the browser fires the `beforeinstallprompt` event, it passes an object that the app uses later to prompt the user to install the app. This code just defers the installation and puts it in the hands of the app through the Install button.

In the terminal window, press Ctrl-C to kill the server process, then execute the `http-server` command again (this reloads the modified code into the server). Next, refresh the Tip Calculator page in the browser and you should see the Install button appear. Remember, the browser shows the installation prompt when the app encounters a user engagement heuristic, which means it may take a while to show the prompt. When the prompt appears, use it to install the app locally, then close the browser and open the installed shortcut to see how it works.

Some operating systems install the app on the desktop (Windows), while others install the app in an apps area in the browser. In my testing on Windows, Chrome installs the PWA in `chrome://apps` as well as on the desktop. Figure 2.14 shows the Chrome Apps page with the installed Tip Calculator app.

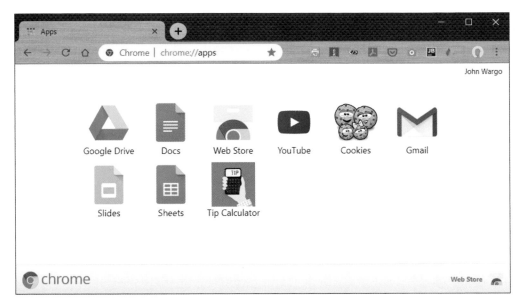

Figure 2.14    Chrome Apps Page

Deleting the PWA from the apps page (right-click and select **Remove from Chrome...**, as shown in Figure 2.15) also removes it from the desktop. The new Edge browser (based on Chromium) from Microsoft installs the app in the apps area but not on the desktop.

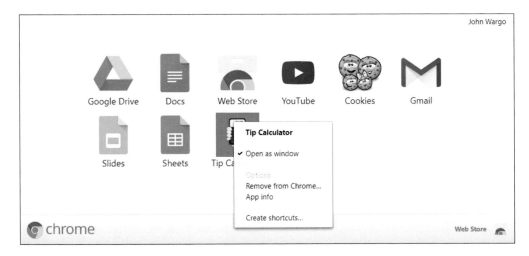

Figure 2.15    Chrome Removing an Installed PWA

The browser fires one additional event during the installation process: the `appinstalled` event. At the bottom of the project's `js/main.js` file, add the following event listener:

```
// register an event listener for after the app installs
window.addEventListener('appinstalled', (event) => {
  console.log('App Installed');
});
```

An app uses this event to perform any post-installation cleanup or anything else it wants to do after the installation completes.

Finally, do you remember when I mentioned that you could pass an extra query parameter when launching the installed PWA? We set this up using the `start_url` in the manifest file:

```
"start_url": "/index.html?source=pwa",
```

This configures the installed shortcut to pass `?source=pwa` on the query string when launching the PWA. If you add the following code to the project's `main.js` file, it changes the Tip Calculator page title when it runs as an installed PWA:

```
// did we launch as a PWA?
var urlParams = new URLSearchParams(window.location.search);
// look for the source parameter, if it's `pwa` then it's installed
if (urlParams.get('source') === 'pwa') {
  console.log('Launched as PWA');
  // add the PWA moniker to the title
  let theTitle = document.getElementById('title');
  theTitle.innerHTML = theTitle.innerHTML + ' (PWA)';
}
```

Listing 2.3 lists the complete source for the project's `main.js` file.

Listing 2.3   **Tip Calculator `main.js` File**

```
// @ts-check

// borrowed from https://flaviocopes.com/how-to-format-number-as-currency-javascript/
const formatter = new Intl.NumberFormat('en-US', {
  style: 'currency',
  currency: 'USD',
  minimumFractionDigits: 2
})

function updateTipAmounts() {
  // grab the meal cost from the page
  let mealCost = document.getElementById("mealCost").value;
  // populate the table with tip amounts
  document.getElementById('tip10').innerHTML =
    formatter.format(mealCost * 0.10);
  document.getElementById('tip15').innerHTML =
    formatter.format(mealCost * 0.15);
```

```
    document.getElementById('tip18').innerHTML =
      formatter.format(mealCost * 0.18);
    document.getElementById('tip20').innerHTML =
      formatter.format(mealCost * 0.20);
    document.getElementById('tip22').innerHTML =
      formatter.format(mealCost * 0.22);
}

function doInstall() {
  // we've tapped the install button, so hide it
  installButton.style.display = 'none';
  // execute the deferred installation prompt
  deferredPrompt.prompt();
  // wait for the response from the deferred prompt
  deferredPrompt.userChoice.then((res) => {
    // did the user approve installation?
    if (res.outcome === 'accepted') {
      console.log('doInstall: accepted');
    } else {
      console.log('doInstall: declined');
    }
    // clear the deferred prompt object so we can only do
    // this once
    deferredPrompt = null;
  });
}

// register the event listener for the input field
document.getElementById('mealCost').oninput = updateTipAmounts;

// did we launch as a PWA?
var urlParams = new URLSearchParams(window.location.search);
// look for the source parameter, if it's `pwa` then it's installed
if (urlParams.get('source') === 'pwa') {
  console.log('Launched as PWA');
  // add the PWA moniker to the title
  let theTitle = document.getElementById('title');
  theTitle.innerHTML = theTitle.innerHTML + ' (PWA)';
}

// get a handle to the install button
let installButton = document.getElementById('installButton');
// now set the click handler for the install button
installButton.onclick = doInstall;

// create an object we'll use to hold a reference to the PWA
// install event
let deferredPrompt;
```

```
// add an event listener to respond to the event. right
// before the browser installs the PWA, it fires the
// beforeinstallprompt event. here, we'll manage the
// installation ourselves
window.addEventListener('beforeinstallprompt', (event) => {
    // don't allow the browser to do its install, we want to do
    // it when the user taps our install button
    event.preventDefault();
    // stash the event object so we can use it later (when the
    // user taps the install button)
    deferredPrompt = event;
    // now unhide the Install button so the user can tap it!
    installButton.style.display = 'block';
});

// register an event listener for after the app installs
window.addEventListener('appinstalled', (event) => {
  console.log('App Installed');
});
```

> **Tip**
>
> Notice that comment at the top of the source listing with @ts-check? Remember when I said that Visual Studio Code added a special feature that enabled me to write better code? With that directive in a .js file, Visual Studio Code applies the TypeScript compiler to the code as I type, looking for errors in real time—even when I'm editing a JavaScript file instead of a TypeScript file. This means that I get the benefits of TypeScript without using TypeScript for my app. You can read more about this feature here: https://code.visualstudio.com/docs/nodejs/working-with-javascript#_type-checking-javascript.

## Troubleshooting

Browsers don't tell you much when processing a PWA for installation. Basically, it works or it doesn't work, and to pop up warnings and errors would only confuse users. So, with that in mind, adding a manifest and service worker to an app to make it installable either works or it doesn't.

There are some things you can do to debug the process. One of the simplest is to put breakpoints in the code, and watch the process through the browser developer tools. I'm also a big fan of adding a bunch of console.log() calls in my code so I can watch it run through the console.

Most modern browsers offer developer tools that understand manifest files and service workers. Figure 2.16 shows the App Manifest pane in the Chrome Developer tools. Whenever an app links a manifest file, information about the manifest appears in this pane. When the browser encounters an error parsing the manifest, or the manifest doesn't meet minimum requirements to make an app installable, it will display error messages like the ones you see in the figure. In this case, I configured the scope property incorrectly and had some error with my service worker, which had me scratching my head.

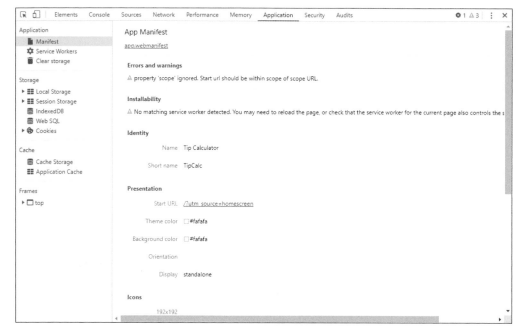

Figure 2.16    Chrome Developer Tools: App Manifest Pane

# Manifest Generation and More

Even though Apple doesn't fully support them on iOS or Safari, PWAs have been around for a while, so there are a lot of nice tools around to help make your life easier. I cover some tools in Chapter 8, "Assessment, Automation, and Deployment," but here's a list of some free tools available online to help you configure web app manifests for your PWA:

- PWA Builder: https://www.pwabuilder.com

- Web App Manifest Generator: https://app-manifest.firebaseapp.com

- (another) Web App Manifest Generator: https://tomitm.github.io/appmanifest

- PWA Fire Developer: https://pwafire.org/developer/tools/get-manifest

Google also publishes the pwcompat library,[8] which brings web app manifest support to noncompatible browsers, enabling a PWA-like experience on older browsers.

# Wrap-Up

In this chapter, I showed you how to add a manifest file to a web app to make it installable on compatible browsers. In the next chapter and beyond, we'll dig into all the cool things you can do with service workers.

---

8.  https://github.com/GoogleChromeLabs/pwacompat

# 3

# Service Workers

If building Progressive Web Apps (PWAs) is like building a house, the web app manifest file is like a real estate agent working to get people interested in buying your house and prepping it so that it's move-in ready for buyers. Service workers, on the other hand, are live-in general contractors working behind the scenes to make sure the house has a solid foundation and all the walls stay up after the buyer moves in.

This chapter introduces service workers and shows how to use them to enable cool background processing in your web app. Here we build a foundation of what service workers do and how they do it, starting with simple web app resource caching and the service worker lifecycle. In the chapters that follow, I show how to add additional functionality to an app's service worker to give the app some pizazz.

## PWA News

For this and the next few chapters of the book, you'll work with the PWA News web app shown in Figure 3.1. The app is publicly available at https://pwa-news.com, but you'll run a version of the app on a local server as you work through the chapter. I'd like to give a special shout out to my friend Scott Good who created the app UI and, through the application of some masterful styling, made it into the beautiful app you see in the figure.

The app is a simple news site, aggregating news articles on PWAs from sites around the world. The app's server process uses the Microsoft Bing News Search API[1] to locate articles with the keyword *PWA* and displays the top 20 results. The app hosts a simple About page describing the site (and promoting the book) plus a Feedback page that renders data about how people feel about the site. You'll play with that one in a later chapter. In Chapter 5, "Going the Rest of the Way Offline with Background Sync," we'll add the ability for visitors to submit their feedback when we talk about going offline.

---

1. https://azure.microsoft.com/en-us/services/cognitive-services/bing-news-search-api/

Figure 3.1   PWA News Web Site

# Introducing Service Workers

A service worker is a block of JavaScript code a web app installs in the browser under certain conditions and runs when the browser needs it to (based on events that fire). Web apps use service workers to add additional capabilities to the app, capabilities that aren't generally available to web apps but are available in many mobile apps.

For install conditions, a browser installs a service worker if

- The browser supports service workers.
- The browser loaded the web app using a TLS (HTTPS) connection or from the system's localhost address (referring to the local device running the browser).
- The web app loads the service worker code within the same context (from the same server location) as the web app for which it's associated.

Unlike with web app manifest files, most modern browsers support service workers; you can check the current support matrix on Can I Use.[2] As I write this, the following browsers support service workers: Chrome (Google), Edge (Microsoft), Firefox (Mozilla), Opera (Opera), and Safari (Apple).

---

2. https://caniuse.com/#feat=serviceworkers

Many other browsers support them as well; check first if you know your app's target audience prefers a specific browser that's not in that list.

Depending on how web developers take advantage of service workers in their apps, service workers:

- **Cache app content.** Google calls service workers *programmable network proxies*; as you'll see in this chapter and the next, you have a lot of options for controlling which resources the browser caches and which ones are pulled from the server when requested by the app. You can even replace requested resources (files or data) dynamically at runtime using a service worker.

- **Perform background processing.** Web apps use service workers to deliver background data synchronization and offline support. Service workers install in the browser, they're associated with the web app, but they run in the browser's execution context. This means they're available to do work whenever the browser is open, even when the app is not loaded. You'll learn more about this in Chapter 5, "Going the Rest of the Way Offline with Background Sync" and Chapter 6, "Push Notifications."

- **Receive push notifications.** With the right protocols and a backend server to send notifications, web apps use the background processing capabilities of service workers to enable the processing and display of push notifications sent to the app. You'll learn more about this in Chapter 7, "Passing Data between Service Workers and Web Applications."

The primary reasons browsers require a TLS connection to install and enable a service worker are those included in the bulleted list you just read through. Considering all you can do with the capabilities described in that list, the service worker has complete control over data coming in and out of the app. Browsers require the TLS connection to enforce that the web app and service worker load from the same location.

Without a TLS connection and the requirement that the service worker loads from the same context as the web app, hackers could compromise a site and load service worker code from another location and take complete control of the app. A rogue service worker could redirect all requests to alternate servers, capture auth and push tokens, and more.

### The Dreadful Application Cache

Earlier, I said, "Web apps use service workers to add additional capabilities to the app, capabilities that aren't generally available to web apps," but that wasn't exactly true. Web developers have been able to implement resource caching in web apps for some time now, through an old feature in many browsers called the Application Cache[3] (or just AppCache).

Unfortunately, AppCache is a pretty horrible technology, as famously described in Jake Archibald's "Application Cache Is a Douchebag."[4] It's so bad that the AppCache page at the above link starts with two warnings against using it in your apps. Furthermore, it also warns that the technology has been removed from many browsers and that the feature may cease to work at any time. How's that? Don't use it.

---

3. https://developer.mozilla.org/en-US/docs/Web/HTML/Using_the_application_cache
4. https://alistapart.com/article/application-cache-is-a-douchebag/

> Developers used it because AppCache support was built into many browsers, but few developers were happy with it. Writing your own cache implementation was problematic as well, because, for performance reasons, it must run on a separate thread, which was challenging in web apps as well.
>
> The CacheStorage[5] API described in Chapter 4, "Resource Caching," was the community's attempt to fix AppCache, and it's one of the key technologies that make PWAs interesting and useful today. My apologies for lying to you, but hopefully now you see why I did.

Of course, service workers have limitations:

- Service workers don't run unless the browser is open. The web app doesn't have to be open, but the browser does.

- Service workers don't have access to the web app's document object model (DOM), but we'll discuss workarounds for this in Chapter 7.

The first limitation may not be a big deal depending on the browser and operating system (OS). On many mobile devices, the browser always runs, so it's there to run the service worker. On desktop systems, some browsers run in the background as well or can be configured to do so. Chrome exposes an advanced setting. Continue running background apps when Google Chrome is closed, as highlighted in Figure 3.2.

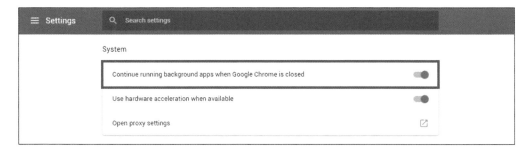

Figure 3.2    Chrome Advanced Settings

I'll show you more about what service workers can do and how they do it as we work through the rest of the chapter.

## Preparing to Code

Throughout the remainder of the chapter, you'll start with a base version of the PWA News site and add a service worker to it. Then we'll tweak and tune the service worker to demonstrate its capabilities. Before we do that, you must configure your local development environment with the components you'll need.

---

5. https://developer.mozilla.org/en-US/docs/Web/API/CacheStorage

## Prerequisites

Before we start modifying code to enhance the PWA News app, you must install some software prerequisites you'll use as you follow along. Who knows, you may already have them installed (you should). This setup is different from previous chapters, so please don't skip ahead until you've ensured that you have everything you need in place.

### Node.js

I built the PWA News site using Node.js and Express (a web framework for Node.js). It hosts the static PWA News web site plus the application programming interface (API) used by the web app. If your development workstation already has Node.js installed, then skip ahead to the next section. If not, hop over to https://nodejs.org and follow the instructions to install the client on your development workstation.

To confirm that you have Node.js installed, open a new terminal window and execute the following command:

```
node -v
```

If the terminal returns a version number (mine reports v10.16.0), then Node.js is properly installed. If you see an error message, then you have some work to do resolving the error before continuing.

### TypeScript

With Node.js installed, now it's time to install the TypeScript compiler. In the terminal window, execute the following command:

```
npm install -g typescript
```

This installs the tsc command you'll use many times through the remainder of the book to compile the web server app TypeScript code into JavaScript.

### Git Client

I published the source code for the book in a GitHub repository at https://github.com/johnwargo/learning-pwa-code. The easiest way to get the code, and to update your local copy when I publish changes, is through Git. If your development workstation already has Git installed, then you're good. If not, hop over to https://git-scm.com and follow the instructions to install the client on your development workstation.

To confirm that you have Git installed, open a new terminal window and execute the following command:

```
git --version
```

If the terminal returns a version number (mine reports git version 2.22.0.windows.1), then Git is properly installed. If you see an error message, then you have some work to do resolving the error before continuing.

With Git installed, open a terminal window or command prompt, navigate to the folder where you want to store the book's code, and then execute the following command:

```
git clone https://github.com/johnwargo/learning-pwa-code
```

Once the cloning process completes, navigate the terminal into the cloned project's `\learning-pwa-code\chapter-03\` folder. This folder contains the PWA News server app, and that's where we'll work.

While we're here, we might as well install all the dependencies required by the app. In the terminal window pointing to the project folder (`\learning-pwa-code\chapter-03\`), execute the following command:

```
npm install
```

This command uses the Node Package Manager (npm) to install Node.js modules used by the server.

### Visual Studio Code

I use Visual Studio Code as my primary code editor for most projects; this is not because I work for Microsoft (I do), but because it's a very capable editor, and the large catalog of available extensions enables me to configure the editor environment with some really cool capabilities to make coding easier. If you haven't tried it out yet, hop over to https://code.visualstudio.com/ and give it a try.

## Navigating the App Source

The folder structure for the PWA News app source is shown in Figure 3.3. The `public` folder shown in the figure holds the web app files we'll use in this chapter. The code you're looking at is for a web server app, and the `public` folder is where the web server looks for the static files it serves.

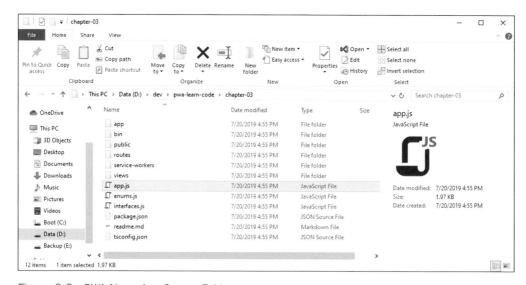

Figure 3.3   PWA News App Source Folder

I wrote server code (the APIs the web app uses) using TypeScript,[6] a typed superset of JavaScript. Using TypeScript allowed me to define types for all my app's variables and more easily find errors (based on that typing). TypeScript code compiles to JavaScript using the TypeScript Compiler (`tsc`), so the `.js` files you see in the figure are compiled versions of my code located in the project's `app` folder.

If you decide you want to make changes to how the server and API work, you must make your modifications in the app folder. Once you're ready to apply your changes, open a terminal window, navigate to the root project folder (the one shown in Figure 3.3), and execute the following command:

```
tsc
```

This compiles the server's `.ts` files into the `.js` files you see in the root folder shown in the figure. You'll see some errors and warnings from the code's references to some of the objects, but the unmodified code runs as is, so look for errors from the code you modified.

## Configuring the Server API

The server process consumes the Bing News Search API from Microsoft Azure to collect the news data displayed in the app. You'll need an Azure account and a Bing API key to work with the code in this chapter.

If you already have an Azure account, log in to your account at https://portal.azure.com. If you don't have an account, create a free one at https://azure.microsoft.com/en-us/free/. Once you've created the account, log in to the portal using your new account at https://portal.azure.com.

To use the Bing Search API, you must first generate an API key for the service. The key is free, and you can use up to 3,000 searches per month in the free tier. Point your browser of choice to https://portal.azure.com/#create/Microsoft.CognitiveServicesBingSearch-v7 and log in. Populate the form with the following information:

- **Name:** Enter a name for the resource (use something such as Learning PWA, or PWA News).

- **Subscription:** Select Pay-As-You-Go.

- **Location:** Select an Azure Region from the drop-down. It doesn't matter which one you pick; I suggest you pick one near your current location (I selected East US).

- **Pricing Tier:** Select the free tier.

- **Resource Group:** Create a new one, and give it any name you want (use something such as RG-PWA or RG-PWA-News).

Click the Create button when you're done with the form.

---

6. https://www.typescriptlang.org/

> **Note**
>
> Microsoft Azure offers a robust free tier you can use as you work through this chapter. The free tier gives customers three transactions per second (up to 3,000 per month), so in your testing of this app, you're unlikely to exceed the free plan limits. To help even further, I coded the server app to restrict how often it connects to Bing to get news articles. By default, it only checks every 15 minutes, no matter how often a client hits the server API. If you do the math, you'll see there's no way for the server to ever exceed that free limit.

When you get to the page shown in Figure 3.4, click the copy icon to the far right of either the KEY 1 or KEY 2 field to copy the selected key to the clipboard. You'll need one of these keys in the next step.

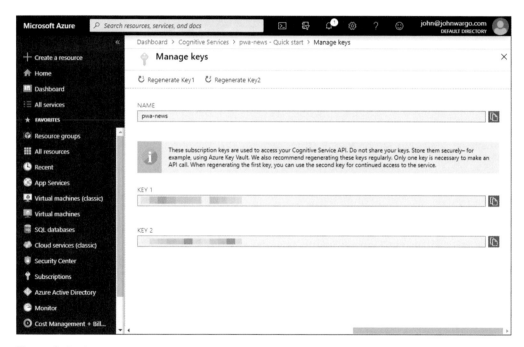

Figure 3.4   Azure Portal

Next, in the project source code folder, open the project's `app/congfig.ts` file. This file exports a single property, the `BING_ACCESS_KEY` shown in Listing 3.1. Paste the key you just copied to the clipboard between the empty quotes in the file.

Listing 3.1   **PWA News app/`config.ts` File**

```
export const config = {
  // enter your private Bing Search API access key
  BING_ACCESS_KEY: ''
};
```

For example, you'll change

```
BING_ACCESS_KEY: ''
```

to something like this:

```
BING_ACCESS_KEY: 'your-super-secret-api-key'
```

Save the file, then open a terminal window, navigate to the root project folder (the one shown in Figure 3.3), and execute the following command:

```
tsc
```

This step invokes the TypeScript compiler to compile the `config.ts` file into a new `config.js` file in the project root folder (not shown in Figure 3.3). With this in place, you're all set to start the server process and begin interacting with the app.

You'll need this same `config.js` file as you work through the code in subsequent chapters, so I included a batch file and shell script to automate copying the compiled file to the other project folders. If your development system runs Windows, in the terminal window pointing to `\learning-pwa-code\chapter-03\`, execute the following command:

```
copy-config.cmd
```

If your development system runs macOS, in the terminal window pointing to `\learning-pwa-code\chapter-03\`, execute the following command:

```
./copy-config.sh
```

At the end of either process, you should see the `config.js` file copied into the root project folder for each chapter folder that uses the PWA News app.

## Starting the Server

With all the parts in place, it's time to start the server. If you don't have a terminal window open pointing to the project folder, open one now, and navigate to the `\learning-pwa-code\chapter-03\` folder. Once there, execute the following command:

```
npm start
```

If everything's set up properly in the code, the server will respond with the following text in the terminal:

```
pwa-news-server@0.0.1 start D:\learning-pwa-code\chapter-03
node ./bin/www
```

At this point, you're all set—the server is up and running and ready to serve content. If you see an error message, you must dig through any reported errors and resolve them before continuing.

To see the web app in its current state, open Google Chrome or one of the browsers that supports service workers and navigate to

```
http://localhost:3000
```

After a short delay, the server should render the app as shown in Figure 3.1. When you look in the terminal window, you should see the server process start, then log messages as it serves the different parts of the app, as shown here:

```
> pwa-news-server@0.0.1 start D:\learning-pwa-code\chapter-03
> node ./bin/www

2019-07-29T22:27:25.054Z GET / 304 8.365 ms - -
2019-07-29T22:27:25.075Z GET /css/custom.css 304 2.004 ms - -
2019-07-29T22:27:25.079Z GET /img/bing-logo.png 304 0.935 ms - -
2019-07-29T22:27:25.104Z GET /js/sw-reg.js 304 0.746 ms - -
2019-07-29T22:27:25.114Z GET /js/utils.js 304 0.756 ms - -
2019-07-29T22:27:25.115Z GET /js/index.js 304 0.731 ms - -
Router: GET /api/news
2019-07-29T22:27:26.376Z GET /sw-34.js 404 1132.392 ms - 565
2019-07-29T22:27:26.381Z GET /app.webmanifest 304 1.766 ms - -
2019-07-29T22:27:26.420Z GET /icons/android-icon-192x192.png 404 20.681 ms - 565
Returning result (1)
2019-07-29T22:27:26.788Z GET /api/news 200 1645.317 ms - 12222
```

The server hosts the app at port 3000 by default (the port number is the numeric value after the last colon in the example), but if your system has another process listening on that port, then it's not going to work. To change the port number used by the app, open the project's `bin/www` file and look for the following line:

```
var port = normalizePort(process.env.PORT || '3000');
```

Change the `'3000'` to another port (hopefully an available one), save your changes, then restart the server and access the site at the new port. You can also set the port using local environment variables[7] if you want.

## Registering a Service Worker

Web apps follow a specific process to install a service worker; there's no automatic way to do it today. The app basically executes some JavaScript code to register the service worker with the browser. In the Tip Calculator app in Chapter 1, "Introducing Progressive Web Apps," I added the code to do this directly in the app's `index.html` file. For the PWA News app, we use a different approach.

In this section, you'll modify the project's existing `public/index.html` file plus add two JavaScript files: `public/js/sw-reg.js` and `public/sw.js`.

In the `<head>` section of the project's `public/index.html` file, add the following code:

```
<!-- Register the service worker -->
<script src='js/sw-reg.js'></script>
```

---

7. https://stackoverflow.com/questions/18008620/node-js-express-js-app-only-works-on-port-3000

This tells the web app to load a JavaScript file that registers the service worker for us. Next, let's create that file. Create a new file called `public/js/sw-reg.js` and populate the file with the code shown in Listing 3.2.

Listing 3.2    **PWA News `sw-reg.js` File**

```javascript
// does the browser support service workers?
if ('serviceWorker' in navigator) {
  // then register our service worker
  navigator.serviceWorker.register('/sw.js')
    .then(reg => {
      // display a success message
      console.log(`Service Worker Registration (Scope: ${reg.scope})`);
    })
    .catch(error => {
      // display an error message
      let msg = `Service Worker Error (${error})`;
      console.error(msg);
      // display a warning dialog (using Sweet Alert 2)
      Swal.fire('', msg, 'error');
    });
} else {
  // happens when the app isn't served over a TLS connection (HTTPS)
  // or if the browser doesn't support service workers
  console.warn('Service Worker not available');
}
```

The code here isn't very complicated; it all centers around the call to `navigator.serviceWorker.register`. The code first checks to see if the `serviceWorker` object exists in the browser's `navigator` object. If it does, then this browser supports service workers. After the code verifies it can register the service worker, it does so through the call to `navigator.serviceWorker.register`.

The `register` method returns a promise, so the code includes `then` and `catch` methods to act depending on whether the installation succeeded or failed. If it succeeds, it tosses a simple message out to the console. If the call to `register` fails (caught with the `catch` method), we warn the user with an alert dialog.

Two potential error conditions exist here: if the browser doesn't support service workers and if service worker registration fails. When the browser doesn't support service workers, I log a simple warning to the console (using `console.warn`). I don't do anything special to warn the user because this is progressive enhancement, right? If the browser doesn't support service workers, the user just continues to use the app as is, with no special capabilities provided through service workers.

On the other hand, if registration fails, then the code is broken (because we already know the browser supports service workers), and I want to let you know more obnoxiously with an alert dialog. I did this because you're learning how this works, and I wanted the error condition to be easily recognized. I probably wouldn't do this for production apps because if the service worker doesn't register, the app simply falls back to the normal mode of operation.

Service workers don't start working until the next page loads anyway, so to keep things clean, you can defer registering the service worker until the app finishes loading, as shown in Listing 3.3.

Listing 3.3    **PWA News `sw-reg.js` File (Alternate Version)**

```
// does the browser support service workers?
if ('serviceWorker' in navigator) {
  // Defer service worker installation until the page completes loading
  window.addEventListener('load', () => {
    // then register our service worker
    navigator.serviceWorker.register('/sw.js')
      .then(reg => {
        // display a success message
        console.log(`Service Worker Registration (Scope: ${reg.scope})`);
      })
      .catch(error) => {
        // display an error message
        let msg = `Service Worker Error (${error})`;
        console.error(msg);
        // display a warning dialog (using Sweet Alert 2)
        Swal.fire('', msg, 'error');
      });
  })
} else {
    // happens when the app isn't served over a TLS connection (HTTPS)
    // or if the browser doesn't support service workers
    console.warn('Service Worker not available');
}
```

In this example, the code adds an event listener for the `load` event and starts service worker registration after that event fires. All this does is defer the additional work until the app is done with all its other startup stuff and shouldn't even be noticeable to the user.

Next, let's create a service worker. Create a new file called `public/sw.js` and populate it with the code shown in Listing 3.4. Notice that we created the service worker registration file in the project's `public/js/` folder, but this one goes into the web app's root folder (`public/`); I'll explain why in "Service Worker Scope" later in this chapter—I'm just mentioning it now to save you a potential problem later if you put it in the wrong place.

Listing 3.4    **First Service Worker Example: `sw-34.js`**

```
self.addEventListener('fetch', event => {
  // fires whenever the app requests a resource (file or data)
  console.log(`SW: Fetching ${event.request.url}`);
});
```

> **Note**
>
> To save you typing in all the service worker example code, I've placed each service worker example, named using the listing number, in a folder called `public/service-workers`. You can see the file name in the listing heading above: `sw-34.js` for Listing 3.4.

This code is simple as well. All it does is create an event listener for the browser's `fetch` event, then logs the requested resource to the console. The `fetch` event fires whenever the browser, or an app running in the browser, requests an external resource (such as a file or data). This is different from the JavaScript `fetch` method, which enables an app's JavaScript code to request data or resources from the network. The browser requesting resources (such as a JavaScript or image file referenced in an HTML `script` or `img` tag) and a web app's JavaScript code requesting a resource using the `fetch` method will both cause the `fetch` event to fire.

This is the core functionality of a service worker, intercepting `fetch` events and doing something with the request—such as getting the requested resource from the network, pulling the requested file from cache, or even sending something completely different to the app requesting the resource. It's all up to you: your service worker delivers as much or as little enhancement as needed for your app.

With this file in place, refresh the app in the browser and watch what happens. Nothing, right? There's not much to see here since, everything happens under the covers. In this example, the service worker does nothing except log the event; as you can see in the browser, the app loaded as expected, so the app's still working the same as it did before.

Open the browser's developer tools and look for a tab labeled **Application** (or something similar) and a side tab labeled **Service Workers**. If you did everything right, you should see your service worker properly registered in the browser, as shown in Figure 3.5 (in Google Chrome).

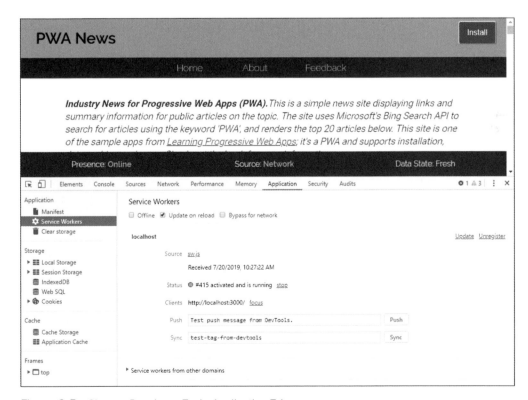

Figure 3.5    Chrome Developer Tools Application Tab

If the browser can't register the service worker, it displays error messages in this panel to let you know.

In the latest Chrome browser and the Chromium-based Edge browser, you can also open a special page that displays information about all service workers registered in the browser. Open the browser and enter the following value in the address bar:

```
chrome://serviceworker-internals/
```

The browser opens the page shown in Figure 3.6, listing all registered service workers.

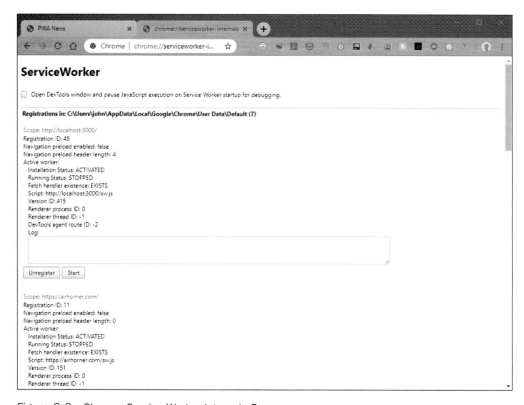

Figure 3.6   Chrome Service Worker Internals Page

The one thing missing from the service worker as it stands today is for it to actually do something with the fetch request. Listing 3.5 adds an additional line of code to our existing service worker:

```
event.respondWith(fetch(event.request));
```

This code instructs the browser to go ahead and get the requested file from the network. Without this statement in the event listener, the browser was doing this anyway. Since the event listener didn't act on the request and return a promise telling the browser it was dealing with it, then the browser goes ahead and gets the file anyway. That's why the app works without this line. Adding the line just completes the event listener.

Listing 3.5    **Second Service Worker Example: sw-35.js**

```
self.addEventListener('fetch', event => {
  // fires whenever the app requests a resource (file or data)
  console.log(`SW: Fetching ${event.request.url}`);
  // next, go get the requested resource from the network,
  // nothing fancy going on here.
  event.respondWith(fetch(event.request));
});
```

The browser passes the `fetch` event listener an `event` object service workers query to determine which resource was requested. Service workers use this mechanism to determine whether to get the resource from cache or request it from the network. I cover this in more detail later (in this chapter and the next), but for now this extra line of code simply enforces what we've already seen the browser do—get the requested resource from the network.

The browser fires two other events of interest to the service worker developer: `install` and `activate`. Listing 3.6 shows a service worker with event listeners for both included.

Listing 3.6    **Third Service Worker Example: sw-36.js**

```
self.addEventListener('install', event => {
  // fires when the browser installs the app
  // here we're just logging the event and the contents
  // of the object passed to the event. the purpose of this event
  // is to give the service worker a place to setup the local
  // environment after the installation completes.
  console.log(`SW: Event fired: ${event.type}`);
  console.dir(event);
});

self.addEventListener('activate', event => {
  // fires after the service worker completes its installation.
  // It's a place for the service worker to clean up from
  // previous service worker versions.
  console.log(`SW: Event fired: ${event.type}`);
  console.dir(event);
});

self.addEventListener('fetch', event => {
  // fires whenever the app requests a resource (file or data)
  console.log(`SW: Fetching ${event.request.url}`);
  // next, go get the requested resource from the network,
  // nothing fancy going on here.
  event.respondWith(fetch(event.request));
});
```

The browser fires the install event when it completes installation of the service worker. The event provides the app with an opportunity to do the setup work required by the service worker. At this point, the service worker is installed but not yet operational (it doesn't do anything yet).

The browser fires the activate event when the current service worker becomes the active service worker for the app. A service worker works at the browser level, not the app level, so when the browser installs it, it doesn't become active until the app reloads in all browser tabs running the app. Once it activates, it stays active for any browser tabs running the app until the browser closes all tabs for the app or the browser restarts.

The activate event provides service workers with an opportunity to perform tasks when the service worker becomes the active service worker. Usually, this means cleaning up any cached data from a previous version of the app (or service worker). You'll learn a lot more about this in Chapter 4, "Resource Caching"; for now, let's add this code to our existing service worker and see what happens.

Once you've updated the code, reload the page in the browser, then open the developer tools console panel and look for the output shown in Figure 3.7. Chances are, you won't see it—that's because the previous version of the service worker is still active. You should see the install event fire but not the activate event.

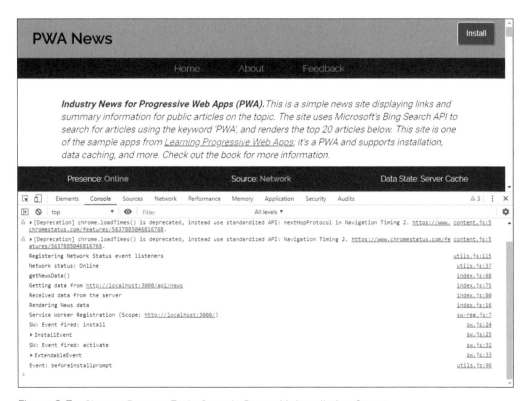

Figure 3.7    Chrome Browser Tools Console Pane with Installation Output

You have several options for activating this new service worker. I explain two here and cover programmatic options in "The Service Worker Lifecycle" later in the chapter. One option is to close and reopen the browser, then reload the app; this automatically enables the registered service worker.

Another option is to configure the browser developer tools to automatically activate the new service worker once it registers the service worker; this approach is useful only when debugging or testing a PWA. At the top of the service workers pane shown in Figure 3.5 is a checkbox labeled **Update on reload**; when you enable (check) this checkbox, the browser automatically updates and activates new service workers every time you reload the page with a new service worker.

Force the browser to activate the new service worker, then look at the console page. You should now see the output shown in Figure 3.8 with each network request logged to the console.

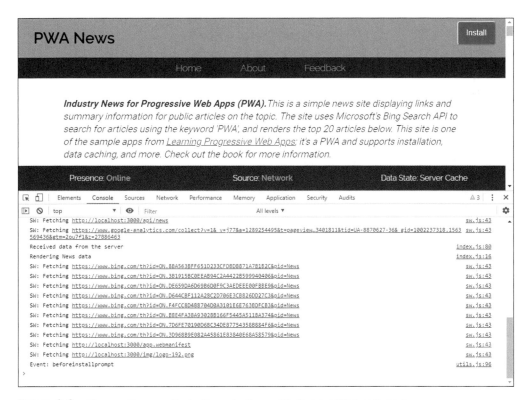

Figure 3.8    Chrome Browser Tools Console Pane with Service Worker Output

At this point, the app has a functioning service worker listening for all relevant events and fetching all requested resources from the network. In the next sections, we talk about service worker scope (as promised) and the service worker lifecycle; then I'll show you more you can do with service workers.

## Service Worker Scope

Remember early on when I said that one of the requirements for PWAs was that the browser accesses the app using a TLS (HTTPS) or localhost connection? This layer of security helps protect apps from rogue agents loading a service worker from another location.

As another layer of security, the location of the service worker file matters. When an app registers a service worker, by default the service worker can work only with resources hosted in the same folder location and below; anything higher up in the folder structure is ignored.

If you remember the code that registers the app's service worker (Listing 3.2), when registration completes successfully, the code executes the following line:

```
console.log(`Service Worker Registration (Scope: ${reg.scope})`);
```

This lets the developer know that the service worker registered correctly, and it outputs the contents of the `reg` object's `scope` property:

```
Service Worker Registration (Scope: http://localhost:3000/)
```

This scope defines the service worker's operational domain, the part of the web app over which the service worker has providence. In this example, the service worker scope begins at `localhost` and covers anything available under that host.

If your app includes content and code in subfolders, for example, `app1` and `app2`, and you want to register a separate service worker for each, you can easily do that. One option is to place the appropriate service worker in each folder; they automatically inherit scope from the folder where the service worker code is hosted when you register the service worker.

Another option is to set the scope for the service worker during registration; as an example, look at the following code:

```
navigator.serviceWorker.register('/sw1.js', {scope: '/app1/'})
```

This example registers the `sw1.js` service worker and sets the scope for the service worker to the `app1` folder. With this in place, this service worker will process fetch requests only for resources located in the `app1` folder and below (subfolders).

## The Service Worker Lifecycle

Each service worker cycles through multiple states from the moment the browser calls `navigator.serviceworker.register` until it's discarded or replaced by the browser. The states defined in the service worker specification are

- Installing
- Waiting
- Active

When an app registers a service worker, the browser

- Locates the service worker (requests it from a server)
- Downloads the service worker
- Parses and executes the service worker

If the browser can't download or execute the service worker, it discards the service worker (if it has it) and informs the code that called `navigator.serviceworker.register`. In Listing 3.3, that means that the `catch` clause executes and whatever code is there executes.

If the browser successfully downloads the service worker, it executes the service worker, and that's how the service worker registers the `install` and `activate` event listeners in the service worker code.

At this point, the `install` event listener fires; that's where a service worker creates its local cache and performs any additional setup steps. A representation of the service worker (version 1) at the Installing state is shown in Figure 3.9.

Figure 3.9    Service Worker 1 Installing

If a service worker isn't currently registered, the service worker transitions to the Active state, and it's ready to process fetch requests the next time the app reloads, as shown in Figure 3.10.

Figure 3.10    Service Worker 1 Active

If the web app attempts to install a new version of the service worker (version 2, for example), then the process starts all over again for the new service worker. The browser downloads and executes service worker v2, the v2 `install` event fires, and it completes its initial setup.

At this point, the app is still active and has an active service worker (v1) in play. Remember, the current service worker remains active until you close the browser (or at least all tabs running the web app) or the browser is configured to force reloading the service worker. With an existing service worker active, service worker v2 goes into a waiting state, as shown in Figure 3.11.

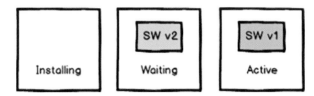

Figure 3.11   Two Service Workers in Play

Once the user closes all browser tabs running the app or restarts the browser, the browser discards service worker v1 and sets service worker v2 to active as shown in Figure 3.12.

Figure 3.12   Service Worker V2 Active

When you update the service worker and a user navigates to the app, the browser attempts to download the service worker again. If the newly downloaded service worker is as little as one byte different from the one currently registered, the browser registers the new service worker and the activation process kicks off again. Regardless of whether or not it has changed, the browser downloads the service worker every time the page reloads.

## Forcing Activation

Earlier I described ways to force the browser to activate a service worker by reloading the page or enabling the Reload option in the browser developer tools. Both of those options are great but require some action by the user. To force the browser to activate a service worker programmatically, simply execute the following line of code somewhere in your service worker:

```
// force service worker activation
self.skipWaiting();
```

You'll typically perform this action during the `install` event, as shown in Listing 3.7.

Listing 3.7   **Fourth Service Worker Example: `sw-37.js`**

```
self.addEventListener('install', event => {
  // fires when the browser installs the app
  // here we're just logging the event and the contents
  // of the object passed to the event. the purpose of this event
  // is to give the service worker a place to setup the local
  // environment after the installation completes.
  console.log(`SW: Event fired: ${event.type}`);
```

```
      console.dir(event);
      // force service worker activation
      self.skipWaiting();
});

self.addEventListener('activate', event => {
      // fires after the service worker completes its installation.
      // It's a place for the service worker to clean up from previous
      // service worker versions
      console.log(`SW: Event fired: ${event.type}`);
      console.dir(event);
});

self.addEventListener('fetch', event => {
      // fires whenever the app requests a resource (file or data)
      console.log(`SW: Fetching ${event.request.url}`);
      // next, go get the requested resource from the network,
      // nothing fancy going on here.
      event.respondWith(fetch(event.request));
});
```

## Claiming Additional Browser Tabs

In some cases, users may have multiple instances of your app running in separate browser tabs. When you register a new service worker, you can apply that new service worker across all relevant tabs. To do this, in the service worker's activate event listener, add the following code:

```
// apply this service worker to all tabs running the app
self.clients.claim()
```

A complete listing for a service worker using this feature is provided in Listing 3.8.

Listing 3.8  **Fifth Service Worker Example: sw-38.js**

```
self.addEventListener('install', event => {
      // fires when the browser installs the app
      // here we're just logging the event and the contents
      // of the object passed to the event. the purpose of this event
      // is to give the service worker a place to setup the local
      // environment after the installation completes.
      console.log(`SW: Event fired: ${event.type}`);
      console.dir(event);
      // force service worker activation
      self.skipWaiting();
});
```

```
self.addEventListener('activate', event => {
    // fires after the service worker completes its installation.
    // It's a place for the service worker to clean up from previous
    // service worker versions
    console.log(`SW: Event fired: ${event.type}`);
    console.dir(event);
    // apply this service worker to all tabs running the app
    self.clients.claim()
});

self.addEventListener('fetch', event => {
    // fires whenever the app requests a resource (file or data)
    console.log(`SW: Fetching ${event.request.url}`);
    // next, go get the requested resource from the network,
    // nothing fancy going on here.
    event.respondWith(fetch(event.request));
});
```

## Observing a Service Worker Change

In the previous section, I showed how to claim service worker control over other browser tabs running the same web app after a new service worker activation. In this case, you have at least two browser tabs open running the same app, and in one tab a new version of the service worker was just activated.

To enable the app running in the other tabs to recognize the activation of the new service worker, add the following event listener to the bottom of the project's sw.js file:

```
navigator.serviceWorker.addEventListener('controllerchange', () => {
  console.log("Hmmm, we're operating under a new service worker");
});
```

The service worker controllerchange event fires when the browser detects a new service worker in play, and you'll use this event listener to inform the user or force the current tab to reload.

## Forcing a Service Worker Update

In the world of single-page apps (SPAs), browsers load the framework of a web app once, and the app then swaps in the variable content as often as needed while the user works. These apps don't get reloaded much because users simply don't need to. This is kind of a stretch case, but if you're doing frequent development on the app or know you're going to update your app's service worker frequently, the service worker's registration object (reg in all the source code examples so far) provides a way to request an update check from the app's code

To enable this, simply execute the following line of code periodically to check for updates:

```
reg.update();
```

The trick is that you must maintain access to the registration object long enough that you can do this. In Listing 3.9, I took the service worker registration code from Listing 3.2 and modified it a bit.

First, I created a variable called `regObject`, which the code uses to capture a pointer to the `reg` object exposed by the call to `navigator.serviceWorker.register`. Next, I added some code to the registration success case (the `.then` method) that stores a pointer to the `reg` object in the `regObject` variable and sets up an interval timer for every 10 minutes. Finally, I added a `requestUpgrade` function that triggers every 10 minutes to check for a service worker update.

Listing 3.9   **Alternate Service Worker Registration: `sw-reg2.js`**

```
// define a variable to hold a reference to the
// registration object (reg)
var regObject;

// does the browser support service workers?
if ('serviceWorker' in navigator) {
  // then register our service worker
  navigator.serviceWorker.register('/sw.js')
    .then(reg => {
      // display a success message
      console.log(`Service Worker Registration (Scope: ${reg.scope})`);
      // Store the `reg` object away for later use
      regObject = reg;
      // setup the interval timer
      setInterval(requestUpgrade, 600000);
    })
    .catch(error => {
      // display an error message
      let msg = `Service Worker Error (${error})`;
      console.error(msg);
      // display a warning dialog (using Sweet Alert 2)
      Swal.fire('Registration Error', msg, 'error');
    });
} else {
  // happens when the app isn't served over a TLS connection
  // (HTTPS) or if the browser doesn't support service workers
  console.warn('Service Worker not available');
  // we're not going to use an alert dialog here
  // because if it doesn't work, it doesn't work;
  // this doesn't change the behavior of the app
  // for the user
}

function requestUpgrade(){
  console.log('Requesting an upgrade');
  regObject.update();
}
```

You could even trigger execution of this code through a push notification if you wanted to force the update only when you publish updates by sending a special notification message whenever you publish a new version of the service worker.

### Service Worker ready Promise

There's one final service worker lifecycle topic I haven't covered yet. The serviceWorker object has a read-only ready property that returns a promise that never rejects and sits there waiting patiently until the service worker registration is active. This gives your service worker registration code a place to do things when a page loads with an active service worker.

We already have the install and activate events, both of which get involved during service worker registration and replacement. If your app wants to execute code only when a service worker is active, use the following:

```
if ('serviceWorker' in navigator) {
  navigator.serviceWorker.ready.then((reg) => {
    // we have an active service worker working for us
    console.log(`Service Worker ready (Scope: ${reg.scope})`);
    // do something interesting...

  });

} else {
  // happens when the app isn't served over a TLS connection (HTTPS)
  console.warn('Service Worker not available');
}
```

You'll see an example of this in action in Chapter 6.

# Wrap-Up

In this chapter, we covered a lot about service workers and have one running in our app. You learned all about the service worker lifecycle and the special events and methods the service worker provides developers.

Unfortunately, the service worker we have doesn't do much. In the next chapter, we'll expand the capabilities of the service worker and explore many ways to manage caching the resources used by the app.

# 4

# Resource Caching

In Chapter 3, "Service Workers," we added a service worker to a web app and learned all about the service worker lifecycle. The service worker didn't do much of anything, but at least we got one working in the app. In this chapter, we cover many of the ways you can cache web app content using a service worker.

Web apps use a cache for two reasons: to speed up app loading and so the app, or parts of the app, function when the system running the app does not have network connectivity. Launching a web app using cached resources is one of the things that makes Progressive Web Apps (PWAs) perform more like native mobile apps. When the app UI appears quickly, users don't mind too much if it takes a little longer to populate the page with data, whereas users get frustrated when it takes a long time to load the app UI and then even longer to load its data.

The caching strategy you pick depends on the nature of the web app you're writing and how much of it you want available when the browser running the app is offline.

## Service Worker Cache Interface

One of the core capabilities enabling service workers is the browser's Cache Interface.[1] This cache provides service workers with a built-in way to cache resources used by a web app. The cache is a local repository of request/response pairs; the request is an object representing the resource request from the web app, and the response is an object representing the response from the server for that specific resource.

With a properly populated cache, a service worker can respond to resource requests from the cache and the app doesn't know any better; as far as the app is concerned, those resources came directly from the web server. The cache doesn't just cache the resource files (for example, .css, .html, or .js files), it caches the full server response for the requested resource (which includes headers, other stuff, plus the actual requested file).

---

1. https://developer.mozilla.org/en-US/docs/Web/API/Cache

> **Note**
>
> The cache is an interface included with a browser's support for service workers, but you can use the cache outside of a service worker if you need for other parts of your application.

> **JavaScript and Promises**
>
> One of the things we haven't spent any time discussing is modern JavaScript development approaches and promises.[2] Stuffy old JavaScript used callbacks to enable asynchronous operation: when an app called an asynchronous function or method (which took some time to complete), the app passed in a function it wanted executed when the time-consuming process completed. When you had asynchronous tasks calling other asynchronous tasks, things became quite messy. This created a situation commonly known as *callback hell*[3] and created some very hard-to-read JavaScript code.
>
> Recent work by the JavaScript community introduced the concept of promises, a construct that fixes much of this problem. The reason JavaScript promises is important is that service workers and their associated cache mechanisms make heavy use of promises. In previous chapters, any function or method we called that used promises were easily handled by the `.then` and `.catch` methods tacked on to the end of the function or method call.
>
> In this chapter, we dig into topics that make much heavier use of promises, so you're going to have to be up to speed on how they work. This book isn't about promises, and there are a lot of great resources online that cover the topic better than I can. So, if you're not familiar and comfortable working with promises, why don't you put the book down for a little while and do some external reading on promises before picking this back up again?

The `Cache` interface exposes the following methods:

- `add`—Retrieves the requested resource from the network and adds the request (and associated response) to the cache.

- `addAll`—For an array of request objects, retrieves the requested resource represented by each object in the array and adds each result to the cache.

- `delete`—Deletes the specified request entry from the cache.

- `keys`—Returns a promise that resolves to an array of keys from the cache; keys in this case are request objects.

- `match`—Returns a promise that resolves to the response for the first matching request in the cache. Basically, the app passes in a request object, and this method returns the first matching response from the cache.

- `matchAll`—Returns a promise that resolves to an array of all request responses matching the specified request in the cache.

- `put`—Adds a request/response object pair to the cache.

We use most of these methods throughout the remainder of this chapter.

---

2. https://developers.google.com/web/fundamentals/primers/promises

3. http://callbackhell.com/

# Preparing to Code

The work we do in this chapter revolves around the code for the server app available in the book's GitHub repository at https://github.com/johnwargo/learning-pwa-code. I provided complete instructions for how to download the code and configure your development environment in the section "Preparing to Code" in Chapter 3. If you haven't already completed those steps, go there and complete them first before picking up here again.

> **Note**
>
> I'm writing most of this book on Windows (not because I work for Microsoft but because that's my primary development system). Consequently, all the file path examples in this chapter and beyond use the backslash (\) character as a path delimiter. If you're following these examples on a system running Linux or macOS, please just replace the backslash characters in the folder path examples with forward slashes (/), and everything will be OK.

Open a terminal window and navigate the terminal into the cloned project's `\learning-pwa-code\chapter-04\` folder. This folder contains the Chapter 4 version of the PWA News server app (which has all the code changes you were supposed to make in Chapter 3).

Install all the dependencies required by the app by executing the following command:

```
npm install
```

This command uses the Node Package Manager (npm) to install Node.js modules used by the server.

If you ran the `copy-config` command during the setup process in Chapter 3, you're good—skip ahead to running the `npm` command after the next paragraph. If not, copy the `config.ts` file from `\learning-pwa-code\chapter-03\app\` to `\learning-pwa-code\chapter-04\app\`. This copies the configuration file holding the Bing API key you used in Chapter 3. With the file copied, execute the following command:

```
tsc
```

This compiles the server's `.ts` files (including the copied `config.ts` file) into the `.js` files you see in the project root folder. You'll see some errors and warnings from the code's references to some of the objects in the code, but you should be OK if it all worked in Chapter 3.

With all the parts in place, it's time to start the server; in the terminal window, execute the following command:

```
npm start
```

If everything's set up properly in the code, the server will respond with the following text in the terminal:

```
pwa-news-server@0.0.1 start D:\learning-pwa-code\chapter-04
node ./bin/www
```

At this point, you're all set—the server is up and running and ready to serve content. If you see an error message, you must dig through any reported errors and resolve them before continuing.

To see the web app in its current state, open Google Chrome or a browser that supports service workers and navigate to

`http://localhost:3000`

After a short delay, the server should render the app as shown in Figure 3.1.

> **Tip**
>
> In this chapter, we're making a lot of changes to a node-based server app while the server runs.
>
> Rather than forcing you to kill the server and restart it every time you make changes, you can use nodemon[4] to automatically restart the node server process whenever you make changes to the server's web app.
>
> To use the module, follow the installation instructions on the module's home page, then use it to start the server by executing the following command:
>
> ```
> nodemon node bin/www
> ```
>
> instead of the npm start command described earlier.

## Caching Application Resources

One option for enabling app resource caching in a PWA is to preload the app with all the resources the app needs to launch. In the case of the PWA News app, it means caching the app UI and other required parts, then letting the app's code reach out to the server to get the latest data once the UI completes loading.

To do this, you can use a simple array like the following:

```
var urlList = [
  '/',
  '/app.webmanifest',
  '/index.html',
  '/css/custom.css',
  '/img/bing-logo.png',
  '/js/index.js',
  '/js/sw-reg.js',
  '/js/utils.js'
];
```

In this example, I built the array from the files I knew I had to have to render the app's home page in the browser. The first entry in the array is probably a surprise. When I tested this app against my local server, as you soon will, I found the server accepts either / or /index.html to load the app, so I had to accommodate both options in the cache.

---

4.  https://www.npmjs.com/package/nodemon

You don't need the app.manifest file either, since it doesn't matter when the app is already installed. I added it here to avoid the error the index.html file generates when loading the app offline and it tries to load the manifest.

Let's add this to the service worker and use it to cache some data. Open the project's service worker file (sw.js) located in \learning-pwa-code\chapter-04\public\sw.js. Copy the urlList array code from the previous example to the top of the file.

Next, update the install event listener to cache the web resources during service worker installation. Copy or type the following code to replace the existing install event in the sw.js file:

```
self.addEventListener('install', event => {
  console.log(`SW: ${event.type} event fired`);
  // the service worker is installing, so it's our chance
  // to set up the app. In this case, we're telling
  // the browser to wait until we've populated the cache
  // before considering this service worker installed
  event.waitUntil(
    // create a local cache for our app resources
    caches.open('pwa-learn-cache')
      // Once it's open...
      .then(cache => {
        console.log('SW: Cache opened');
        // cache all the resources from the array
        return cache.addAll(urlList);
      })
      .catch(error => {
        console.error(error);
      })
  );
});
```

What this code does is use the service worker event object's waitUntil method to instruct the browser to hold off completing the service worker installation process until the code in the parentheses completes. The method expects a promise, so internally it doesn't do anything until the promise resolves.

The code opens the cache, but other interesting stuff happens inside as well:

- The call to caches.open opens the pwa-learn-cache cache and returns a promise

- When the cache opens, the .then method of caches.open calls the cache's addAll method, which returns a promise

- The cache's addAll method uses the urlList array to request all the resources needed by the app. Given an array of URLs, addAll retrieves each target URL and adds the resulting response object for each to the cache. Our array doesn't look like an array of URLs, but from the scope of the running web app, it is.

At the end of all this code, the app has a new cache populated with the response objects for each element in the urlList array.

This code is just the first example of why I mentioned in the sidebar that you must understand promises to work with service workers and caches. The code is a lot less complicated than it would be with callbacks, but there's still a lot going on. Keeping your code's `.then` methods with the right promise or making sure you're returning a promise when you should will save you some troubleshooting time later.

Finally, update the `fetch` event listener so it looks to the cache first before reverting to the network for requested resources. Copy or type the following code to replace the existing `fetch` event in the project's `sw.js` file:

```
self.addEventListener('fetch', event => {
  console.log(`SW: ${event.type} ${event.request.url}`);
  // fires whenever the app requests a resource (file or data)
  event.respondWith(
    // check to see if it's in the cache
    caches.match(event.request)
      .then(response => {
        // if it is, then return the cached response
        // object from the cache
        if (response) {
          console.log(`SW: Return Cache ${event.request.url}`);
          return response;
        }
        // otherwise, tell the browser to go get the
        // resource from the network
        console.log(`SW: Return Network ${event.request.url}`);
        return fetch(event.request);
      })
  );
});
```

In this event listener, the code responds to the request with a promise; in this case, it is the promise from the call to `caches.match`. The `match` method returns a promise that should resolve to a `fetch` response. If the call to `match` finds the request, the code returns the `response` object from the cached request (essentially the result of the same request processed during the `install` event).

If the requested resource is not in the cache, the code returns a promise from the call to `fetch` to get the requested resource from the network. When the fetch completes, the code returns the result of the fetch (a response object containing the requested resource or an error) to the browser for processing.

Listing 4.1 shows the complete listing for this version of the service worker. The file is in the project's `\learning-pwa-code\chapter-04\public\service-workers` folder along with any other service worker files we create in this chapter.

Listing 4.1    **First Service Worker Example: sw-41.js**

```
var urlList = [
  '/',
  '/app.webmanifest',
  '/index.html',
  '/css/custom.css',
  '/img/bing-logo.png',
  '/js/index.js',
  '/js/sw-reg.js',
  '/js/utils.js',
];

self.addEventListener('install', event => {
  console.log(`SW: ${event.type} event fired`);
  // the service worker is installing, so it's our chance
  // to setup the app. In this case, we're telling
  // the browser to wait until we've populated the cache
  // before considering this service worker installed
  event.waitUntil(
    // create a local cache for our app resources
    caches.open('pwa-learn-cache')
      // once it's open...
      .then(cache => {
        console.log('SW: Cache opened');
        // cache all of resources from the array
        return cache.addAll(urlList);
      })
      .catch(error => {
        console.error(error);
      })
  );
});

self.addEventListener('activate', event => {
  // fires after the service worker completes its
  // installation. It's a place for the service worker
  // to clean up from previous service worker versions
  console.log(`SW: ${event.type} event fired`);
});

self.addEventListener('fetch', event => {
  console.log(`SW: ${event.type} ${event.request.url}`);
  // fires whenever the app requests a resource (file or data)
  event.respondWith(
    // check to see if it's in the cache
    caches.match(event.request)
      .then(response => {
        // if it is, then return the cached response
```

```
      // object from the cache
      if (response) {
        console.log(`SW: Return Cache ${event.request.url}`);
        return response;
      }
      // otherwise, tell the browser to go get the
      // resource from the network
      console.log(`SW: Return Network ${event.request.url}`);
      return fetch(event.request);
    })
  );
});
```

If you launched the app after you started the server, you have an existing service worker active for the app. Unregister the current service worker, as shown in Figure 3.5, then reload the app in the browser. When you open the developer tools pane and switch to the **Console** tab, you'll see that the cache opened, as shown in Figure 4.1.

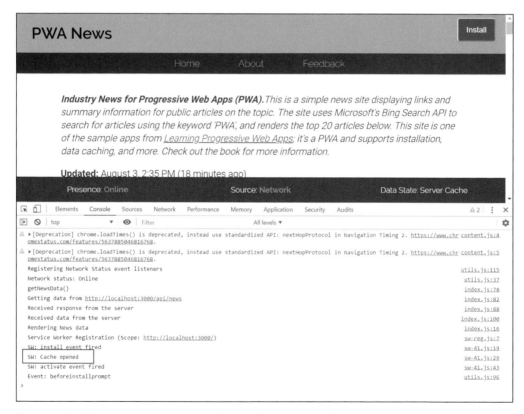

Figure 4.1   Chrome Developer Tools—Service Worker Cache Opened

The service worker doesn't activate until you reload the app again, so do that now and look at the output. You should see the service worker grabbing files from the cache or the network, depending on the resource, as shown in Figure 4.2.

Figure 4.2    Chrome Developer Tools—Service Worker Activated

Now, if you navigate to the Developer Tools **Cache Storage** tab, shown in Figure 4.3, you'll see the cache we created as well as the contents of the cache. As you work with different caching strategies and test out your apps, you can use this tool to view cached resources, delete the cache, and even delete individual cached resources.

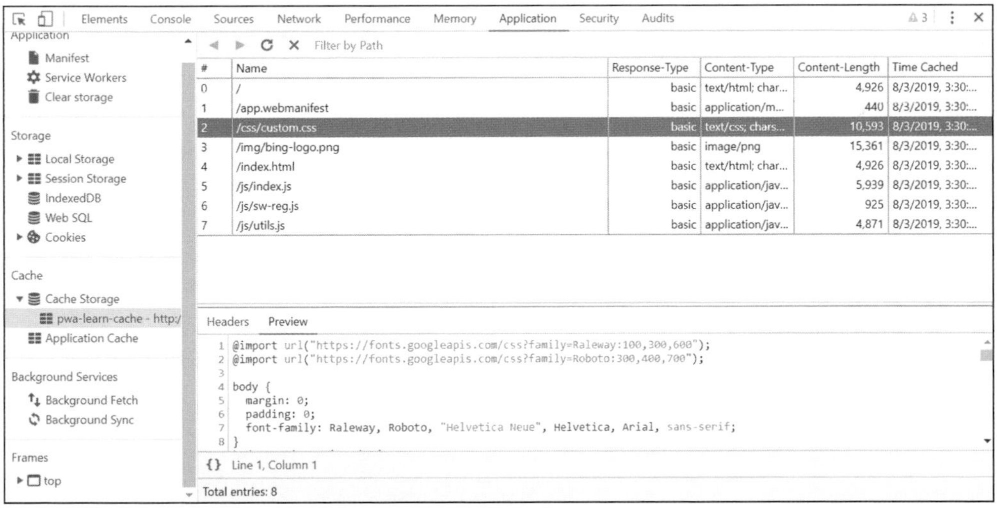

Figure 4.3    Chrome Developer Tools—Cache Storage

Earlier, I mentioned that many cache methods return response objects instead of just the cached resource (such as an HTML, a CSS, or a JavaScript file). Each column shown in the figure maps to the individual properties of the response object.

Let's take the app offline and see how the code works; there are three ways to do this:

- Stop the server by pressing Ctrl-C in the terminal window.

- Enable the Offline checkbox in the browser, as shown in the top-left corner of the Developer Tools **Service Workers** panel highlighted in Figure 4.4.

- Change the network status from Online to Offline in the Developer Tools **Network** pane highlighted in Figure 4.5.

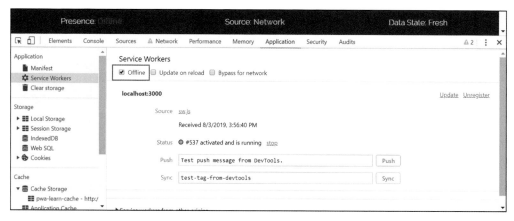

Figure 4.4   Chrome Developer Tools—Service Workers Panel

| Name | Status | Type | Initiator | Size | Time | Waterfall |
|---|---|---|---|---|---|---|
| index.html | 200 | fetch | sw.js:61 | 5.3 KB | 12 ms | |
| custom.css | 200 | fetch | sw.js:61 | 10.8 KB | 14 ms | |
| bing-logo.png | 200 | fetch | sw.js:61 | 15.5 KB | 17 ms | |
| index.js | 200 | fetch | sw.js:61 | 6.3 KB | 17 ms | |
| sw-reg.js | 200 | fetch | sw.js:61 | 1.4 KB | 19 ms | |
| utils.js | 200 | fetch | sw.js:61 | 5.2 KB | 19 ms | |
| android-icon-192x192.png | 200 | png | Other | 13.8 KB | 4 ms | |

37 requests   285 KB transferred   366 KB resources   Finish: 780 ms   DOMContentLoaded: 190 ms   Load: 584 ms

Figure 4.5   Chrome Developer Tools—Network Panel

Take the browser offline, then reload the page. When you look at the console output, you should see many of the app's resources loaded from cache and network errors for a bunch of other resources. That's good, that's what we expected.

Next, look at the page; it should appear as expected except that there's no data from Bing displayed. All you see is an error message, but we can probably do better than that. When you try to load the app's About and Feedback pages, you get the browser's default "Can't find that page" error message. We can do better there too. I'll show you how to fix those issues, but only after I show you first how to manage an app's caches.

## Offline Awareness

When Scott and I created the PWA News site, I knew we'd take the app online and offline as we tested different caching strategies, so I wanted to show in the app whether the app was online or offline—to make it as easy as possible for you to tell. The good news is that the browser makes this easy to implement.

If you look in the project's \public\js\utils.js file, you'll find the following:

```
// register event listener for both online and offline events
// so we can make sure the UI updates accordingly and it always
// understands the current state
console.log('Registering Network Status event listeners');
window.addEventListener("offline", setNetworkStatus);
window.addEventListener("online", setNetworkStatus);

function setNetworkStatus() {
    // what's our network status?
    let netStatus = (navigator.onLine) ? ONLINE_STR : OFFLINE_STR;
    // tell the developer (just for fun)
    console.log(`Network status: ${netStatus}`);

    // get a handle to the page body, offline status is page(body)
    // wide, just in case
    let body = document.querySelector('body');
    // remove the online class (if it's there)
    body.classList.remove(ONLINE_STR.toLowerCase());
    // remove the offline class (if it's there)
    body.classList.remove(OFFLINE_STR.toLowerCase());

    // set the presence value (text)
    document.getElementById('presenceValue').textContent = netStatus;
    // add the status class to the object
    body.classList.add(netStatus.toLowerCase());
}
```

The PWA News app registers event listeners for both the online and offline states, then updates content in the footer whenever the app enters either state. This is something you can easily add to your PWAs to let app users know in which mode the app is operating.

## Cache Management

We updated our service worker so it caches the main resources the app uses, but what do you do when you update your app? How do you get the new versions of the app's resources into the cache? In this section, we discuss strategies for managing your local cache before we get back into caching strategies in the sections that follow.

The first question we must answer as we address the issue of cache management is, How can the app recognize that there's a new version of the web app? In Chapter 2, "Web App Manifest Files," I mentioned that the browser downloads the service worker every time you reload the app and checks to make sure it is the same as the one currently installed in the browser. If it's different (if it changes by at least one byte), the browser parses the service worker, executes it, and completes the installation and activation process for the downloaded service worker. This process gives us a useful option: at the top of the service worker file, add a simple variable or constant like this:

```
// service worker version number
const SW_VERSION = 1;
```

This constant defines a simple service worker version identifier, and when you publish a new version of the app, you simply increment this value. With that in place, the browser detects the new service worker version, installs the updated service worker, and rebuilds the cache with the new resources for the app.

> **Note**
>
> The browser doesn't detect the service worker version change because it reads that variable. It detects the service worker version change because it does a byte comparison between the active service worker and the one loaded by the app. If they're different, the browser knows there's a new version to register. You could just as easily toggle the constant between two values every time you update your service worker to get the same result.

What if the new app version uses different file names for app resources? What do you do now? Well, one option is to simply cache the new resources and ignore the old ones using the code we already have in place in Listing 4.1. The problem with that approach is that you'll be caching data you'll never need again, and that's wasteful (especially on mobile devices).

Thinking out loud here for a while (no changes for you to make to the app), you could delete the cache using something like the following:

```
caches.delete('pwa-learn-cache').then(() => {
  console.log('SW: Cache deleted');
  // do something else here...

});
```

From the service worker lifecycle, we know that the current service worker is active and still using this cache. If we delete the cache under the current service worker, who knows what would happen (probably something bad). No, there must be a better way.

You could extend the earlier example to something like this:

```
// service worker version number
const SW_VERSION = 1;
// generates a custom cache name per service worker version
const CACHE_NAME = `pwa-learn-cache-v${SW-VERSION}`;
```

This generates a custom name for each app cache version: pwa-learn-cache-v1, pwa-learn-cache-v2, pwa-learn-cache-v3, and so on. Every time the swVersion value changes, the code generates a new cacheName and therefore a new cache. This requires a small change to the service worker's install event handler, replacing the original version's

```
caches.open('pwa-learn-cache')
```

with

```
caches.open(CACHE_NAME)
```

Here's the complete listing for the new event handler:

```
self.addEventListener('install', event => {
  console.log(`SW: ${event.type} event fired`);
  event.waitUntil(
    // create a local cache for our app resources
    caches.open(CACHE_NAME)
      // once it's open...
      .then(cache => {
        console.log('SW: Cache opened');
        // cache all of resources from the array
        return cache.addAll(urlList);
      })
      .catch(error => {
        console.error(error);
      })
  );
});
```

Well, this gets us part way there. We've created and populated a new cache for this new service worker version, but we left behind the previous cache. This would work, but we're still leaving around cached files we'll never use again. Users would never notice, but it would bother me.

OK, so what do we do? Well, the service worker activate event fires after the service worker installs and just as the service worker becomes the active service worker. At this point, the previous service worker is no longer active, so this seems like a perfect place for us to clean up the earlier cache. The following code shows an updated service worker activate event that deletes all caches that don't match the name of the current service worker's cache:

```
self.addEventListener('activate', event => {
  // fires after the service worker completes its installation.
  // it's a place for the service worker to clean up from
  // previous service worker versions
  console.log(`SW: ${event.type} event fired`);
```

```
// don't complete the activation until all the code runs
event.waitUntil(
  // get the list of cache keys (cache names)
  caches.keys().then(cacheList => {
    // don't stop until all complete
    return Promise.all(
      cacheList.map(theCache => {
        // is the cache key different than the
        // current cache name?
        if (CACHE_NAME !== theCache ) {
          // if yes, then delete it.
          return caches.delete(theCache);
        }
      })
    );
  })
);
});
```

The problem with this code is that it whacks all caches except for the current one used by the service worker. That's fine if the app has only one cache, but if the app opened other caches, this process would delete all caches except for the only one the service worker cares about.

In the following example, I added a CACHE_ROOT constant the service worker uses to build the cache name. We can use this to identify all versions of the service worker cache separately from all others:

```
// service worker version number
const SW_VERSION = 1;
// the root name for our cache
const CACHE_ROOT = 'pwa-learn-cache'
// generates a custom cache name per service worker version
const CACHE_NAME = `${CACHE_ROOT}-v${SW_VERSION}`;
```

All it requires is a slight change to the if statement buried deep within the activate event listener:

```
if ((CACHE_NAME !== theCache) && (theCache.startsWith(CACHE_ROOT))) {
```

Here's the complete listing for the event listener:

```
self.addEventListener('activate', event => {
  // fires after the service worker completes its installation.
  // it's a place for the service worker to clean up from previous
  // service worker versions
  console.log(`SW: ${event.type} event fired`);
  // don't complete the activation until all the code runs
  event.waitUntil(
    // get the list of cache keys (cache names)
    caches.keys().then(cacheList => {
      // don't stop until all complete
      return Promise.all(
```

```
        cacheList.map(theCache => {
          // is the cache key different than the
          // current cache name and has the same root?
          if ((CACHE_NAME !== theCache) && (theCache.startsWith(CACHE_ROOT))) {
            // if yes, then delete it.
            console.log(`SW: deleting cache ${theCache}`);
            return caches.delete(theCache);
          }
        })
      );
    })
  );
});
```

With this in place, the service worker creates a new cache during the `install` event and whacks all its older caches during the `activate` event, leaving other caches alone.

Listing 4.2 shows the complete code listing for this updated service worker. Take a moment to update the app's service worker with the code shown in Listing 4.2 and check it out. Make sure to check the contents of the local cache in the browser's Developer Tools (refer to Figure 4.3) to validate correct operation.

Listing 4.2    **Second Service Worker Example: sw-42.js**

```
// service worker version number
const SW_VERSION = 1;
// the root name for our cache
const CACHE_ROOT = 'pwa-learn-cache';
// generates a custom cache name per service worker version
const CACHE_NAME = `${CACHE_ROOT}-v${SW_VERSION}`;

var urlList = [
  '/',
  '/app.webmanifest',
  '/index.html',
  '/css/custom.css',
  '/img/bing-logo.png',
  '/js/index.js',
  '/js/sw-reg.js',
  '/js/utils.js',
];

self.addEventListener('install', event => {
  console.log(`SW: ${event.type} event fired`);
  // the service worker is installing, so it's our chance
  // to setup the app. In this case, we're telling
  // the browser to wait until we've populated the cache
  // before considering this service worker installed
  event.waitUntil(
    // create a local cache for our app resources
    caches.open(CACHE_NAME)
```

```
          // once it's open...
          .then(cache => {
            console.log('SW: Cache opened');
            // cache all of resources from the array
            return cache.addAll(urlList);
          })
          .catch(error => {
            console.error(error);
          })
      );
    });

    self.addEventListener('activate', event => {
      // fires after the service worker completes its installation.
      // it's a place for the service worker to clean up from previous
      // service worker versions
      console.log(`SW: ${event.type} event fired`);
      // don't complete the activation until all the code runs
      event.waitUntil(
        // get the list of cache keys (cache names)
        caches.keys().then(cacheList => {
          // don't stop until all complete
          return Promise.all(
            cacheList.map(theCache => {
              // is the cache key different than the
              // current cache name and has the same root?
              if ((CACHE_NAME !== theCache) &&
                (theCache.startsWith(CACHE_ROOT))) {
                // if yes, then delete it.
                console.log(`SW: deleting cache ${theCache}`);
                return caches.delete(theCache);
              }
            })
          );
        })
      );
    });

    self.addEventListener('fetch', event => {
      console.log(`SW: ${event.type} ${event.request.url}`);
      // fires whenever the app requests a resource (file or data)
      event.respondWith(
        // check to see if it's in the cache
        caches.match(event.request)
          .then(response => {
            // if it is, then return the cached response
            // object from the cache
            if (response) {
```

```
            console.log(`SW: Return Cache ${event.request.url}`);
            return response;
        }
        // otherwise, tell the browser to go get the
        // resource from the network
        console.log(`SW: Return Network ${event.request.url}`);
        return fetch(event.request)
    })
  );
});
```

## Return a Data Object on Error

In the app's current state, when the browser can't fetch news data from the server, the page displays the generic error highlighted above the footer in Figure 4.6. The app knows it received an error retrieving the data, so it correctly updates the status in the bottom-right corner of the page, but we can do better. Since we have a service worker working on our behalf, let's let it manage dealing with the fetch error.

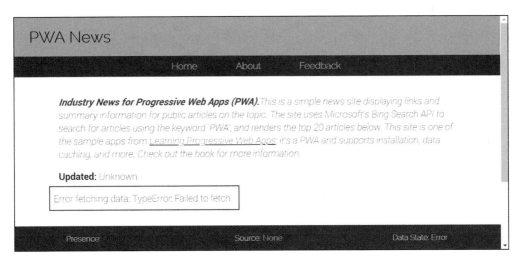

Figure 4.6   PWA News Data Fetch Error

What we want to do is to make the service worker return an empty data set plus the error code the app needs to update the footer. To do this, first add the following constant to the top of the project's public/sw.js file:

```
const EMPTY_NEWS_OBJECT = {
  "status": 3,
  "lastUpdated": 0,
  "items": []
};
```

What this does is create a generic `results` object the service worker serves up when it can't fetch the data live from the server. Next, update the `fetch` event listener so it deals differently with data requests than with the other resources used by the app. Start by refactoring the existing event listener so it looks like the following:

```
self.addEventListener('fetch', event => {
  console.log(`SW: ${event.type} ${event.request.url}`);
  // is the request for news data?
  if (event.request.url == `${location.origin}/api/news`) {
    console.log('SW: Data request detected');

  } else {
    // non-data request, so respond with fetch results
    event.respondWith(
      // check to see if it's in the cache
      caches.match(event.request)
        .then(response => {
          // if it is, then return the cached response
          // object from the cache
          if (response) {
            console.log(`SW: Return Cache ${event.request.url}`);
            return response;
          }
          // otherwise, tell the browser to go get the
          // resource from the network
          console.log(`SW: Return Network ${event.request.url}`);
          return fetch(event.request);
        })
    );
  }
});
```

The `if` clause checks to see whether the requested resource is the call to the server's News API. The `else` clause includes the original code from the initial event listener. If you load the app now, it should work exactly as it did before, even when offline, as all we've really done is add a log item for the special data case.

Now, in the event listener's `if` clause, after the log item, copy in the following code:

```
event.respondWith(
  // then see if you can get the data
  fetch(event.request)
    // oops, error, can't complete the fetch
    .catch(() => {
      // return the empty news object
      return new Response(JSON.stringify(EMPTY_NEWS_OBJECT),
        { "status": 200, "statusText": "Dummy data!" });
    })
);
```

The code tries to get the data from the server; if it can't, the `catch` method kicks in and responds with the empty news object we added at the top of the file. Now when you try to load the page while offline, you'll get the friendlier message already built into the app, as shown in Figure 4.7.

Figure 4.7    Delivering a Nicer Offline Error Message

Here's the complete source code listing for the new event handler:

```
self.addEventListener('fetch', event => {
  console.log(`SW: ${event.type} ${event.request.url}`);
  // is the request for news data?
  if (event.request.url == `${location.origin}/api/news`) {
    console.log('SW: Data request detected');
    event.respondWith(
      // then see if you can get the data
      fetch(event.request)
        // oops, error, can't complete the fetch
        .catch(() => {
          // return the empty news object
          return new Response(JSON.stringify(EMPTY_NEWS_OBJECT),
            { "status": 200, "statusText": "Dummy data!" });
        })
    );
  } else {
    // non-data request, so respond with fetch results
    event.respondWith(
      // check to see if it's in the cache
```

```
      caches.match(event.request)
        .then(response => {
          // if it is, then return the cached response
          // object from the cache
          if (response) {
            console.log(`SW: Return Cache ${event.request.url}`);
            return response;
          }
          // otherwise, tell the browser to go get the
          // resource from the network
          console.log(`SW: Return Network ${event.request.url}`);
          return fetch(event.request);
        })
    );
  }
});
```

You can easily tweak this code to deliver a different data object for each type of data request.

> **Note**
>
> I'm not going to show this here, because I think it's a silly example, but you could also use this approach to tweak an app's content or styling on the fly based on some condition in the app. Using the online/offline example from the earlier sidebar, you could code your service worker so it delivers different CSS styling depending on whether the app is online or not.
>
> I bring this up because most books and articles start their coverage of this topic showing how to return a flipped version of an image or setting a different background color for a page via CSS on the fly, and I didn't want you to wonder why I never mentioned these approaches. ☺

The complete service worker code for this example is in the project folder's `public\service-workers\sw-43.js` file.

## Adding an Offline Page

At the beginning of this chapter, I omitted the app's other pages, About and Feedback, from the list of cached resources. I did this not because I hate those pages but because I needed some pages to not be available offline for this section of the chapter.

When you take the browser offline and try to load the About or Feedback page, you'll see an error page like the one shown in Figure 4.8. This isn't the best experience for the user, as it's a stark change from the look and style of our app and doesn't say much about what really happened. The browser tries to explain some of the possible causes for the current error condition but fails rather spectacularly.

**This site can't be reached**

The webpage at **http://localhost:3000/about.html** might be temporarily down or it may have moved permanently to a new web address.

ERR_FAILED

Figure 4.8    Browser Page Error

We, on the other hand, know a lot more about why the pages didn't appear and can give the user a better experience through service workers. There are a lot of different options for doing this, ranging from simple to complex. I'll highlight a few here and leave it up to you to figure out some others.

One option is to use the approach taken in the previous section and return custom content whenever a fetch request fails. Rather than return a data object as we did in the previous section, you return text or HTML content.

Here's an example of a `fetch` event listener that does just that:

```
self.addEventListener('fetch', event => {
  console.log(`SW: ${event.type} ${event.request.url}`);
  event.respondWith(
    // check to see if it's in the cache
    caches.match(event.request)
      .then(response => {
        // if it is, then return the cached response
        // object from the cache
        if (response) {
          console.log(`SW: Return Cache ${event.request.url}`);
          return response;
        }
        // otherwise, tell the browser to go get the
        // resource from the network
        console.log(`SW: Return Network ${event.request.url}`);
        return fetch(event.request)
        .catch(() => {
```

```
            return new Response("Hmmm, I can't seem to access that page.");
        })
      })
  );
});
```

In this case, when the fetch fails, the code creates a new `Response` object with the content and returns it as the response for the fetch operation. When you try this in a browser in offline mode, you get the page shown in Figure 4.9.

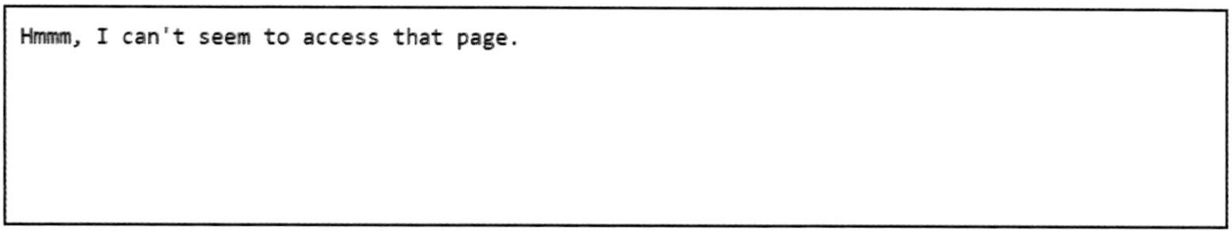

```
Hmmm, I can't seem to access that page.
```

Figure 4.9    Custom Content in Response to an Error

Now, you can get fancy and return HTML in the response; the affected portion of the code would look like this:

```
return fetch(event.request)
  .catch(() => {
    return new Response(
      "<!DOCTYPE html><html><body>" +
      "<h1>Access Error</h1>" +
      "<p>Hmmm, I can't seem to access that page.</p>" +
      "</body></html>",
      { headers: { "Content-Type": "text/html" } }
    );
  })
```

The code returns an HTML page to the browser, but the browser doesn't recognize it as an HTML page until you add the headers as a parameter when creating the `response` object. When you load the page in an offline browser, you get a slightly better experience because the resulting page has a formal heading and some styling around the body, as shown in Figure 4.10.

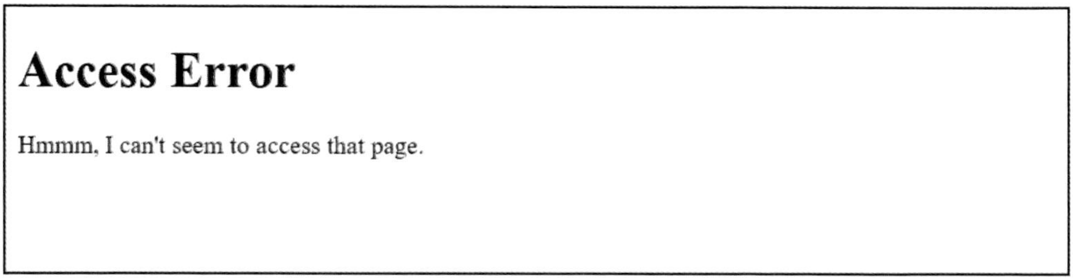

# Access Error

Hmmm, I can't seem to access that page.

Figure 4.10    An HTML Response to an Error

Now, you can spruce the content up with styling and other bells and whistles, but you're still generating HTML on the fly in your service worker, and that's not efficient. Another issue is that this is a rather brute-force approach, as it affects any requested resource even though the browser is already quite capable of dealing with missing images, CSS files, and other stuff. What we need is something that returns HTML only when the request says it can handle HTML, like this:

```
if (event.request.headers.get('accept').includes('text/html')) {
  // do something cool

}
```

Here's a full implementation with the accepts check and generated HTML content:

```
return fetch(event.request)
  .catch(() => {
    if (event.request.headers.get('accept').includes('text/html')) {
      return new Response(
        "<!DOCTYPE html><html><body>" +
        "<h1>Access Error</h1>" +
        "<p>Hmmm, I can't seem to access that page.</p>" +
        "</body></html>",
        { headers: { "Content-Type": "text/html" } }
      );
    }
  })
```

This approach limits when the service worker responds with HTML, but we're still sending generated HTML. What we should do is send a custom HTML page that looks like the rest of our site. We've already cached the site's CSS file, so all we need to do is add the page we want returned when the app is offline, or the browser can't locate the page.

The app already has this offline page located at the project's public\offline.html. Let's add the file to the cache using a slightly different approach. First, add the following line to the top of the project's sw.js file:

```
const OFFLINE_PAGE = '/offline.html';
```

This creates a reference to the offline file we'll use when we serve it up when a resource can't be found. Next, update the urlList array by adding OFFLINE_PAGE as the last item in the array:

```
var urlList = [
  '/',
  '/app.webmanifest',
  '/index.html',
  '/css/custom.css',
  '/img/bing-logo.png',
  '/js/index.js',
  '/js/sw-reg.js',
  '/js/utils.js',
  OFFLINE_PAGE
];
```

With this in place, the app knows about the offline file and will cache it during service worker installation. Finally, in the `fetch` event listener, add the following code to the end of the event listener when the service worker knows the resource isn't in the cache:

```
return fetch(event.request)
  .catch(() => {
    if (event.request.headers.get('accept').includes('text/html')) {
      return caches.match(OFFLINE_PAGE);
    }
  })
```

At this point, the service worker has given up; it knows the requested resource isn't in the cache, and it tried to fetch it from the network and failed. All that's left to do is serve up the offline file if it happens to be in the cache. Here's the complete event listener code:

```
self.addEventListener('fetch', event => {
  console.log(`SW: ${event.type} ${event.request.url}`);
  // is the request for news data?
  if (event.request.url == `${location.origin}/api/news`) {
    console.log('SW: Data request detected');
    event.respondWith(
      // then see if you can get the data
      fetch(event.request)
        // oops, error, can't complete the fetch
        .catch(() => {
          // return the empty news object
          return new Response(JSON.stringify(EMPTY_NEWS_OBJECT),
            { "status": 200, "statusText": "Dummy data!" });
        })
    );
  } else {
    // non-data request, so respond with fetch results
    event.respondWith(
      // check to see if it's in the cache
      caches.match(event.request)
        .then(response => {
          // if it is, then return the cached response
          // object from the cache
          if (response) {
            console.log(`SW: Return Cache ${event.request.url}`);
            return response;
          }
          // otherwise, tell the browser to go get the
          // resource from the network
          console.log(`SW: Return Network ${event.request.url}`);
          return fetch(event.request)
            .catch(() => {
              if (event.request.headers.get('accept')
```

```
                        .includes('text/html')) {
                        return caches.match(OFFLINE_PAGE);
                    }
                })
            })
        );
    }
});
```

Bring the app back online, reload the page in the browser, then go offline again. When you try to load the About page while the browser is offline, you get the much prettier page, shown in Figure 4.11, which includes the app header, menu, and footer, just like the rest of the app's pages. This is a much better user experience, don't you agree?

Figure 4.11   Serving an Offline Page from Cache

The complete service worker code for this example is in the project folder's `public\service-workers\sw-44.js` file.

## Implementing Additional Caching Strategies

Up to this point, we've built a powerful set of skills you can use to make your web apps more resilient to network issues. Our service worker example from the previous chapter delivered a service worker that merely logged each request and then went to the network for the latest version of every resource (no big deal). In this chapter so far, you've seen different variations on a service worker caching strategy that caches resources just in case they're not available from the network but gets the latest from the network whenever possible. Where a resource can't be dragged from the network and isn't in the cache, I've shown you several ways to soften the blow for your app users.

In this section, I expand coverage to include additional caching strategies you can use in your PWAs. This will by no means be complete coverage of all possible options, but with these as a base, you can probably cobble together any weird or obscure caching strategy you want for your own apps. What you implement for your apps depends on the app and how frequently app resources change.

For the following examples, I don't expect you to update the app with the different caching strategies shown. You can if you want to, but the purpose of the remainder of the chapter is to simply highlight other options for you to use.

## Cache-Only

For an installed PWA, especially simple apps such as the Tip Calculator from Chapter 2, the app is entirely static; there's no dynamic content in the app. You can easily build a URL array into the service worker and use it to cache all app resources at startup, as I showed in an earlier example. With that in place, the app works regardless of whether the browser has network connectivity.

In the PWA News app, only parts of the app rarely change. To enable the app to run even if the device running the app doesn't have network connectivity, you can update the urlList array from our recent service worker examples to contain every possible static resource needed by the app. With that in place, you can implement the cache-only approach highlighted in the following fetch event listener:

```
self.addEventListener('fetch', event => {
  console.log(`SW: ${event.type} ${event.request.url}`);
  // fires whenever the app requests a resource (file or data)
  event.respondWith(
    // check to see if it's in the cache
    caches.match(event.request)
      .then(function (response) {
        // if it is, then return the cached response
        // object from the cache
        if (response) {
          console.log(`SW: Return Cache ${event.request.url}`);
          return response;
        }
      })
  );
});
```

If the resource isn't in the cache, the code does nothing; the service worker lets the browser deal with its failure. In this case, the browser displays the generic resource-not-found error page shown in Figure 3.8. You can add an offline file to the resource array, as shown in an earlier example, which is needed only if you forget to put a file in the resource array. The `fetch` event listener code looks like the following:

```
self.addEventListener('fetch', event => {
  console.log(`SW: ${event.type} ${event.request.url}`);
  // fires whenever the app requests a resource (file or data)
  event.respondWith(
    // check to see if it's in the cache
    caches.match(event.request)
      .then(function (response) {
        // if it is, then return the cached response
        // object from the cache
        if (response) {
          console.log(`SW: Return Cache ${event.request.url}`);
          return response;
        }
        // otherwise check to see that the request accepts HTML
        if (event.request.headers.get('accept').includes('text/html')) {
          // then return the offline page
          console.log(`SW: serving offline page ${OFFLINE_PAGE}`);
          return caches.match(OFFLINE_PAGE);
        }
      })
  );
});
```

For this approach, I had to make sure every file the app needed to run was in the cache. What caused me the most pain was figuring out that I also needed the service worker file even though it was already installed. Remember, the browser requests the service worker file every time the page loads, regardless of whether the service worker changed.

The complete service worker code for this example is in the project folder's `public\service-workers\sw-45.js` file.

## Network First, Then Cache

For many apps, especially ones that display dynamic data, you want the app to always pull content from the network if possible, then fall back to the cache when the device running the app is offline.

Like the cache-only example from the previous section, with this approach, you build the list of static resources and use it to populate the cache at service worker activation. The service worker attempts to pull requested resources from the network and serves them from the cache if the network version is not available.

For dynamic sites, your cache of local files is a little different. What you need in the cache is all the resources required to render the app UI plus cached data or some extra content to explain why there's no data. You can spoof the data as we did earlier in the chapter, or, in the next chapter, I'll show you how to cache data for offline use.

With the list of cached resources in place, the following `fetch` event listener shows how to implement a network-first, cache-next approach:

```
self.addEventListener('fetch', event => {
  console.log(`SW: ${event.type} ${event.request.url}`);
  // fires whenever the app requests a resource (file or data)
  event.respondWith(
    // try to get the file from the network
    fetch(event.request)
      .catch(() => {
        // rats, network resources are not available
        // do we have it in the cache?
        console.log(`SW: Trying Cache ${event.request.url}`);
        return caches.match(event.request)
          .then(response => {
            // if it is, then return the cached response
            // object from the cache
            if (response) {
              console.log(`SW: Return Cache ${event.request.url}`);
              return response;
            }
          })
      })
  );
});
```

The complete service worker code for this example is in the project folder's `public\service-workers\sw-46.js` file.

## Network First, Update Cache

In all the examples so far, the cache we used was static, populated during service worker installation and never updated again. That's not very exciting, is it? This approach forces the service worker to manually rebuild the cache with every version, even if the file didn't change or wasn't used again.

Another approach is to let the service worker build the cache as the app runs, automatically populating the cache with every resource requested by the app. This one's a little tricky, so hold on while I lay it all out for you.

For the Tip Calculator app from Chapter 2, this is the perfect caching strategy. Every request the app makes is automatically cached. So, if you install the app or later try to hit the app while the device is out of network connectivity, the app will load, in its entirety, from cache.

When I implemented this caching strategy for the PWA News app, I was a little worried about the app's news data. The way that Bing structures its news results, the data comes back as a JSON object with URLs pointing to any images associated with the articles (typically thumbnail images). I didn't want to cache those images because they'd change with every news update and I didn't want to fill up the cache with unused images, nor did I want to figure out a way to clean them up either.

As I tested the code I'll share with you in a minute, I noticed that everything was taken care of automatically for me. Woohoo! Let me explain.

The following code implements a service worker `fetch` event listener that caches every request made by the server. What I found in my testing was that it cached every resource request, even the API request to the server to retrieve new data. What it didn't do was cache the image files—automatically, not because I did anything special to make that happen. Not only did it not cache the image files for me, the web app still displayed the image files for me when I disabled the network and reloaded the page. Surprised? Yeah, me too. Take a moment to look through the code, and I'll explain everything on the other side.

```
self.addEventListener('fetch', event => {
  console.log(`SW: ${event.type} ${event.request.url}`);
  // fires whenever the app requests a resource (file or data)
  event.respondWith(
    // try to get the file from the network
    fetch(event.request)
      // whew, we got it
      .then(response => {
        // do we have a valid response?
        if (response && response.status == 200) {
          // clone the response; it's a stream, so we can't
          // write it to the cache and return it as well
          let responseClone = response.clone();
          // try to open the cache
          caches.open(CACHE_NAME)
            // if we successfully opened the cache
            .then(function (cache) {
              console.log(`SW: Adding ${event.request.url} to the cache`);
              // then write our cloned response to the cache
              cache.put(event.request, responseClone);
            });
          // return the original response
          return response;
        } else {
          // return whatever error response we got from the server
          return response;
        }
      })
      .catch(() => {
        // rats, network resources not available
        // do we have it in the cache?
        console.log(`SW: Trying Cache ${event.request.url}`);
        return caches.match(event.request)
          .then(response => {
            // if it is, then return the cached response
            // object from the cache
            if (response) {
              console.log(`SW: Return Cache ${event.request.url}`);
              return response;
            }
          })
      }) // catch
  );
});
```

The complete service worker code for this example is in the project folder's
`public\service-workers\sw-47.js` file.

All right, for every resource request, this service worker does the following:

- Tries to retrieve the resource from the network.
- If it gets a response, it
  - Checks to see if the response is a valid response and not an error.
  - Clones the response (responses are streams, so the service worker can't pass a response to the browser and write it to the cache at the same time).
  - Writes the cloned response to the cache.
  - Returns the original response to the requestor.
  - If the response is not an HTTP response of 200 (success), it returns whatever it has to the requestor for the requestor to process the error.
- If it gets an outright error, it
  - Checks the cache to see if it has the resource there.
  - If it does, it returns the cached resource.
  - Otherwise, it does nothing and lets the requestor deal with the problem (usually by showing the page shown in Figure 4.8).

As it processes all of the app's requests, the requests return with different response types[5] depending on how the browser views the resource origin based on security settings in the browser and in the app. Remember, service workers are all about security, so if you request a resource that's not from the same origin as the page requesting the resource, the service worker's going to complain. The way it complains here is by not caching the resource.

The service worker checks to see if the response is valid using the following code:

```
if (response && response.status == 200)
```

Some examples you see online do it this way:

```
if (response && response.status == 200 && response.type == 'basic')
```

What I learned while testing this code is that the service worker will cache only resources with a `type` of `basic`. There's no need to check the type before caching. All the same origin requests arrive as `basic`, but the image requests, because their origin is Bing and not the local API server, are ignored and not added to the cache. To prove this, look at Figure 4.12; it shows the complete resource cache generated by this `fetch` event listener.

---

5. https://developer.mozilla.org/en-US/docs/Web/API/Response/type

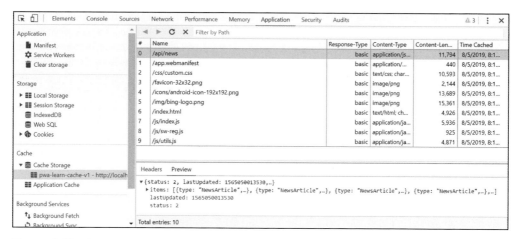

Figure 4.12    Populated PWA News Cache

I mentioned that when I disabled the network, the news thumbnail image files appeared properly in the app anyway. Why is that? Well, even though I have a service worker managing my cache for me, the browser still respects the cache headers[6] in the response headers. If you look at a Bing image request response header in Fiddler,[7] as shown in Figure 4.13, you'll see that Bing sets a Cache-Control max-age header for the resource in the highlighted portion of the image. This tells the browser it can hold onto the image for 1,209,600 seconds if it wants to.

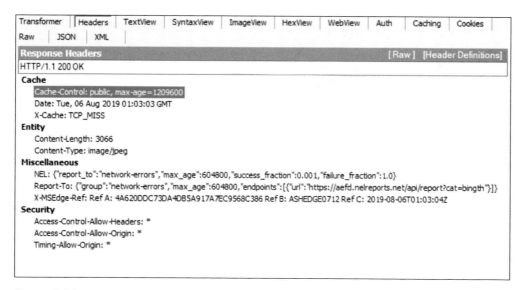

Figure 4.13    Bing Image Headers in Fiddler

6. https://developer.mozilla.org/en-US/docs/Web/HTTP/Headers/Cache-Control

7. https://www.telerik.com/fiddler

So, even though you think the service worker has complete control over the cache, it doesn't; it has complete control over cache storage, but the browser controls the HTTP cache. If you're testing away and notice that things aren't refreshing properly for you, that's because the browser may be interfering. You may have to clear the browser cache for your latest resources to show.

Now, I'm not saying you couldn't configure the cross-origin resource sharing (CORS) settings for the app and allow the service worker to cache resources from another origin—you probably can. My point is that this extra security protection worked in my favor as I implemented this service worker caching example.

## Wrap-Up

In this chapter, I demonstrated many ways to build service workers to cache resources for a PWA. I didn't show you every possible caching strategy, but I did give you a strong foundational skill set to use when you're building your own PWAs.

In the next chapter, I'll demonstrate how to use other capabilities of the browser to cache web app data and deliver a different sort of offline operation than what I showed here.

# 5

# Going the Rest of the Way Offline with Background Sync

In Chapter 4, "Resource Caching," I showed multiple ways to use service workers and the browser cache to cache web app resources, including application data. That approach works well, because the browser is great at fetching resources and displaying them. All we did was add a manager in the middle to enable our code to control what's cached and what isn't. In this chapter, we take app resource caching to the next level, using service workers to enable offline mode in a web app.

We do this using the PWA News app's Feedback page, shown in Figure 5.1. This page currently displays randomly generated feedback from imaginary site visitors. As we work through the concepts in this chapter, we'll add an input form to the page to capture visitor sentiment and use the service workers background sync capabilities to ensure that the feedback is delivered to the server when the browser has a network connection to the server.

The version of the app used in this chapter is a little different than the one from previous chapters. In this version, I added the ability to submit sentiment to the server and update the graph shown in the figure. In the coding examples for this chapter, we'll make that functionality work even when the browser is offline, uploading recorded sentiment when the browser goes back online.

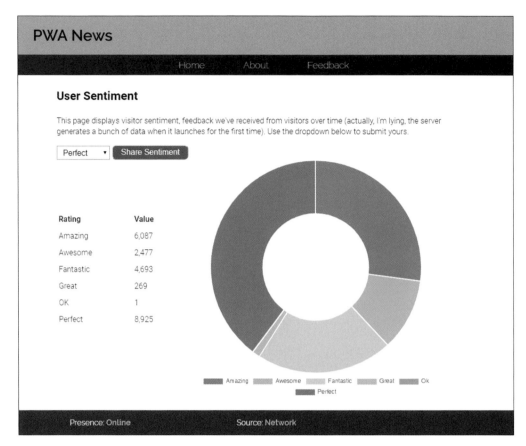

Figure 5.1   PWA News Feedback Page

# Introducing Background Sync

Background sync is a feature of service workers that enables web apps to ensure that user actions aren't lost even if the browser loses network connectivity or the user switches to another app or closes the browser or the current tab. By user actions, I mean things such as:

- Sending an email.
- Subscribing to a newsletter.
- Sending a chat message.
- Submitting a form.

These actions are essentially any data created or updated in the web app that must be sent to the server. The ability to fire and forget application actions and know they'll complete whenever the app (or the browser running the app) regains network connectivity is one of the most powerful mobile app features enabled by PWAs. Web apps do this using service workers.

Developers have two options for implementing this functionality. The first option uses the background sync process described in this chapter, and the other uses the browser's ability to send data between a service worker and a web app, as described in Chapter 7, "Passing Data between Service Workers and Web Applications." The difference between these two approaches is that background sync accommodates scenarios in which service workers can't send the data to the server immediately; instead, the service worker retries the action whenever the browser comes back online (described later). The options described in Chapter 7 enable a web app to pass data between the two entities (the web app and the service worker) and is really only useful for real-time operations.

To make background sync work, web apps share data with service workers through a local database shared by both processes:

- The service worker and the web app both open the same local database. The web app writes action data to the database. The service worker reads action data from the database, then deletes the action data once it's successfully processed.

- When the web app invokes background sync to process an action, it writes the action's data to the database and then fires off a sync event to the service worker to process the action.

- When the service worker's sync event listener receives the event, code in the event listener reads the action data from the local database and does whatever it needs to do with the data.

- If the browser (and therefore the service worker) has network connectivity and can perform the action immediately, it does so. If the action succeeds, the service worker deletes the action's data from the local database. If it fails, it leaves the data there for the service worker to try again the next time the sync event fires.

- If the browser doesn't have network connectivity, the browser queues up the event to try it again later.

- This can't go on forever. After some time, the action must be allowed to pass on to greener pastures. In this case, the browser warns the service worker that it's done trying to complete the action and the service worker must remove the data from the queue.

Figure 5.2 illustrates the process, highlighting the roles the browser and service worker play in the process.

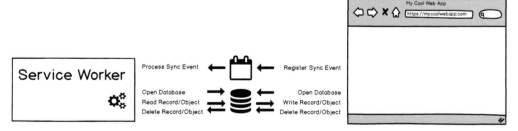

Figure 5.2   Service Worker Background Sync Overview

To trigger a sync, a web app registers a sync event using the following code:

```
navigator.serviceWorker.ready.then(reg => {
  reg.sync.register('doThatSyncThing');
});
```

The call to `navigator.serviceWorker.ready` returns the current service worker's registration object (`reg` in the example) that the code uses to register the sync event.

You can also register a sync event inside of a service worker using the following code:

```
self.registration.sync.register('doThatSyncThing');
```

Passed to the `register` method is an event tag identifying the sync event to the service worker. You can use as many event tags as you want in your app; all that matters is that your service worker has code ready to recognize and process the events (through their tags) as they come in.

The browser keeps track of all registered sync events for the service worker and fires the service worker's sync event listener repeatedly until the sync event resolves. How a browser manages processing sync events varies depending on the browser, but in general it works like this:

- If the browser is online, the sync event fires immediately, and the service worker attempts to complete the action.
- If the action fails, the browser waits a while before trying again. It should implement an exponential backoff strategy whereby easy subsequent retry occurs after a longer delay.
- If the browser status changes from offline to online, the browser tries again.
- Eventually, the browser gives up, since it knows it's likely never going to complete the action—how long that takes is up to the browser.

Inside the service worker, an event listener listens for the sync event, then executes the code associated with the event tag passed with the sync event:

```
self.addEventListener('sync', event => {
  if (event.tag == 'doThatSyncThing') {
    // do something...

  }
});
```

Tags play an interesting role in this process. In general, an app uses tags in a way that enables them to group actions together. For example, a chat app may use something like the following:

- AddContact
- DeleteMessage
- SendMessage
- SetStatus

Then, in the service worker, the app processes each type of event using separate blocks of code. When the app registers a sync event, and there's already a sync event queued up with the same tag, the browser's SyncManager doesn't add a new event to the queue using the duplicate tag; it sees that there's already an event registered with that tag and ignores the new one, assuming the service worker code processing the event will deal with all queued data for that particular event.

Earlier I mentioned that the browser will eventually give up on processing a sync event after it tried a bunch of times without success. When this happens, it stops processing that event until another sync event fires with the same tag. To protect itself from the impact of this, a web app could generate a unique tag for each event, as shown here:

```
navigator.serviceWorker.ready.then(reg => {
  reg.sync.register('doThatSyncThing-1');
});
```

Then, when processing events, the service worker processes all events that match the specific pattern, as shown here:

```
self.addEventListener('sync', event => {
  if (event.tag.startsWith('doThatSyncThing')) {
    // do something...

  }
});
```

Like everything else with service workers, background sync makes heavy use of promises, so if you didn't feel comfortable with promises in the previous chapter, you should probably sharpen your promises skills now before continuing.

## Offline Data Sync

Service workers don't offer capabilities for managing offline data in web apps. Service workers run in the browser but don't run all the time, and this limitation prohibits their use for real background data synchronization. The browser wakes the service worker up only when there's work for it to do, using the event interfaces shown in previous chapters. Unfortunately, there is no option for data events or timer events in service workers (today anyway; apparently, Google has periodic background sync[1] as a feature, but it's not mainstream).

If your app requires data synchronization, you should use one of the many sync software development kits (SDKs) available in the market, such as the ones from Amazon,[2] Couchbase,[3] and Firebase.[4] Don't write your own—it's been done many times already by people smarter than both of us.

---

1. https://www.chromestatus.com/feature/5689383275462656
2. https://aws.amazon.com/appsync/
3. https://www.couchbase.com/
4. https://firebase.google.com/

There is, in some cases, a simple workaround for this limitation. The PWA News app pulls data from a server process, and users can't make any updates to the news data, so a service worker–based sync process can be easily implemented. The approach uses browser push and the poke-and-pull method (illustrated in Figure 5.3):

- Update the service worker so it creates a local database to host the news data and populates it on activation.

- Modify the web app so it looks for its news data in the database rather than getting it from the server.

- Update the server process so it sends a push notification (the poke) to the app whenever there's new news data available. Push notifications are covered in Chapter 6, "Push Notifications."

- Add a push event listener to the service worker so it requests a news update from the server (the pull) whenever it receives a specific push notification from the server.

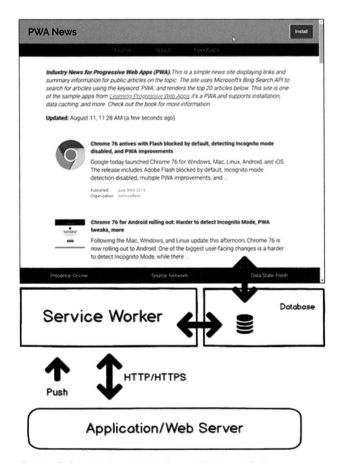

Figure 5.3    Service Worker-Based Poke and Pull

The code in the web app that loads the news data from the local database must have a fallback process that pulls the data from the server when it runs on a browser that doesn't support service workers. Remember, PWAs are progressively enhanced web apps, so they must work even when service workers aren't supported.

Is the poke-and-pull method the best approach for this app? No, probably not. But, for certain types of apps, it is a reasonable approach. For example, many chat apps are built this way, using push notifications or web sockets to let client applications know about new data.

# Choosing a Sync Database

As I showed in an earlier section, browsers don't provide a direct mechanism for a web app to send data to service workers for background sync. You must create a shared store accessible by both the web app and the service worker. The web app queues data to the store then notifies the service worker to pick it up and process it via the sync event.

There are many different ways you can implement this cache store in your web apps, but Google recommends, and pretty much all background sync examples on the Internet use, the browser's IndexedDB[5] database. The reason, described in *Live Data in the Service Worker*[6] and *Offline Storage for Progressive Web Apps*[7] is that IndexedDB is asynchronous and available to service workers. Other available options have limitations (synchronous instead of asynchronous, limits in data types, etc.). With that in mind, we'll use an IndexedDB database for the PWA News sync queue.

I'm not going to provide a detailed primer on IndexedDB; there's a lot of good material available online that I'm not inclined to duplicate. I will, however, share some core examples here to get us both on the same page before we jump into enhancing the PWA News app for background sync. If you're already familiar with IndexedDB, feel free to skip ahead to the next section.

IndexedDB provides an outdated approach to asynchronous operation. Instead of using the modern promise approach, it uses callbacks to handle asynchronous operations. This approach leads quickly to the callback hell described in Chapter 4. To help developers avoid this problem, the community responded with several promise-based wrappers around the IndexedDB API; you can use these libraries to simplify the readability of your IndexedDB code. For this book, I decided not to arbitrarily point you to a third-party library and instead to show you the old-school callback hell way to interact with an IndexedDB database, but in the enhancements to the PWA News application, I'll implement a promise-based approach.

## Create Database

To create an IndexedDB database, a web app must execute the following code:

```
var theDB = window.indexedDB.open(DATABASE_NAME, 1);
```

5.  https://developer.mozilla.org/en-US/docs/Web/API/IndexedDB_API
6.  https://developers.google.com/web/ilt/pwa/live-data-in-the-service-worker
7.  https://developers.google.com/web/fundamentals/instant-and-offline/web-storage/offline-for-pwa

This creates a `theDB` object pointing to an open database. If the database doesn't exist when this code executes, the browser creates the database. Service workers don't have access to the browser's `window` object, so to create/open an IndexedDB database, use the following code:

```
var theDB = self.indexedDB.open(DATABASE_NAME, 1);
```

We want code that runs in both locations, because both the web app and the service worker must open the database, so we'll use the latter example for the PWA News app.

Remember, there are no promises here, so to report or act on database operation success or failure, you must create callback functions. For IndexedDB operations, the two you'll care the most about are the `onsuccess` and `onerror` callbacks:

```
theDB.onsuccess = function (event) {
  console.log('Open Success');
  // get a handle to the database
  let db = event.target.result;

};

theDB.onerror = function (event) {
  console.log('Open Error');

};
```

The `onsuccess` callback gets an `event` object you can use to get a handle to the database object, as shown in the example. If you keep a reference to the `theDB` object, you can also access the database later from

```
let db = theDB.result;
```

The database object also supports other callback options:

```
theDB.onclose = function (event) {
  console.log('Closing database');

}

theDB.abort = function (event) {
  console.log('Aborting...');

}
```

You may have noticed that I passed a number to the call to the IndexedDB open method. That parameter specifies the version number for the database. When you open an IndexedDB database, the browser checks the version number you provided against an existing database; if they're different, as will be the case when you create a new database, the browser fires the `onupgradeneeded` callback. This callback gives the app an opportunity to make any database changes required by the new version.

```
theDB.onupgradeneeded = function (event) {
  console.log('Database upgrade needed');
  // do something interesting

}
```

## Create Store

IndexedDB groups related data into stores;[8] you'll need at least one store to manage data for an application. The database's onupgradeneeded callback is the perfect place to create it:

```
const STORE_NAME = 'my-store';
theDB.onupgradeneeded = function (event) {
  console.log('Database upgrade needed');
  // does the store already exist?
  if (!db.objectStoreNames.contains(STORE_NAME)) {
    // no? Then create it
    console.log('creating store');
    var storeOptions = { keyPath: "idx", autoIncrement: true };
    var theStore = db.createObjectStore(STORE_NAME, storeOptions);
  } else {
    console.log('Store already exists');
  }
}
```

As you can probably tell from the name, IndexedDB is an indexed database, so you can create multiple indexes in a store and use them to more easily locate objects in the store. In this example, I simply created an index called idx that the IndexedDB engine automatically increments for me. This gives the app a unique identifier it can use to locate and work with every object in the store.

## Add Data

Using the previous examples as a base, an app adds a data object to a store by executing the following code:

```
// get a handle to the db
let db = theDB.result;
let transaction = db.transaction([STORE_NAME], "readonly");
// get a handle to the store
let store = transaction.objectStore(STORE_NAME);
// finally, add the record
let request = add({ key1: 'value1', key2: 'value2' });
```

That's a lot of intermediate variables, right? Well, you can simplify this using the following:

```
// get a handle to the db
let db = theDB.result;
let request = db.transaction([STORE_NAME], "readwrite")
  .objectStore(STORE_NAME)
  .add({ key1: 'value1', key2: 'value2' });

request.onsuccess = function (event) {
  console.log('Add successful');

};
```

---

8. https://developer.mozilla.org/en-US/docs/Web/API/IDBObjectStore

```
request.onerror = function (event) {
  console.error('Add failure');

}
```

And, of course, we have the standard callback functions for success and failure.

IndexedDB is a transactional database system, so an app must make database updates through transactions that you can later abort using the `transaction` object's abort method. IndexedDB is also an indexed object store, so in this last example, the code added an object to the store.

To see the results of this code, you must use the browser's developer tools, as shown in Figure 5.4. In this figure, I opened the developer tools, then selected the **Application** tab across the top. Next, I expanded the IndexedDB option in the left navigator. Chrome doesn't automatically refresh the contents of this pane, so I had to right-click on **IndexedDB** and select **Refresh IndexedDB** before I could see my database and store.

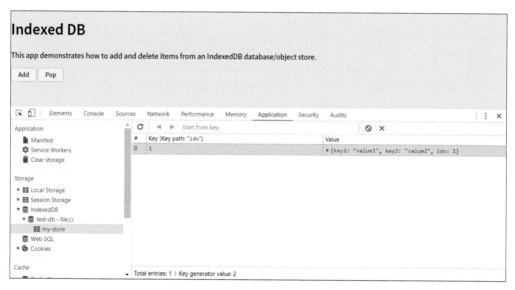

Figure 5.4   Chrome Developer Tools: IndexedDB Data

In the figure, you can see the generated key plus the data object associated with the key. Notice that the code didn't include the `idx` object in the call to add, but IndexedDB added it there automatically for you.

## Delete Objects

To delete an object from an IndexedDB store, an app needs the index for the object and the following code:

```
// get a handle to the db
let db = theDB.result;
let idx = 3;
```

```
let request = db.transaction([STORE_NAME], "readwrite")
  .objectStore(STORE_NAME)
  .delete(idx);

// success!
request.onsuccess = function (event) {
  console.log('Item ${idx} deleted');

}

// ugh, error
request.onerror = function (event) {
  console.log('Unable to delete item ${idx}');

}
```

## Iterating through Data Using Cursors

To loop through objects in a store, IndexedDB uses cursors. A web app opens a cursor and, if the cursor is not null, uses it to retrieve the data object from the store:

```
// get a handle to the db
let db = theDB.result;
var request = db.transaction([STORE_NAME], "readonly")
  .objectStore(STORE_NAME)
  .openCursor();

// success!
request.onsuccess = function (event) {
  // get a handle to the cursor
  var cursor = event.target.result;
  // do we have a valid cursor?
  if (cursor) {
    // get the object value from the cursor
    item = cursor.value;
    // do something with the item's data

    // Move onto the next item in the object store
    cursor.continue();
  } else {
    // no valid cursor, so must be at the end

  }
};

// ugh, error
request.onerror = function (event) {
  console.error(request.error);
  // do something with the error

}
```

In the example, `item` points to the object {key1: "value1", key2: "value2", idx: 1}. The app accesses object values through `item.key1`, `item.key2`, and `item.idx`.

When the app's done processing the data accessible through the cursor, it makes a call to `cursor.continue`, which moves the cursor to the next object in the store. This creates a loop where the cursor moves through all the store objects until it's done, at which point the code drops into the `else` clause to wrap up the process.

This is basically everything you need to know about IndexedDB to add background sync to the PWA News app. In the following sections, we'll take the PWA News app's existing process of directly POSTing user sentiment data to the server and update it to use service worker background sync instead. I'll fill in all the details about how background sync works through the code we add to the PWA News app.

## Preparing to Code

The work we do in this chapter revolves around the code for the server app available in the book's GitHub repository at https://github.com/johnwargo/learning-pwa-code. I provided complete instructions for how to download the code and configure your development environment in the section "Preparing to Code" in Chapter 3, "Service Workers." If you haven't already completed those steps, go there and complete them before picking up here again.

Open a terminal window and navigate the terminal into the cloned project's `\learning-pwa-code\chapter-05\pwa-news\` folder. This folder contains the Chapter 5 version of the PWA News server application (which has all the code changes you were supposed to make in Chapter 4).

Install all the dependencies required by the application by executing the following command:

```
npm install
```

This command uses the Node Package Manager (npm) to install Node.js modules used by the server.

If you ran the `copy-config` command during the setup process in Chapter 3, you're good. Skip ahead to running the `npm` command after the next paragraph. If not, copy the `config.ts` file from `\learning-pwa-code\chapter-03\app\` to `\learning-pwa-code\chapter-05\pwa-news\app\`. This copies the configuration file holding the Bing API key you used in Chapter 3. With the file copied, execute the following command:

```
tsc
```

This compiles the server's `.ts` files (including the copied `config.ts` file) into the `.js` files you see in the project root folder. You'll see some errors and warnings from the code's references to some of the objects in the code, but you should be OK if it all worked in Chapter 3.

With all the parts in place, it's time to start the server. In the terminal window, execute the following command:

```
npm start
```

If everything's set up properly in the code, the server will respond with the following text in the terminal:

```
pwa-news-server@0.0.1 start D:\learning-pwa-code\chapter-05\pwa-news
node ./bin/www
```

At this point, you're all set—the server is up and running and ready to serve content. If you see an error message, you must dig through any reported errors and resolve them before continuing.

To see the web app in its current state, open Google Chrome or a browser that supports service workers and navigate to:

```
http://localhost:3000
```

After a short delay, the server should render the app as shown in Figure 3.1. At this point, you're ready to code.

# Enhancing the PWA News Application

The PWA News app's Feedback page displays a chart showing visitor sentiment for the site. There's also a select dropdown and a button that visitors can use to submit their feedback about the site. At this point in our chapter progression, the app's service worker has code to cache all app resources, including the feedback page, so the app will run using cached data even when the device running the app is outside of network coverage. What the app can't do, which we'll fix in this chapter, is accept visitor feedback when offline. We'll use background sync and some complicated code writing to accomplish this goal. Ready?

For the rest of this chapter, we'll work with the web app code found in the book's GitHub repository's chapter-05\pwa-news\public\ folder.

## Preparing the Service Worker for Background Sync

Start by opening the project's public\sw.js file; the service worker doesn't know anything about sync events, so we're going to fix that first. At the bottom of the file, add the following code:

```
self.addEventListener('sync', event => {
  // process the Submit Feedback action items
  if (event.tag == 'feedback') {
    console.log('SW: Processing Feedback sync');

  } else {
    console.log(`SW: Unrecognized sync event: (${event.tag})`);
  }
});
```

This code registers the event listener for the sync event discussed earlier in the chapter. It doesn't do anything right now except log the event; we'll add code later to act on feedback requests. For now, we just need a place in the service worker to validate the changes we'll make next in the feedback page.

> **Tip**
>
> Remember, the service worker registers from the project's `index.html` file, so if you make any changes to the service worker, you must refresh the service worker from the app's home page, then switch to the Feedback page to see the results.

## Updating the Web App to Use Background Sync

Now we need to implement changes to the web app's Feedback page so it uses background sync to upload visitor sentiment to the server.

Open the project's `public\js\feedback.js` file. If you look toward the bottom of the file, you'll find the following code:

```
function submitFeedback(event) {
  console.log('submitFeedback()');
  // get the selected item from the form
  var theSelect = document.getElementById("sentiment");
  let selectedSentiment = theSelect.options[theSelect.selectedIndex].value;
  console.log(`Selected Sentiment: ${selectedSentiment}`);
  // do we have a sentiment value? We should.
  if (selectedSentiment) {
    // post it to the server using fetch
    postFeedback(selectedSentiment);
  }
}
```

This is the function that starts the process of sending visitor feedback to the server. The code checks to see that there's a sentiment value selected on the page, then calls the file's `postFeed-back` function to POST it to the server using `fetch`. There should always be one value selected on the form, but I prefer to make few assumptions when it comes to user input.

> **Note**
>
> I could easily have added the code to POST the feedback to the server in this same function, and the first version of this code did that, but I knew I'd be expanding the capabilities of this function in this chapter, so I broke the POST process into a separate function to make things cleaner for you later.

Now, replace the call to `postFeedback` with the following code:

```
if ('serviceWorker' in navigator && 'SyncManager' in window) {
  // yes, save the feedback to the database

} else {
  // service worker or background sync not supported
  // so we'll do this the old-fashioned way
  postFeedback(selectedSentiment);
}
```

This is an `if` statement that checks to see if the browser supports service workers and the `SyncManager`. If they are supported, IndexedDB should be available as well, and we can create a database and use background sync to submit visitor sentiment to the server. You could also check for `indexedDB` if you wanted to be completely thorough.

This code moves the call to `postFeedback` to the `else` clause of the `if` statement. It is our fallback to regular operation when a visitor uses a browser that doesn't support service workers. If you omit this fallback, users on older browsers will curse you because their sentiment never seems to make it to the server no matter how many times they click the button.

The last piece of this is to add the code that opens the local IndexedDB database and writes the selected sentiment value to the store. Now, the code we're about to add refers to functions that don't exist yet, so don't panic when your integrated development environment (IDE) or editor starts to complain about some of the code. Add the following code inside the `if` clause of the `if/then` statement we just added a minute ago; I'm hoping it's clear what the code does, but I'll explain it anyway on the other side.

```
openIDB()
  .then(db => {
    queueFeedback(db, selectedSentiment)
      .then(() => {
        console.log('submitFeedback: Successfully queued feedback');
      })
      .catch(error => {
        console.error(error);
        Swal.fire('Sync Error', error, 'error');
      })
  })
```

All right, what's happening here is that we're calling a function called `openIDB` (which we haven't written yet), and when the promise it returns resolves, we're calling another function called `queueFeedback` (another function we haven't written yet) that adds the selected sentiment value to the database we just opened. Both functions return promises, so that's why there are so many `thens` and `catches` in the code. The call to `openIDB` returns a handle to the database that was just created or opened. The code then passes that value to the call to `queueFeedback` so it doesn't have to figure out where it's writing its stuff.

Here's the complete listing for the new `submitFeedback` function:

```
function submitFeedback() {
  // the user tapped the Share Sentiment button
  console.log('submitFeedback()');
  // get the selected item from the form
  var theSelect = document.getElementById("sentiment");
  let selectedSentiment = theSelect.options[theSelect.selectedIndex].value;
  // do we have a sentiment selected? we should
  if (selectedSentiment) {
    console.log(`submitFeedback: '${selectedSentiment}' selected`);
    // is IndexedDB supported?
    if ('serviceWorker' in navigator && 'SyncManager' in window) {
      // yes, save the feedback to the database
```

```
    openIDB()
      .then(db => {
        queueFeedback(db, selectedSentiment)
          .then(() => {
            console.log('submitFeedback: Successfully queued feedback');
          })
          .catch(error => {
            console.error(error);
            Swal.fire('Sync Error', error, 'error');
          })
      })
  } else {
    // service worker or sync not supported
    // so do this the old-fashioned way
    postFeedback(selectedSentiment);
  }
 }
};
```

The call to Swal refers to SweetAlert2,[9] an open source library for generating visually pleasant alert dialogs in web apps. The first quoted string is the title for the alert dialog. The second parameter (error) is the error message returned from the call to queueFeedback, and the final 'error' tells SweetAlert2 to display an error dialog.

The complete feedback code for this example is in the project folder's \public\chapter-code\feedback-5.js file.

With that code in place, it's time to start writing the code that interacts with the local IndexedDB database. If you remember the description of how the sync process works, both the web app and the service worker access the database at different times. The web app accesses the database with write capabilities when it queues up the sentiment value for processing. The service worker accesses the database with read and write capabilities when it processes the queue of sentiment data. The service worker requires read and write access because it uses read to read the data from the store and write when it deletes the value after successful processing.

If you're thinking the way I do about the code I just described, you probably realized that both processes probably run some of the same code to do what they do. To minimize typing the same code in both the web app and service worker, we're going to put all of it in the same file and access it from both processes. Add a new file to the project called \public\js\db.js, then open it for editing.

At the top of the file, add the following constants:

```
// IndexedDB DB and Store Properties
const DB_NAME = 'pwa-news';
const DB_VERSION = 1;
const STORE_NAME = 'feedback-store';
```

---

9.  https://sweetalert2.github.io/

The module code references the store name in several places, so I moved the value into a constant so I wouldn't have to type it everywhere. I pulled the database version into a constant here because I may change this value with every app version, and I wanted the value in an easy place to find later. It's used only once, but putting it at the top of the file makes it very easy to change later. Finally, I moved the database name into a constant here just because; I had everything else here, so it made sense to have the database name here as well.

Next, add the `openIDB` function, shown next, to the new file. The function uses the concepts described earlier in the chapter to open the IndexedDB database and return the database object to the calling function so it can use it later to interact with the open database.

```
function openIDB() {
  // open the indexedDB database used by the app
  return new Promise((resolve, reject) => {
    // open the feedback database
    var theDB = self.indexedDB.open(DB_NAME, DB_VERSION);

    // success, callback
    theDB.onsuccess = function (event) {
      console.log('openIDB: Successfully opened database');
      // success, return the db object result
      resolve(event.target.result);
    };

    // define the database error callback
    theDB.onerror = function (event) {
      let msg = `Database error ${theDB.error}`;
      console.error(`openIDB: ${msg}`);
      Swal.fire('Database Error', msg, 'error');
      // reject the promise, we failed
      // include the error message with the failure
      reject(msg);
    };

    theDB.onupgradeneeded = function (event) {
      console.log('openIDB: Database upgrade needed');
      // get a handle to the database
      var db = event.target.result;
      // does the store already exist?
      if (!db.objectStoreNames.contains(STORE_NAME)) {
        // no? Then create it
        console.log(`openIDB: Creating store ${STORE_NAME}`);
        // first create the configuration options for the store
        var storeOptions = { keyPath: "idx", autoIncrement: true };
        // then create the store
        var theStore = db.createObjectStore(STORE_NAME, storeOptions);
      };
    };
  });
};
```

When you open an IndexedDB database, and it doesn't already exist, the act of opening it creates it for you.

In the onupgradeneeded callback, the code checks to see if the store we need already exists and creates it if it's not already there.

The last piece of this is the code that follows. It takes the selected sentiment and stores it in the database inside the feedback-store store. Like the generic example shown earlier, this function adds a data object (in this case, { timestamp: Date.now(), sentiment: feedback }) to the store, then registers the sync event that tells the service worker there's data there for it to process. I added a timestamp to the data object thinking I might display the submission date in the console as the service worker processed each queued feedback item. I never got around to doing that, but if you want, it's there for you to use in your version of the app.

Add the following function to the project's db.js file:

```javascript
function queueFeedback(db, feedback) {
  console.log('queueFeedback()');
  return new Promise((resolve, reject) => {
    let request = db.transaction([STORE_NAME], "readwrite")
      .objectStore(STORE_NAME)
      .add({ timestamp: Date.now(), sentiment: feedback });

    request.onsuccess = function (event) {
      console.log('queueFeedback: Successfully added feedback');
      navigator.serviceWorker.ready.then(reg => {
        console.log('queueFeedback: Registering sync event');
        // fire off the sync request
        // to the service worker
        reg.sync.register('feedback')
          .then(() => {
            // tell the user
            Swal.fire({
              type: 'info',
              title: 'Request Queued',
              text: 'Your sentiment rating was queued for ' +
                'submission to the server.',
              footer: 'Please refresh the page.'
            });
            // and resolve the promise
            resolve();
          })
          .catch(() => {
            // I can't think of why this would happen
            reject();
          })
      });
    };
  });
};
```

```
    request.onerror = function (event) {
      // unable to create transaction
      reject(db.error);
    };
  });
};
```

### Refresh on Success

In the `submitFeedback` function in `feedback.js`, the code automatically refreshes the feedback data after successfully POSTing the data to the server. The function can do this because the code submitting the data to the server and refreshing the feedback data are both available to the Feedback page. When we switch the app to use background sync for this, we lose the ability to refresh the page because the page never knows that the data was successfully submitted. The service worker does, but it can't directly refresh the page on success (more on this later).

In the background sync version of the app, the success dialog suggests a page refresh after queueing the data in the hope that the data will upload by the time the user refreshes the page. If the browser is offline or there's some other issue with data upload, then refreshing the page is a waste of time.

There are other options.

What I could have done, but chose not to, was check for network connectivity when the user clicks the Share Sentiment button, then call `postFeedback` if there's network connectivity and `queueFeedback` when there isn't. This approach would give the app an online/offline feel, and it's probably the best solution, but as this chapter is all about going offline, I decided to go all in on offline.

I mentioned earlier that the browser can't directly refresh the page, and that was almost a lie (sorry). In the next chapter, you'll learn about a mechanism that allows service workers to send messages to a browser window, and you could easily use this feature to send a refresh message to the web app after uploading data. I left that topic out of this chapter because it makes more sense in the next chapter and would have thoroughly complicated this chapter. If you want extra credit, after finishing the next chapter, come back here and implement it and post your results somewhere for others.

The complete service worker code for this example is in the project folder's `\public\chapter-code\db.js` file.

Finally, we need the Feedback page to load this new JavaScript file. Open the project's `public\feedback.html` and add the following lines to the bottom of the page's body section, along with the other script tags.

```
<!-- Add the indexedDB module -->
<script src='js/db.js'></script>
```

Save your changes to both files and refresh the Home page, then switch to the Feedback page. Remember, the service worker loads from the project's `index.html` file but reigns over all pages of the app. You must refresh the Home page to load the updates to the service worker, then switch to the Feedback page to load the other half of our code changes.

Select one of the sentiments from the dropdown field and click the Share Sentiment button. The app should immediately display the queue dialog shown in Figure 5.5. At this point, we think we queued some data for processing by the service worker—let's check.

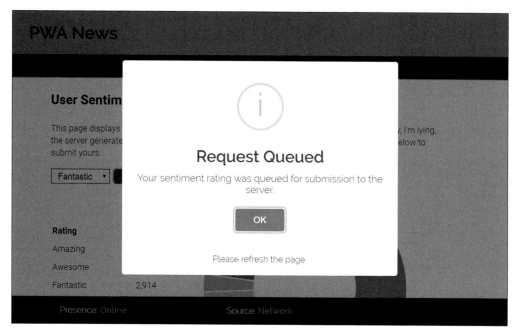

Figure 5.5   Submitting Feedback

Open the browser's developer tools and switch to the **Application** tab. In the left navigator, expand the **IndexedDB** option and refresh the content. You should see the feedback data queued up, as shown in Figure 5.6.

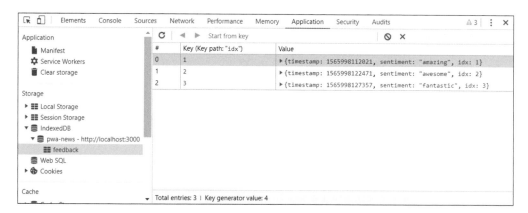

Figure 5.6   Feedback Data Queued for Processing by the Service Worker

The data is still there because we haven't added any code to the service worker to process it; we'll do that in the next section.

## Finishing the Service Worker

Our final step is to complete the enhancements to the service worker so it knows how to process the feedback queue. In this section, we

- Add a reference to the new db.js file in the service worker.
- Finish the code in the service worker's sync event listener.
- Add two functions to the project's db.js file.

Open the project's public\sw.js file and add the following lines of code to the top of the file:

```
// the server feedback API endpoint
const FEEDBACK_URL = `${self.location.origin}/api/sentiment`;
```

This service worker will use this constant to connect to the server when processing feedback.

Next, add the following line to the install event listener before the call to skipWaiting():

```
self.importScripts('./js/db.js');
```

Remember, the service worker runs in a separate process from the web application, so it doesn't know you've already loaded the database library in the feedback page. You must explicitly load it in the service worker as well.

The result should look like this:

```
self.addEventListener('install', event => {
  // fires when the browser installs the app
  // here we're just logging the event and the contents
  // of the object passed to the event. the purpose of this event
  // is to give the service worker a place to set up the local
  // environment after the installation completes.
  console.log(`SW: Event fired: ${event.type}`);
  console.dir(event);
  self.importScripts('./js/db.js');
  // Force service worker activation
  self.skipWaiting();
});
```

All right, now it's time to tell the service worker how to process the queued feedback. The code we're about to work through is probably the most complicated code we've looked at so far. To explain it as cleanly as I can, I've identified the high-level steps in Table 5.1.

Table 5.1   **Service Worker Queue Processing**

| Step | Method | Description |
|---|---|---|
| 1 | `event.waitUntil()` | Instruct the service worker to stay active (not shut down) until everything completes. |
| 2 | `getFeedbackItems()` | Get the feedback items from the data store. |
| 3 | `Promise.all()` and `data.items.map()` | Loop through each of the feedback items. |
| 4 | `fetch()` | POST the data to the server. |
| 5 | `deleteFeedback()` | Delete processed feedback from the data store. |

Everything the service worker does here is asynchronous, so I'm using promises everywhere. Update the existing `sync` event listener in the project's service worker; I'll explain the code after you're done reading it:

```
self.addEventListener('sync', event => {
  console.log('SW: Sync event fired');
  if (event.tag === 'feedback') {
    console.log('SW: Processing Feedback sync');
    event.waitUntil(
      getFeedbackItems()
        .then(data => {
          return Promise.all(
            // loop through the items array
            data.items.map(function (feedbackItem) {
              // update the server if you can
              return fetch(FEEDBACK_URL, {
                method: 'post',
                headers: { 'Content-Type': 'application/json' },
                body: JSON.stringify({
                  sentiment: feedbackItem.sentiment
                })
              })
                .then(() => {
                  // successfully posted,
                  // so whack the record at idx
                  return deleteFeedback(data.db, feedbackItem.idx)
                })
                .catch(error => {
                  // ruh roh, something went wrong
                  console.error(`SW: Sync Error: ${error}`);
                })
            })
          );
        }));
```

```
  } else {
    // this should never happen
    console.log(`SW: Unrecognized sync event (${event.tag})`);
  }
});
```

Here's what the code does:

- We don't want the browser to shut down the service worker until it's done processing the queue, so the code starts with a call to `event.waitUntil()` that instructs the browser's `SyncManager` to wait until we're done.

- `waitUntil` expects a promise, so `getFeedbackItems` creates one (we'll add that code in a minute) then gets to work.

- `getFeedbackItems` connects to the database and builds an array of all the feedback items, then returns it as the result of the promise.

- The code loops through the feedback item array. It uses `Promise.all()` to say it's about to make a bunch of promises, and it will resolve (success) if they all succeed or reject (failure) if one fails.

- Inside that `Promise.all()`, it uses the `array.map()` method to execute a function against each element in the array.

- The `map` method makes a call to `fetch()` to POST the data to the server for each item in the array. The `fetch` method returns a promise, so that makes `Promise.all()` happy.

- When the POST completes successfully, the code calls `deleteFeedback()`, which deletes the processed item from the store (we'll add that code in a minute). Oh, and `deleteFeedback` returns a promise too.

The result is that if the feedback item is successfully uploaded to the server (using `fetch`), the processed item is deleted from the store. That was a lot of code to accomplish that simple act, wasn't it?

The reason promises are so important here is because promises give the code an easy way to filter results back up through the cascading method calls I just explained. If just one part of the process fails, for whatever reason, we want everything left in place for the next time the service worker wakes up to process the queue. Promises give us an easy way to manage that.

The complete service worker code for this example is in the project folder's `\public\chapter-code\sw-5.js` file.

Most browser developer tools provide a way to send sync messages to a service worker directly from the browser (rather than having to do it via code). In Google's Chrome browser, open the developer tools, switch to the **Application** tab, then select the Service worker panel, as shown in Figure 5.7. Look for the Sync input field highlighted in the figure. Enter the sync tag, then click the Sync button to send the tag to the `sync` event listener in the service worker.

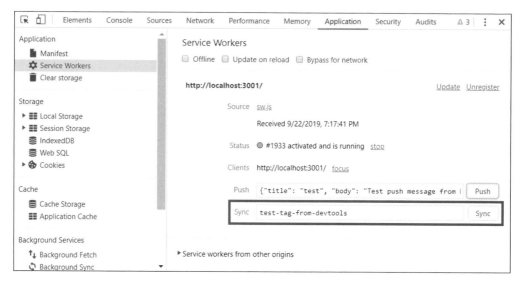

Figure 5.7   PWA News Feedback Page

With the service worker all sorted out, open the project's `public/js/db.js` file. At the bottom of the file, add the following function:

```
function getFeedbackItems() {
  console.log('DB: getFeedbackItems()');

  // will hold the array of feedback items
  let items = [];

  return new Promise((resolve, reject) => {
    // yes, save the feedback to the database
    openIDB()
      .then(db => {
        let request = db.transaction([STORE_NAME], "readonly")
          .objectStore(STORE_NAME)
          .openCursor();

        // success!
        request.onsuccess = function (event) {
          // get a handle to the cursor
          var cursor = event.target.result;
          // do we have a valid cursor?
          if (cursor) {
            // add the feedback item to the array
            items.push(cursor.value);
            // move onto the next item in the object store
            cursor.continue();
          } else {
```

```
            // no valid cursor, so must be at the end
            resolve({ db: db, items: items });
          }
        };

        // ugh, error
        request.onerror = function (event) {
          console.error(request.error);
          reject(request.error);
        }
      })  // openIDB()
      .catch(error => {
        console.error(request.error);
        reject(request.error);
      }); // openIDB()
  });
};
```

The getFeedbackItems function

- Creates a promise (of course).

- Opens the IndexedDB database.

- Opens a cursor in the feedback-store store.

- Loops through each object in the store using the cursor.

- Adds each object to the items array.

- Returns the database object and items array.

The code returns the database object so the next function we'll add can use it. It simplifies the code by not forcing me to create an ugly global variable to hold the database object.

Finally, add the following function to the bottom of the db.js file:

```
function deleteFeedback(db, idx) {
  console.log(`DB: deleteFeedback: Processing index ${idx}`);

  return new Promise((resolve, reject) => {
    // create a transaction
    let request = db.transaction([STORE_NAME], "readwrite")
      .objectStore(STORE_NAME)
      .delete(idx);

    // success!
    request.onsuccess = function (event) {
      console.log(`DB: deleteFeedback: Item ${idx} deleted`);
      resolve(idx);
    }
```

```
    // ugh, error
    request.onerror = function (event) {
      console.log(`DB: deleteFeedback: Unable to delete item ${idx}`);
      console.error(transaction.error);
      reject(transaction.error);
    }
  });
};
```

The deleteFeedback function

- Gets the database object and the index of the feedback item being deleted as parameters passed to the function.

- Creates a promise (of course).

- Using the database object, creates a transaction for managing the changes to the data store.

- Deletes the selected item (using its index as a pointer to the feedback item being deleted).

The complete service worker code for this example is in the project folder's \public\chapter-code\db.js file.

At this point, we're done with code changes. Save all the changes to the files, switch to the browser, and refresh the Home page. Remember, the service worker loads from the project's index.html file but reigns over all pages of the app. You must refresh the Home page to load the updates to the service worker, then switch to the Feedback page to load the other half of our code changes.

Go ahead and submit a new feedback, then switch to the Developer Tools console page. You should see your queued-up feedback items processing, as shown in Figure 5.8.

Figure 5.8   Chrome Developer Tools Console Output Showing Feedback Queue Processing

Try taking the application offline and submitting some feedback. When you turn the network connection back on, the service worker should wake up and immediately process the queued items.

We just went through a lot of code and generated a lot of promises, but we now have a version of the PWA News site that works as expected online or offline.

## Dealing with Last Chances

Early on, I mentioned that if background sync fails, then the browser will retry it again later. What I didn't say, and what is not documented, is how many times the browser will retry until it gets it right. I heard somewhere that browsers use an internal exponential backoff algorithm to control how frequently they retry. Looking around to understand this better, I came across an article titled *Chrome, the Background Sync API and Exponential Backoff*, which looks at this specific question.

Thinking about this problem, you'd think the browser would retry 5, 10, or 20 times before abandoning a sync event, but it turns out that browsers such as Chrome retry the sync only twice before abandoning it. To quote a line from Kevin Kline's character in *A Fish Called Wanda*: "Disappointed!"

For our simple PWA News Feedback page, trying to deliver the data only three times isn't a big deal. For a more transactional app such as a chat app or banking app, I really want more. The good news is that the browser's `SyncManager` at least tells you when it's about to abandon your request. The following listing contains a quick copy and paste of the `event` object passed to the service worker's `sync` event listener. In there you should see the `lastChance` property. It's false now, because it was grabbed from a first pass at processing the sync event.

```
bubbles: false
cancelBubble: false
cancelable: false
composed: false
currentTarget: ServiceWorkerGlobalScope {clients: Clients, registration:
  ServiceWorkerRegistration, onactivate: null, onfetch: null, oninstall: null, ...}
defaultPrevented: false
eventPhase: 0
isTrusted: true
lastChance: false
path: []
returnValue: true
srcElement: ServiceWorkerGlobalScope {clients: Clients, registration:
  ServiceWorkerRegistration, onactivate: null, onfetch: null, oninstall: null, ...}
tag: "feedback"
target: ServiceWorkerGlobalScope {clients: Clients, registration:
  ServiceWorkerRegistration, onactivate: null, onfetch: null, oninstall: null, ...}
timeStamp: 0
type: "sync"
__proto__: SyncEvent
```

When the browser's `SyncManager` has had enough with this sync event, it switches `lastChance` to true so you'll know what's coming next and can act the way that makes the most sense for your app.

In the service worker, you could do something like this:

```
// is this the last time the browser will
// process this event?
if (event.lastChance) {
  console.warn(`SW: ${event.tag.toUpperCase()} sync last chance`);
}
```

This just throws a warning to the console, but the user will never see that, and it doesn't actually do anything. Do you remember earlier when I mentioned that you could register a sync event inside of the service worker? Well, that is one way to keep this sync event alive. If your code learns that the SyncManager is about to abandon this sync event and there's still data to process, simply resubmit the background sync using

```
self.registration.sync.register('feedback')
```

This is a little dangerous in that it forces the service worker to process the event forever, but hey, it works.

So, in our current service worker example, the preceding code would go into the sync event listener:

```
self.addEventListener('sync', event => {
  console.log('SW: Sync event fired');
  // is this the last time the browser will
  // process this event?
  if (event.lastChance) {
    console.warn(`SW: ${event.tag.toUpperCase()} sync last chance`);
  }
  if (event.tag === 'feedback') {
    console.log('SW: Processing Feedback sync');
    event.waitUntil(
      getFeedbackItems()
        .then(data => {
          return Promise.all(
            // loop through the items array
            data.items.map(function (feedbackItem) {
              // update the server if you can
              return fetch(FEEDBACK_URL, {
                method: 'post',
                headers: { 'Content-Type': 'application/json' },
                body: JSON.stringify({
                  sentiment: feedbackItem.sentiment
                })
              })
                .then(() => {
                  // successfully posted,
                  // so whack the record at idx
                  return deleteFeedback(data.db, feedbackItem.idx)
                })
                .catch(error => {
                  // ruh roh, something went wrong
                  console.error(`SW: Sync Error: ${error}`);
```

```
              if (event.lastChance) {
                // do something to handle the last event
                // warn the user, submit the event again
                self.registration.sync.register('feedback');
              }
            })
          })
        );
      }));
    } else {
      // this should never happen
      console.log(`SW: Unrecognized sync event (${event.tag})`);
    }
});
```

All right, back to this exponential fallback algorithm. Because the referenced article was a little old, I thought things might have changed in the browser, so using the article's code as a starting point, I embellished it a bit and ran it in the browser to see how the browser manages fallback. Trust, but verify, right? You can find my complete code listing in \learning-pwa-code\chapter-05\fallback-test.

What I did to test this code was load it in the browser, then stop the server process running in the terminal window. What I learned is highlighted in Figure 5.9.

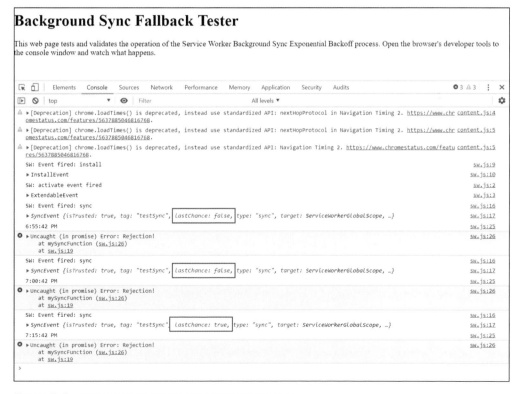

Figure 5.9   Chrome Background Sync Fallback Results

When the `SyncManager` detects that it can't complete processing a sync event, it waits 5 minutes and tries again. If the retry fails, the `SyncManager` waits 15 minutes and tries it again, but this time it switches the `lastChance` property from `false` to `true`. That's not a very sophisticated algorithm; I can't imagine a PhD over at Google spent a lot of time on that one.

Anyway, that's a limitation of background sync you must be aware of and accommodate in your apps. If the data is important, you're going to have to force the browser to retry the sync more than twice using the strategy I presented in this section.

## Wrap-Up

We covered a lot of code in this chapter, and you learned a lot about background sync. Our PWA News app is feature complete; it works while online and offline using resource and data caching plus background sync for data submission. I hope you had as much fun reading this chapter as I had writing it.

In the next chapter, we dig into the last real PWA topic covered in the book: browser notifications.

# 6

# Push Notifications

One of the things that makes mobile apps so engaging is the mobile platform push notification capabilities that enable app developers to send information to the device running the app. Depending on the device OS and the type of notification, the information sent to the device displays in the device's notification area or appears in-app. Notifications expand the scope of the app beyond what's currently available on the device and deliver a clean way to keep app users informed of almost anything.

Service workers give web apps some of the same capabilities. In this chapter, I show how to configure a web app to support notifications plus how to send notifications to subscribed browsers through a server process. Like the previous one, this chapter is chock-full of code, so let's get started.

## Introducing Push Notifications

In web apps, notifications are little pop-up windows browsers display when they receive a notification message. The web app can send notifications to itself, or you can send them to the browser from a remote system, usually an app or web server. Notifications appear only when the target browser is running, but the default browser on many smartphones runs constantly, and Google Chrome has a setting that users can enable to keep that browser running in the background as well. Figures 6.1, 6.2, and 6.3 show the same notification on Windows, macOS, and Android.

Windows notifications appear at the bottom-left corner of the desktop, while macOS notifications appear in the upper-right corner of the desktop. On Android, notifications appear alongside other notifications displayed by the device. If you're wondering why I'm not saying anything about iOS, that's because as I write this, iOS doesn't support browser notifications.

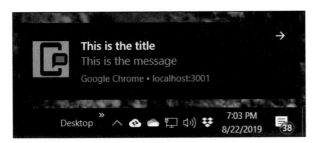

Figure 6.1   A Browser Notification on Windows

Figure 6.2    A Browser Notification on macOS

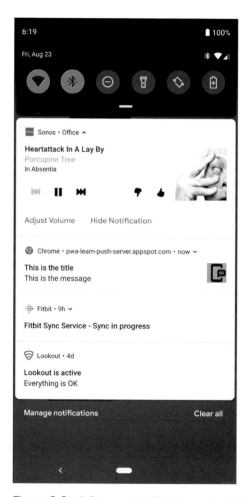

Figure 6.3    A Browser Notification on Android

These are often called *push notifications* because they're usually pushed to the browser over a network connection. I prefer to call them *remote notifications* because they're sent from a remote service. The other type of notification is what I call *local notifications*, that is, notifications sent to the browser by the web app running in that browser. You'll see examples of both in the code we use later in the chapter.

Local notifications work only when the web page requesting them is hosted. If you open the page directly from the file system (rather than using a URL), notifications don't work.

Remote notifications, however, require service workers to function. For notifications sent by a remote system, it's the service worker that processes the notification when it arrives and decides what to do with it.

Before the browser can receive notifications from a web app or a remote system, the browser user must first grant permission to authorize the browser to show notifications on behalf of the app. If the user doesn't grant permission, you can't send notifications to the browser.

You've probably seen this permissions prompt periodically as you surf the web, sites that immediately ask for permission to send notifications to your browser before you even know whether the site contains anything of interest. This approach leads to greatly annoyed users and causes tweets such as the one shown in Figure 6.4.

Figure 6.4    Twitter Complaint about Push Permission Prompts

Web apps should wait until they're certain site visitors are interested in receiving notifications before asking permission to send them. You could gauge interest based on how many pages users visit or how much time they spend on each, then display the permissions prompt only when you're sure they may want them. One option is to use the `beforeinstallprompt` event discussed in Chapter 2, "Web App Manifest Files," to unhide a subscribe button or link. This event only fires once the browser thinks the visitor has shown real interest in the app. In the app we work on in this chapter, the code never prompts automatically; it instead provides a button the visitor must click to subscribe to notifications.

The browser provides several events a web app can listen for to know when the user clicked or closed the notification window. Notifications can even be interactive; you can provide action buttons with your notifications and execute specific code depending on which action button the user clicks or taps. We cover all this and more as we work through the chapter's code.

# Remote Notification Architecture

Before we jump into all the examples and code, let's talk about how push works. The ability to send notifications to browsers requires three things:

1.  A browser capable of receiving, processing, and displaying notifications.

2.  An app to send notifications to one or more browsers. This is your app backend.

3.  Some hardware/software solution to manage delivering notifications to the browser—a push service.

The first one probably makes a lot of sense; the forced split between the second and third requirements causes some confusion.

The browser is a container for running other people's code, and consequently, there's risk that ill-behaved or malicious code could wreak havoc on the user's system. HTML, CSS, and JavaScript are properly sandboxed by the browser, and there are limits on how they can affect anything outside of the current app. Service workers change that, of course, but we already talked about the extra security surrounding them.

Early on, many browser vendors allowed developers to publish extensions that tweaked the inner workings of the browser, but over the years, browsers became increasingly restrictive in what they would allow inside the guts of the browser. To deliver a secure environment for notifications, support for them must be a core component of the browser, available outside of your app's context and able to wake up a service worker when necessary.

Sending notifications to browsers must be streamlined as well. Backend apps won't have direct connections to the browser, especially when the app is not loaded in the browser. The browser requests a page, then closes the connection. Yes, I know you could use WebSockets to do this, but who wants to maintain thousands or millions of socket connections to target browsers? When a browser has ten or more service workers listening for notifications, do you really want each back-end server maintaining a connection into your browser? No, you really don't.

So, to make all this possible and minimize the impact on the browser and the computer system or smartphone running the browser, the push specification uses an intermediate server process to manage subscription and notification delivery. That server runs somewhere in the cloud and typi-cally comes from the browser vendor. When a web app subscribes to notifications, the browser knows exactly where to go to register the subscription—to its own cloud push service.

Now that you know why browser push works like it does, let me show you *how* it works, starting with the subscription process:

- A web app asks the user for permission to display notifications in the browser. Due to the invasive nature of browser notifications, the notification standard requires user approval before any notifications can be sent to the browser.

- If approved, the web app subscribes the app for notifications through the browser's push service.

- The push service subscribes the app/browser combination, stores the information somewhere internally, then returns a subscription object that contains everything a backend app needs to send notifications to this app running on the subscribed browser.

- The subscribing web app sends the subscription object (plus whatever additional information it thinks is pertinent) to the backend app where it's stored away for future use when sending notifications.

The process (except for requesting permission) is highlighted in steps 1 through 3 in Figure 6.5.

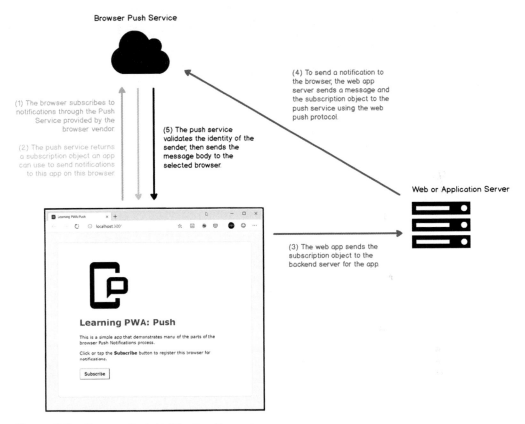

Figure 6.5    Browser Push Notification Process

> **Note**
>
> To protect the user from rogue notifications, the app backend sends all notification requests in encrypted format. To do this, the web app generates a set of encryption keys to use in its inter-action with the push service. The web app includes the public key in the subscription request sent to the push service.
>
> When the web app backend server sends notification requests to the push service, it encrypts the request using the server's private key. Since the push service has the public key (from the subscription request), it can decrypt the message and know for certain the request was sent by the right server.

When the backend app server has information or data to send to a browser, the server

- Encrypts the notification request using the server's private key.
- Sends the request to the push service using the Push API.[1]
- The push service decrypts the request, verifies the identity of the sender, and, if verified, sends the notification to the target browser.
- The browser wakes up the app's service worker to process the notification.

In this book, I do not cover anything related to implementation of the Push API. It's an open standard with community-supported libraries, so I'm going to skip all the hard work and use a popular open source solution for managing delivery of notification requests to a push service. I show how the server uses the open source solution to send notifications at the end of the chapter.

## Preparing to Code

The work we do in this chapter revolves around a new app I created for this chapter (styled by Scott Good, of course). Notifications don't work unless the web app receiving them is hosted somewhere (rather than just loaded from the file system), so I included a server process much like the one used in the previous chapters. The setup process is a little different than what you've seen previously, so don't skip the instructions here or in the next section.

The code for the server app is available in the book's GitHub repository at https://github.com/johnwargo/learning-pwa-code. I provided complete instructions for how to download the code and configure your development environment in the section "Preparing to Code" in Chapter 3, "Service Workers." If you haven't already completed those steps, go there and complete them first before picking up here again.

Open a terminal window and navigate the terminal into the cloned project's `\learning-pwa-code\chapter-06\` folder. This folder contains a relatively empty version of the web app we'll build out as we work through the chapter. Install all the dependencies required by the app by executing the following command:

```
npm install
```

This command uses the Node Package Manager (npm) to install Node.js modules used by the server.

## Generating Encryption Keys

The notification process requires a set of encryption keys: public and private keys used to ensure the integrity of the notification process. Browser notifications use Voluntary Application Server Identification (VAPID) for Web Push[2] encryption keys to encrypt communication with the push service. I don't to go into detail about these keys and how they're made, as knowing that

---

1. https://www.w3.org/TR/push-api/
2. https://datatracker.ietf.org/doc/rfc8292/

information won't help you learn push. The push process uses them, so you must have a set of keys for any web app you create that sends browser notifications.

One of the ways to generate a set of keys is to use the Secure VAPID key generator.[3] The server process included with this chapter's code uses the popular web-push module[4] to manage delivery of notification requests to the browser cloud service. It includes a function that generates the keys automatically, so that's what we'll use.

Open a terminal window, navigate to the cloned project's \learning-pwa-code\chapter-06\ folder, and execute the following command:

```
node generate-keys.js
```

This executes a little node app I wrote that generates a set of VAPID keys and writes them to some configuration files used by the web app. The app calls the web-push modules `webpush.generateVAPIDKeys()` method, which handles the whole process[5] for us.

I mentioned earlier that the client app requires the server's public key and the server uses the private key, so the process generates two files. The first is \chapter-06\app\config.ts, which looks like this:

```
export const Config = {
  GCMAPI_KEY: '',
  VAPID_PUBLIC: 'SUPER-SECRET-PUBLIC-KEY',
  VAPID_PRIVATE: ' SUPER-SECRET-PRIVATE-KEY '
};
```

The server uses this file to provide the private encryption key when sending notification messages through a push service.

The other file is \chapter-06\public\js\config.js, which looks like this:

```
const Config = {
  VAPID_PUBLIC: 'SUPER-SECRET-PUBLIC-KEY',
};
```

The web app uses this file to provide the public encryption key when subscribing to notifications.

> **Note**
>
> You don't have to break your VAPID keys out into separate configuration files as I did here. I did this because I knew the server source code would be publicly available through the book's GitHub repository, and saving the keys to separate files enabled me to omit them from the repository.

As in previous chapters, I coded the server app in TypeScript, so before you can use the server process with the new configuration file, you must open a terminal window, navigate to the project folder, and execute the following command:

```
tsc
```

---

3. https://tools.reactpwa.com/vapid

4. https://www.npmjs.com/package/web-push

5. You can read about the web-push process at https://www.npmjs.com/package/web-push#usage.

This command invokes the TypeScript compiler, which compiles `\chapter-06\app\config.ts` to `\chapter-06\config.js`. With this in place, we're ready to go.

You probably noticed that I neglected to explain the `GCMAPI_KEY` shown in the first file example. Google provided support for browser notifications long before there was a push standard, and Google's implementation used the now-deprecated Google Cloud Messaging (GCM) service. In this chapter, I'm assuming we're targeting modern browsers that support the standard; if your app must support older browsers, you must set up an account in Google's Firebase Cloud Messaging (FCM) service and generate the key required to support older browsers the `GCMAPI_KEY` mentioned earlier. For more information on this topic, refer to Matt Gaunt's "What Is the Deal with GCM, FCM, Web Push and Chrome?"[6] at Google's Web Fundamentals FAQ.

With all the parts in place, it's time to start the server. In the terminal window, execute the following command:

```
npm start
```

If everything's set up properly in the code, the server will respond with the following text in the terminal:

```
learning-pwa-push@0.0.1 start D:\dev\learning-pwa-code\chapter-06
node ./bin/www
```

At this point, you're all set—the server is up and running and ready to serve content. If you see an error message, you must dig through any reported errors and resolve them before continuing.

> **Note**
>
> The server process for this chapter runs on port 3001, which is different from the server for previous chapters. I did this because the browser caches resources for you automatically, and we need a different service worker and associated files for the work we're doing here.
>
> Yes, I know I could provide instructions on how to manually clear the cache and do whatever other cleanup is required, but since I know both of us will be going forth and back between this project and earlier ones, I decided to run them on different ports to keep the browser from getting confused.

To see the web app in its current state, open a browser that supports service workers and navigate to

```
http://localhost:3001
```

After a short delay, the server should render the simple web page shown in Figure 6.6. The app doesn't do anything yet, but we'll fix that soon. When we're done, the app will let users subscribe to notifications, as shown in the figure, and will have a service worker that processes and displays any remote notifications sent to it through the server.

I created the web app for this chapter using the HTML5 Boilerplate[7] template and grabbed a push icon from https://icons8.com/icon/25175/push-notifications. You'll see jQuery and other stuff in the app, but we won't make use of much of it—it's just there because of the template.

---

6. https://developers.google.com/web/fundamentals/push-notifications/faq

7. https://html5boilerplate.com/

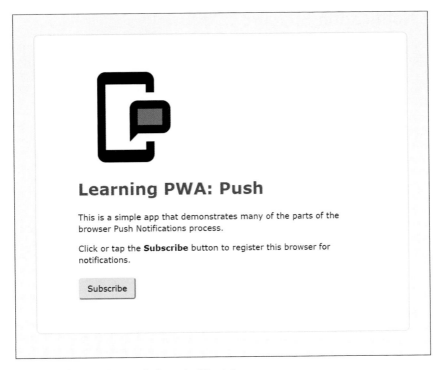

Figure 6.6   The Chapter's Sample Client App

The server also includes an admin app, shown in Figure 6.7. It's available at http://localhost:3001/admin; we'll use it to manage subscriptions (edit and delete them) plus send notifications to selected browsers. We won't make any changes to this app; it's just here to make testing notifications easier.

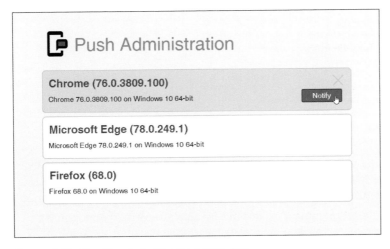

Figure 6.7   The Chapter's Sample Admin App

## Validating Notification Support

Some browsers, such as Safari on iOS, don't support notifications, so before an app does anything with them, the app must first check to see if notifications are even available in the browser. To do this, check for the existence of the Notification object using the following:

```
// does the browser support notification?
if (("Notification" in window)) {
  // yes! Do something interesting

} else {
  // no? Then display a warning message
  // or disable the part of the ui that handles notifications

}
```

This check is a core component of the updateUI function in the project's chapter-06/public/js/index.js. The web app executes this function to update the UI at startup and every time the browser's subscription status changes.

Does your app have to check for notification support before doing anything related to notifications? No, not really. If you don't, any code that uses the Notification object will simply fail on browsers that don't support notifications.

## Checking Notification Permission

Once a web app knows the browser supports notifications, it should check whether the user has granted permission using the Notification object's permission property, as shown in the following code:

```
if (Notification.permission === "granted") {
  console.log('User has approved notifications');

}
```

The supported permission values are

- granted
- denied
- default

A permission value of 'granted' means that the user approved use of notifications for this app. A permission value of 'denied' means the opposite: the user did not grant permission for notifications for this app. Easy, right?

The 'default' value is a weird one as it means that the browser is not sure whether the user approved notifications. In this case, the browser simply assumes the user has not granted permission. This happens when the user closes the permissions prompt dialog without making a selection.

# Getting Permission for Notifications

Now that you know how to check that the browser supports notifications and whether the user has granted permission for notifications, it's time to get the user's permission for notifications. To do this, an app calls the Notification object's requestPermission method, and the browser takes over the approval process from there.

The requestPermission method returns a promise; when the promise resolves, it returns a DOMString containing 'granted', 'denied', and 'default' values described in the previous section.

The following code illustrates the requestPermission method in action. Open the web app project's chapter-06\public\js\index.js file and add the code to the existing doSubscribe function.

```js
Notification.requestPermission().then(result => {
  switch (result) {
    case 'granted':
      // the user gave us permission,
      // so we can go ahead and subscribe

      break;
    case 'denied':
      // code block
      console.error('Denied');
      Swal.fire({
        type: 'info',
        title: 'Subscribe',
        text: 'You denied access to notifications.',
        footer: 'Please try again when you are ready.'
      });
      break;
    default:
      // the user closed the permissions dialog
      // without making a selection
      console.warn('Default');
      Swal.fire({
        type: 'info',
        title: 'Subscribe',
        text: 'Dialog closed without making a selection.',
        footer: 'Please try again later.'
      });
  }
});
```

When an app user clicks or taps the Subscribe button, this code requests permission for notifications, then notifies the user of the result. We'll do more with this result a little later, but for now let's just get this working.

> **Note**
>
> The call to Swal you see in different places in the code refers to SweetAlert2,[8] a popular JavaScript library for displaying cool dialogs in web apps.

I could have checked to see if the user had already granted permission (using the code from the previous section) before requesting it again, but if the user has already granted permission, the call to requestPermission simply returns the previous result.

Save the changes to the file, then switch to a browser and open http://localhost:3001. The browser should display the page shown in Figure 6.6. If it doesn't, then go back and check your code. When it's working correctly, tap the Subscribe button and you should see the notifications prompt shown at the top of Figure 6.8.

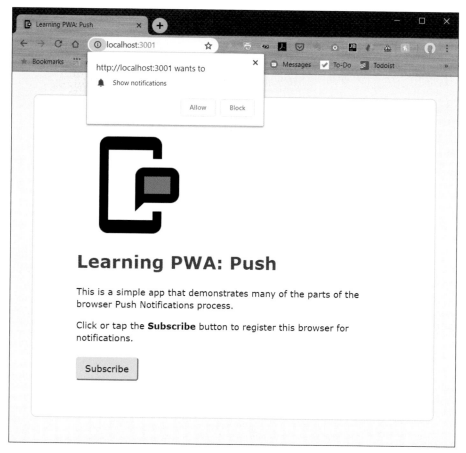

Figure 6.8   Prompting for Notification Permission

Open the browser's developer tools, switch to the **Console** tab, then make a selection in the notifications prompt. You should see the permission result written to the console and, in some cases, dialogs popping up when you don't allow notifications.

---

8. https://sweetalert2.github.io/

One of the things that I learned as I worked through the code for this chapter is that browsers are a little persnickety when you close the notifications prompt without making a selection too many times. After I closed the prompt a few times, Chrome stopped showing me the prompt at all, and a quick trip to the console showed me the following:

> Notifications permission has been blocked as the user has dismissed the permission prompt several times. This can be reset in Page Info which can be accessed by clicking the lock icon next to the URL. See https://www.chromestatus.com/features/6443143280984064 for more information.

Looking at the link provided in the message let me know that Chrome will wait a week before allowing me to attempt to grant permissions for notifications again. The good news is that this is easily fixed; following the instructions in the console message, click the information icon to the left of the URL input field, and change the Notifications option to Ask, as shown in Figure 6.9.

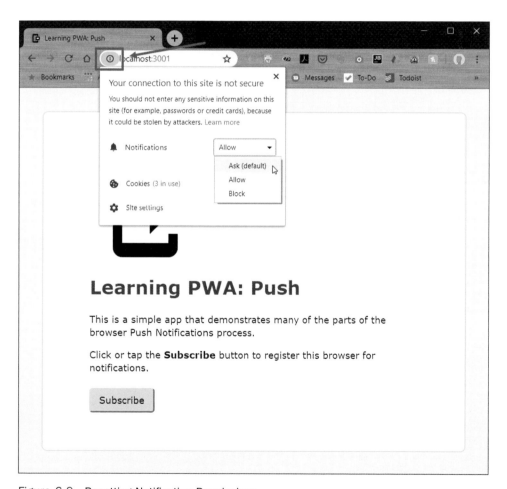

Figure 6.9    Resetting Notification Permissions

> **Note**
>
> You may be asking yourself why I told you to click the information icon when the message clearly said to click the lock icon. That's because we're loading this app from a local server over an HTTP connection, so the lock icon isn't there. If this site were hosted on a server and had a TLS/SSL certificate in place, you would see a lock icon there instead.

## Local Notifications

At this point, when you approve notifications, you can send one to the browser using the following code:

```
let theNotification = new Notification('I read Learning PWA, '
  + 'and all I got was this silly notification!');
```

Add that code to the project's `index.js` file's `doSubscribe` function, in the `granted` case.

When you reload the page and reset notification permissions (using the trick I showed you in Figure 6.9), then click the Subscribe button, you should see something like what is shown in Figure 6.10 pop up somewhere on the screen.

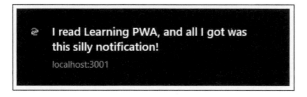

Figure 6.10    Displaying a Local Notification

You've just sent your first notification to a browser. How does it feel?

Notifications can be more robust than I've shown here; we're only passing in a title, which generates the simple notification you see in the figure. You can also pass in a notification options object that enables you to create more sophisticated and interactive notifications. I describe these options in the next section.

The `Notification` object exposes several events that you can handle in your app:

- `onclick`
- `onclose`
- `onerror`
- `onshow`

To handle them in the app, add the following code to the `granted` case, immediately following the definition of the `theNotification` object.

```
theNotification.onclick = function (event) {
  console.log('Notification clicked');
  console.dir(event);
};

theNotification.onclose = function (event) {
  console.log('Notification closed');
  console.dir(event);
}

theNotification.onerror = function (event) {
  console.error('Notification error');
  console.dir(event);
}

theNotification.onshow = function (event) {
  console.log('Notification shown');
  console.dir(event);
}
```

Play around with the different options, making note of the `event` object in the console output. Your app can use data in the object to act according to the user's selection or browser activity.

As fun and exciting as that was, if you try that code on a smartphone, you'll get the error shown in Figure 6.11. Showing notifications that way is supported only on desktop browsers.

To display the same notification on both desktop and mobile browsers, you must let the registered service worker send the local notification for you using the following code:

```
navigator.serviceWorker.ready.then(registration => {
  registration.showNotification('I read Learning PWA, '
  'and all I got was this silly notification!');
});
```

Replace all the notification code (defining the `theNotification` object and its callbacks) you added earlier with the service worker–driven version just shown. With this in place, the notification will work on desktop and mobile browsers. The service worker–compatible version supports notification events as well; you'll see them when we work with the service worker later.

The complete code for the project's `index.js` file up to this point in the chapter is in the project's `chapter-06\public\chapter-code\index-61.js` file.

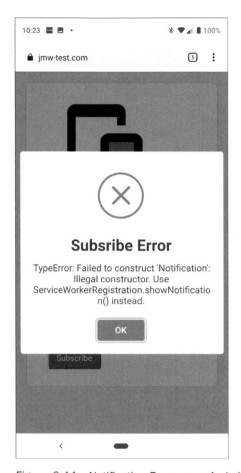

Figure 6.11   Notification Error on an Android Device

## Notification Options

As I explained in the previous section, what you saw in Figure 6.10 was just a simple notification using a title string passed to the `Notification` object's constructor or, in the second example, to the `registration.showNotification` method. The browser is capable of much more.

> **Note**
>
> Since using the `Notification` object is restricted to desktop browsers (today, anyway), I'm going to ignore that form of notification going forward. The good news is that everything I show in the rest of the chapter applies to that type of notification, so if you want to use them in your apps, you can apply the details from this section to it as well.

To take advantage of additional notification options, you must pass an options object to the call to `registration.showNotification`, as shown in the following example:

```
registration.showNotification(title, options);
```

The `options` object is a simple JavaScript object containing one or more of the following properties:

- `actions`: An array of items representing the actions the user can perform with this notification. You'll see an example of this later.

- `badge`: A URL pointing to an image file used to represent the notification when there isn't enough space to display the full notification.

- `body`: The body text for the notification. You'll seen an example of this in use in a minute.

- `data`: An arbitrary data object associated with the notification. The service worker can use this data as it processes the notification.

- `dir`: The notification text display direction. This property defaults to `auto`; additional options are `rtl` (right to left) and `ltr` (left to right).

- `icon`: A URL pointing to an image file displayed in the notification (typically to the left of the notification on Windows and to the right for macOS).

- `image`: A URL pointing to an image file displayed in the notification (typically above the notification).

- `lang`: Specifies the language for the notification.

- `renotify`: A Boolean value (true/false) specifying whether the browser should notify the user when a new notification replaces the previous one. This property defaults to false.

- `requireInteraction`: A Boolean value (true/false) specifying whether the notification should remain active until the user clicks or dismisses it. The default value is false, which directs the browser to close the notification automatically after a few seconds.

- `tag`: A string value identifying the notification. To keep the browser from cluttering up the user's system with notifications, when a new notification comes in with the same tag, it replaces any previous notifications in the queue with the same tag.

- `vibrate`: Specifies a vibration pattern array to use when notifying users of new notifications. The array contains play/pause items specifying number of milliseconds for each. For example, to vibrate for 200 milliseconds, pausing for 100 milliseconds, repeated three times, you would use `[200, 100, 200, 100, 200, 100]`.

A more thorough description of these options plus listing of newer options not currently supported in many browsers can be found in Notification.Notification().[9]

> ## Warning
>
> Many of the options described here work only on Microsoft Windows. macOS especially, but Android as well, do not support all the available notification options. I could not get image files or action buttons to display on anything but Windows.
>
> All I can do is hope that these operating systems (notifications are displayed by the OS, not the browser) continue to add support for other options over time.

---

9. https://developer.mozilla.org/en-US/docs/Web/API/notification/Notification

Now it's time to see some of these in action. The following example sets the body text and an icon for a notification:

```
let options = {
  body: "Isn't this cool?",
  icon: "/img/push-icon-red.png"
};
let title = 'I read Learning PWA, and ' +
  'all I got was this silly notification!'
registration.showNotification(title, options);
```

When you run this in the browser, you'll see the notification shown in Figure 6.12.

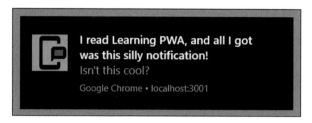

Figure 6.12    A Notification with a Body and Icon

One of my favorites is to include a random image file along with the notification, as shown in the following:

```
let options = {
  body: "Isn't this cool?",
  image: "https://picsum.photos/200/100",
  icon: "/img/push-icon-red.png",
};
let title = 'I read Learning PWA, and ' +
  'all I got was this silly notification!'
registration.showNotification(title, options);
```

This generates the notification shown in Figure 6.13.

You can also include actions for your notifications, as shown in the following example:

```
let options = {
  body: "Isn't this cool?",
  image: "https://picsum.photos/200/100",
  icon: "/img/push-icon-red.png",
  actions: [
    { action: 'like', title: 'Like' },
    { action: 'dislike', title: 'Dislike' }
  ]
};
let title = 'I read Learning PWA, and ' +
  'all I got was this silly notification!'
registration.showNotification(title, options);
```

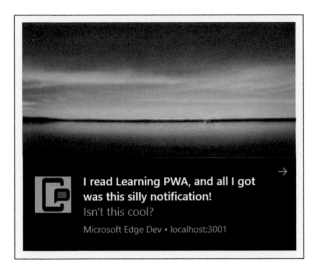

Figure 6.13    A Notification with a Body, Icon, and Random Image

This code generates the notification shown in Figure 6.14.

Figure 6.14    A Notification with a Body, Icon, Random Image, and Actions

Processing the user's interaction with the action buttons requires some additional code in your service worker, which I cover when we get to service workers later in the chapter.

## Subscribing to Notifications

In this section, we subscribe the browser for notifications with the push server and share the subscription details with the server so it can send notifications to the browser later. At this point in the process, we need the server's VAPID public key, which we put in the project's `chapter-06\public\js\config.js` file earlier in the chapter.

Open the project's `chapter-06\public\index.html` file and add the following lines to the bottom of the file's body section

```
<!-- Push configuration file -->
<script src="js/config.js"></script>
```

This makes the file's `Config` object available to the web app.

Next, open the project's `chapter-06\public\js\index.js` file and add the following code to the top of the file (I'll explain later what it's used for):

```
const UUID_KEY = 'subscription-uuid';
```

With those changes in place, let's talk through the subscription process and add the required code to the project's `index.js` file. In the following paragraphs, and through the rest of the chapter, I'll describe the building blocks we need, then ask you to add complete code blocks to the project. I apologize if this is confusing; just use the finished files in the project's `chapter-06\public\chapter-code` folder if that helps.

To subscribe the browser for notifications, the web app must execute the `registration.pushManager.subscribe` method. Getting access to the registration object and setting up the parameters for the method takes a bit of work we must do first.

The browser doesn't have direct access to the `registration` object, but the app's service worker does, so we can get the object through the following:

```
navigator.serviceWorker.ready.then(registration => {

});
```

The subscribe method requires a special set of options defined in the `subOptions` object:

```
var subOptions = {
  userVisibleOnly: true,
  applicationServerKey: urlBase64ToUint8Array(Config.VAPID_PUBLIC)
};
```

The `userVisibleOnly` is the app's promise to the browser that it will display a notification for every push item sent to it. There's only one supported value, and that's `true`. The notification subscription won't work with any other value assigned to the property.

The `applicationServerKey` is a specially formatted version of the server's public key, which we have available through the `Config.VAPID_PUBLIC` property in the project's `config.js` file. The function for converting the VAPID public key into the correct format is borrowed directly from "Using VAPID Key for applicationServerKey"[10] and is shown here:

```
function urlBase64ToUint8Array(base64String) {
  // this code borrowed from:
  // https://www.npmjs.com/package/web-push
  const padding = '='.repeat((4 - base64String.length % 4) % 4);
  const base64 = (base64String + padding)
    .replace(/-/g, '+')
    .replace(/_/g, '/');

  const rawData = window.atob(base64);
  const outputArray = new Uint8Array(rawData.length);

  for (let i = 0; i < rawData.length; ++i) {
    outputArray[i] = rawData.charCodeAt(i);
  }
  return outputArray;
}
```

Add the urlBase64ToUint8Array function to the project's index.js file; we'll need it in a little while.

Putting all of this together, the code to subscribe the browser for notifications is the following:

```
navigator.serviceWorker.ready.then(registration => {
  var subOptions = {
    userVisibleOnly: true,
    applicationServerKey: urlBase64ToUint8Array(Config.VAPID_PUBLIC)
  };
  registration.pushManager.subscribe(subOptions)
    .then(subscription => {
      console.log('Browser subscribed');

    })
  );
```

If the browser successfully subscribes for notifications, the push service returns the subscription object, which looks like this:

```
{
  endpoint: "https://fcm.googleapis.com/fcm/send/some-unique-id"
  expirationTime: null
  options: PushSubscriptionOptions
  applicationServerKey: ArrayBuffer(65) {}
  userVisibleOnly: true
}
```

---

10. https://www.npmjs.com/package/web-push#using-vapid-key-for-applicationserverkey

Remember, we need the `subscription` object on the server to send notifications to the browser later, so next we must upload the object to the server. To accommodate this, add the `postRegistration` function to the project's `index.js` file:

```
function postRegistration(subscription) {
  const serverUrl = `${location.origin}/api/subscribe`;

  return new Promise((resolve, reject) => {
    if (subscription) {
      // build the URL to the app's APIs
      console.log(`Submitting subscription to ${serverUrl}`);

      // the data we're passing to the server
      const data = {
        subscription: subscription,
        name: `${platform.name} (${platform.version})`,
        platformName: platform.name,
        platformVersion: platform.version,
        platformLayout: platform.layout,
        platformOS: platform.os,
        platformDesc: platform.description
      };

      // POST the data to the server
      fetch(serverUrl, {
        method: 'POST',
        headers: { 'Content-Type': 'application/json' },
        body: JSON.stringify(data),
      })
        .then(response => {
          console.log('Received response from the server');
          if (response.status == 201) {
            console.log('Subscription submitted');
            response.json()
              .then(data => {
                console.log(`UUID: ${data.uuid}`);
                localStorage.setItem(UUID_KEY, data.uuid);
                resolve();
              })
          } else {
            // tell the user it failed
            Swal.fire('POST Error', response.statusText, 'error');
            reject(response.statusText);
          }
        });
    } else {
      reject('Missing endpoint value');
    }
  });
}
```

This code sends the `subscription` object to the server along with some additional information about the browser. You'll see an example of this data later when we test out the changes. The code also writes the unique ID for the subscription generated by the server. We'll store this value in the app's local storage (using the `UUID_KEY` we added to the app earlier) so we have it during the unsubscribe process.

The final piece of this is how an app checks the status of a subscription. The app may want to update the UI on the basis of the browser's subscription status; the code to do this is the following:

```
navigator.serviceWorker.ready.then(registration => {
  console.log('Checking subscription');
  // check to make sure the browser isn't already subscribed
  registration.pushManager.getSubscription()
    .then(subscription => {
      if (subscription) {
        // the browser is subscribed

      } else {
        // the browser is not subscribed


      }
    });
});
```

It's finally time to wrap this section up and add the ability to subscribe to notifications to the web app. The following code replaces the entire `granted` case in the existing doSubscribe function in the app. It's a slight variation on the subscription code shown earlier; in this case, it checks to make sure the browser isn't subscribed before subscribing it. Go ahead and add this code to the doSubscribe function in the project's index.js file:

```
case 'granted':
  // the user gave us permission,
  // so go ahead and do the registration
  console.log('Permission granted');
  navigator.serviceWorker.ready.then(registration => {
    console.log('Checking subscription');
    // check to make sure the browser isn't already subscribed
    registration.pushManager.getSubscription()
      .then(subscription => {
        if (subscription) {
          console.log('Browser is already subscribed');
          Swal.fire({
            type: 'info',
            title: 'Subscribe',
            text: 'This browser is already subscribed for notifications'
          });
        } else {
          // subscribe the browser
          console.log('Subscribing the browser');
          var subOptions = {
```

```
                  userVisibleOnly: true,
                  applicationServerKey:
                    urlBase64ToUint8Array(Config.VAPID_PUBLIC)
              };
              registration.pushManager.subscribe(subOptions)
                .then(subscription => {
                  console.log('Browser subscribed');
                  registration.showNotification('I read Learning PWA, and ' +
                    'all I got was this silly notification!');
                  postRegistration(subscription)
                    .then(() => {
                      console.log('Subscription POSTed to server');
                      updateUI();
                      Swal.fire({
                        type: 'info',
                        title: 'Subscribe',
                        text: 'The browser was successfully subscribed for
notifications',
                        timer: 2000
                      });
                    })
                    .catch(error => {
                      console.error(error);
                    })
                })
                .catch(error => {
                  // hmmm, that didn't work
                  console.error(error);
                  // tell the user what we can
                  Swal.fire({
                    type: 'error',
                    title: 'Subscribe Error',
                    text: error
                  });
                });
          }
        });
    updateUI();
  });
  break;
```

Now that we know how to tell if the browser is subscribed, let's update the updateUI function
to hide the subscribe button and unhide the unsubscribe button, depending on the browser's
subscription status:

```
function updateUI() {
  console.log('updateUI()');
  // does the browser support notification?
  if (("Notification" in window)) {
    navigator.serviceWorker.ready.then(registration => {
```

```
    // check to make sure the browser isn't already subscribed
    registration.pushManager.getSubscription()
      .then(subscription => {
        if (subscription) {
          console.log('Browser is already subscribed');
          document.getElementById("subscribeDiv").style.display = 'none';
          document.getElementById("unsubscribeDiv").style.display = 'block';
        } else {
          // no? Then unhide the subscribe div
          document.getElementById("subscribeDiv").style.display = 'block';
          document.getElementById("unsubscribeDiv").style.display = 'none';
        }
      })
  });
  } else {
    // no? Then display a warning
    document.getElementById("noNotificationsWarning").style.display = 'block';
  }
}
```

Go ahead and save your changes and refresh the page in the browser. When you reset the notification permission (shown in Figure 6.9) and then click the Subscribe button, you should see the results shown in Figure 6.15.

For this project, I added a timeout value to the call to SweetAlert2 so the dialog closes automatically after two seconds, so don't be surprised if these dialogs start disappearing.

Figure 6.15   Successful Notification Subscription

The complete code for the project's `index.js` file up to this point in the chapter is in the project's `chapter-06\public\chapter-code\index-62.js` file.

## Unsubscribing from Notifications

Unsubscribing from notifications is much easier than subscribing to them. You still need access to the `registration` object, and you must use the `registration` object to get access to the `subscription` object. Once you have that, it's a simple call to `subscription.unsubscribe` to unsubscribe from notifications.

Of course, everything involved uses promises, so the complete code looks like this:

```
navigator.serviceWorker.ready.then(registration => {
  registration.pushManager.getSubscription()
    .then(subscription => {
      subscription.unsubscribe()
        .then(status => {
          if (status) {
            // successfully unsubscribed

          } else {
            // Failure

          }
        });
    });
});
```

The `status` value returned from `unsubscribe` is a Boolean value (true or false) indicating result of the operation.

For our app, we need a little more than that. We want to tell the user the subscription completed successfully (or not), plus we must remove the subscription from the server so it knows it can't send notifications to this browser again. With that in mind, add the following code to the empty `doUnsubscribe` function in the project's `chapter-06\public\js\index.js` file.

```
navigator.serviceWorker.ready.then(registration => {
  registration.pushManager.getSubscription()
    .then(subscription => {
      subscription.unsubscribe()
        .then(status => {
          console.log(`doUnsubscribe: status: ${status}`);
          if (status) {
            updateUI();
            Swal.fire({
              type: 'info',
              title: 'Unsubscribe',
              text: 'Successfully unsubscribed',
              timer: 2000
            });
```

```
        // get the UUID from storage
        let uuid = localStorage.getItem(UUID_KEY);
        // do we have a UUID?
        if (uuid) {
          // build a server URL using it
          let serverUrl =
           `${location.origin}/api/unsubscribe/${uuid}`;
          // POST the data to the server
          fetch(serverUrl, { method: 'POST' })
            .then(response => {
              console.log(`doUnsubscribe: ${response.status} response`);
            });
        }
      } else {
        Swal.fire({
          type: 'error',
          title: 'Unsubscribe Error',
          text: "I'm not sure what happened here"
        });
      }
    });
  });
});
```

Save the updated code and refresh the app in the browser. The app should now have an awareness of subscription status and display the Subscribe or Unsubscribe button depending on the subscription status. When you click the Unsubscribe button, the app should unsubscribe the browser and display the notification shown in Figure 6.16.

Figure 6.16    Successful Unsubscribe

The complete code for the project's `index.js` file up to this point in the chapter is in the project's `chapter-06\public\chapter-code\index-63.js` file.

At this point, we're done with the web app's `index.js` file. The web app has the UI we need to subscribe and unsubscribe the browser for notifications. All that's left is to set the app up to process remote notifications sent from the server. This work must be done in the project's `sw.js` file.

# Remote Notifications

The browser delivers push notifications to the service worker to process. The browser fires a special push event in the service worker whenever the browser receives a remote browser notification (a notification sent by an external app, routed through the push service).

Earlier, when we created the subscription, we promised the browser's push service that we'd display any notification alert that came from our app's server. Now it's time to deliver the code that does that. In the project's service worker at `chapter-06\public\sw.js`, add the following code to the bottom of the file:

```
self.addEventListener('push', event => {
    console.log('SW: Push event fired');
    console.dir(event);
    const data = event.data.json();
    console.dir(data);
    self.registration.showNotification(data.title, data);
});
```

This adds an event listener for the `push` event and contains all the code you need to respond to notifications sent to the browser by a remote server. When a notification arrives, the code pulls the `title` from the notification data included with the push event, then passes the `title` and the data object to the `showNotification` method.

> ### In-Browser Testing
>
> The browser's developer tools give developers an easy way to test their app's service worker code for processing browser notifications. In the Push section highlighted in Figure 6.17, you can enter the content for a push message, then click the Push button to send it. This delivers the message under the covers; the browser doesn't know it came from the local developer tools.
>
> When the browser receives the notification, it fires the push event (as expected), and the service worker's push event listener executes to process the message.
>
> Normally, you would just send a simple text string to the browser using this feature, and the event listener's code would just create a generic notification like the first one shown in this chapter. For our app, the event listener expects a JSON object in the notification payload, so to make it display the notification using the title plus other options, you must format the notification string as follows:
>
> ```
> {"title": "test", "body": "Test push message from DevTools"}
> ```
>
> This is a quick and easy way to test notifications without involving external tools to send the notification through the browser's push service.

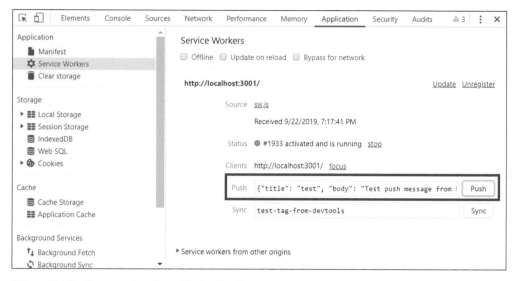

Figure 6.17    Browser Developer Tools: Sending Push Messages

If the notification includes an `actions` array, there's still one more thing you must do: add an event listener for the `notificationclick` event to the `sw.js` file, which looks like this:

```
self.addEventListener('notificationclick', function (event) {
  console.log('SW: Notification clicked');
  console.dir(event);
  if (event.action === 'like' ) {
    event.waitUntil(
      // do something for the like action

    );
  } else {
    event.waitUntil(
      // do something for the dislike action

    );
  }
});
```

Notice that the event listener uses `waitUntil` to let the service worker know not to shut down the event listener until it's done processing the user's action click.

The complete code for the project's `sw.js` file up to this point in the chapter is in the project's `chapter-06\public\chapter-code\sw-62.js` file.

At this point, the web app is ready to test; I'll show you two different ways to test the work we've done so far. We'll start using a third-party developer tool, but also work with the project's admin process (accessible through http://localhost:3001/admin).

Developers building backend apps like the server used in this chapter need some way to test the server's API before they've completed building the frontend app that uses the API. They use tools such as Postman to exercise their APIs as they build them. Download a copy of Postman from https://www.getpostman.com/ and install it on your development workstation. Launch the app and create a new API call, as shown in Figure 6.18:

1. Select GET as the API request method.

2. Enter `http://localhost:3001/api/subscriptions` for the API endpoint.

3. Click the Send button.

With the server running and at least one previous browser subscription completed during our work in this chapter, you should see a subscriptions list like the one shown in the bottom of the figure.

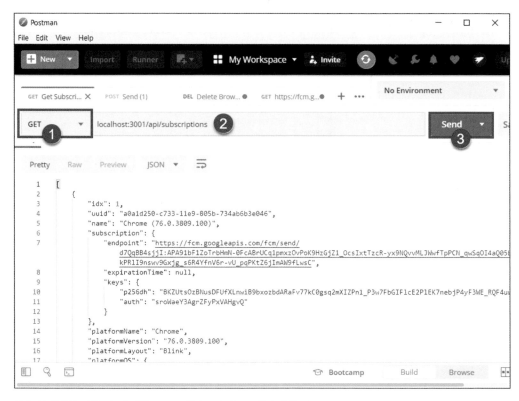

Figure 6.18    Displaying Browser Subscriptions Using Postman

Next, let's try sending a notification like the ones shown earlier in the chapter. Change the configuration of the request in Postman, as shown in Figure 6.19.

1. Start by changing the request type to POST.

2. Change the request URL to `localhost:3001/api/send/1`. Select the **Body** tab, select Raw, and switch the input type to JSON, as shown in the figure.

3. Populate the Body of the request as shown in the figure.

4. Click the Send button.

You should see a notification like the one shown in Figure 6.13 with a slightly different icon.

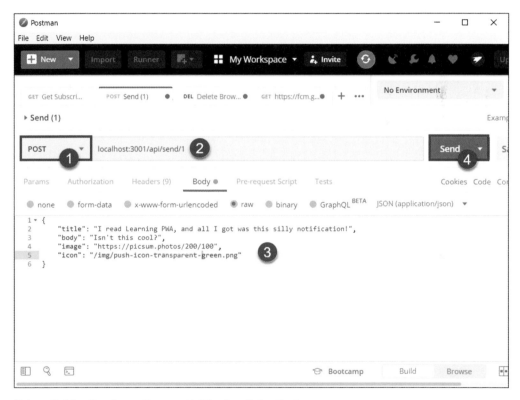

Figure 6.19   Sending a Browser Notification Using Postman

The 1 in the URL refers to the index (represented as `idx` in the subscription list shown in Figure 6.18) of the target browser from the database maintained by the server process. As you subscribe and unsubscribe browsers, that index will change, so make sure you grab the right value from the subscriptions list before trying to send notifications to browsers.

### Lost Subscriptions

One of the things I noticed as I tested the client app used in this chapter was that when I unregistered the service worker to force loading an updated version, then refreshed the page, the Unsubscribe button disappeared and was replaced by the Subscribe button. I didn't expect that and thought there was a problem with the application logic that hid/unhid those buttons.

Remember, subscribing for browser notifications requires service workers, so when I unregistered the service worker, the browser unsubscribed the browser from the push service. Unexpected but cool, right?

You can prove this by unregistering the service worker, then trying to send a notification to the browser using Postman. You'll get a response from the server that looks like this:

```
{
    "msg": "push subscription has unsubscribed or expired.\n"
}
```

Notice that the content we're sending the server is a little different than what you saw in previous examples:

```
{
    "title": "I read Learning PWA, and all I got was this silly notification!",
    "body": "Isn't this cool?",
    "image": "https://picsum.photos/200/100",
    "icon": "/img/push-icon-transparent-green.png"
}
```

This is because we're sending the notification content through the server process and we must pass that content as a big string value to the server. What we're sending is a JavaScript object as a string, so you must put both the keys and values in quotes.

Because I wanted to make it easy for you to test the browser notification process from end to end, Scott Good and I created an admin client you can use to manage subscriptions on the server and send notifications to browsers from a simple interface. You can see an example of this app in Figure 6.7. Open a new tab in the browser and navigate to `localhost:3001/admin`. You should see the list of browser registrations you have so far.

Hover your mouse over one of the browsers listed on the page, then select the Notify button that appears. A popup appears allowing you to edit the content of the notification message, as shown in Figure 6.20. Click the Send Message button highlighted in the figure to send the message to the selected browser.

Use the drop-down on the bottom of the form (highlighted in Figure 6.21) to select from canned notification options available in the app. Click the Reset button when you've completed the selection to copy the selected message content into the editor window.

To adjust the default options, or to add your own, modify the contents of the project's `chapter-06\public\admin\index.html` and `chapter-06\public\admin\js\admin.js` files.

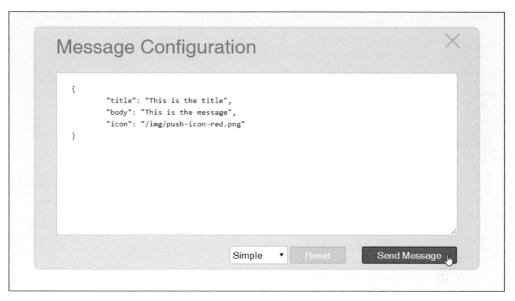

Figure 6.20    Sending a Notification Using the Server's Admin App

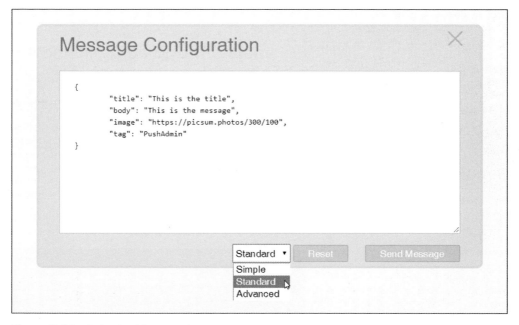

Figure 6.21    Selecting Message Content

## Dealing with Subscription Expiration

One topic we haven't covered yet is what happens when the browser's subscription expires. The browser push services won't hold onto these subscriptions forever, so they eventually whack them and let the browser know. When this happens, the browser fires the pushsubscriptionchange event to which the service worker can react through an event listener:

```
self.addEventListener("pushsubscriptionchange", event => {
  console.log('SW: Push Subscription Change event fired');
  console.dir(event);
  event.waitUntil(
    self.pushManager.subscribe(regOptions)
      .then(subscription => {
        console.log('Browser re-subscribed');
        console.log(subscription)
        // now, send the subscription object to the server
        // just like we did in index.js


      })
      .catch(error => {
        console.error(error);
      })
  );
});
```

In this example, the event listener simply re-subscribes the browser for notifications. In a real-world application, you would probably want to ask users if they want to subscribe again.

You can add this code to your project's sw.js file if you want, but none of your subscriptions will expire as you work through this book.

The complete code for the project's sw.js file up to this point in the chapter is in the project's chapter-06\public\chapter-code\sw-63.js file.


## Sending Notifications to Push Services

The one thing I haven't shown you yet is how the server sends notifications to the browser's push service. This is all done through code in the project's chapter-06\app\routes\api.ts file. If you open the file and look through it, you'll find the following code at the top of the file:

```
// initialize the Web Push Module
// borrowed from https://www.npmjs.com/package/web-push
if (Config.GCMAPI_KEY) {
  // if we have a GCM key, use it
  webpush.setGCMAPIKey(Config.GCMAPI_KEY);
  /* in an early implementation of Push (in 2014)
     Google used Google Cloud Messaging (GCM)
     before any standards were in place. So
     If you're supporting users running
```

```
      really old browsers, then you'll want to
      populate this value in the config file */
}
webpush.setVapidDetails(
  'mailto:john@johnwargo.com',
  Config.VAPID_PUBLIC,
  Config.VAPID_PRIVATE
);
```

This TypeScript code (it doesn't look much different from JavaScript, does it?) reads values from the external config.ts file we created earlier and sets the appropriate configuration values in the web-push module's configuration. Remember, the server uses the third-party web-push module[11] to send notifications through the browser push services, so this code simply initializes that module.

With module configuration out of the way, the server sends notifications using the following code:

```
router.post('/send/:idx', function (req: any, res: any, next: any) {
  // send a notification message
  console.log('Router: POST /send');
  const pushBody = JSON.stringify(req.body);
  // convert the parameter to a number
  let idx = parseInt(req.params.idx, 10);
  // do we have a number in idx?
  if (idx && pushBody) {
    console.log(`Sending notification to Idx: ${idx}`);
    console.log(`Payload: ${pushBody}`);

    storage.getItem(STORAGE_KEY)
      .then(theResult: any => {
        let browsers = theResult ? theResult : [];
        // get the item from the array at idx
        let index = browsers.findIndex(function (subscription: any) {
          return subscription.idx === idx;
        });
        // did we find it?
        if (index > -1) {
          // get the subscriber
          let browser = browsers[index];
          webpush.sendNotification(browser.subscription, pushBody, {})
            .then(result: any => {
              console.log('Notification sent successfully');
              res.json(result);
            })
            .catch(result: any => {
              console.log('Notification failure');
              console.log(result);
```

---

11. https://www.npmjs.com/package/web-push

```
                // does the response have an error code?
                if (result.statusCode) {
                  // then return it to the calling application
                  res.status(result.statusCode).send({ msg: result.body });
                } else {
                  // otherwise who knows?
                  res.status(500).send(result);
                }
              })
          } else {
            console.log('Browser not found');
            res.sendStatus(404);
          }
        })
        .catch(error: any => {
          console.log(error);
          res.sendStatus(500);
        })
  } else {
    res.sendStatus(400);
  }
});
```

This function handles the POST request highlighted in Figure 6.18; this code

- Pulls the browser index off the request's query string.

- Grabs the message content from the request body.

- Makes sure it has an index and message content to send.

- Tries to retrieve the subscription object for the browser specified in `idx`. The subscriptions are stored in a local file using the node-persist module.[12]

- If it has the browser subscription object, it sends it plus the message content to the browser's push service through the call to `webpush.sendNotification(browser.subscription, pushBody, {})`.

The web-push module abstracts away the complexities of the Push API, enabling a server process to reliably send browser notifications with just a few lines of code.

## Wrap-Up

Well, this was a big chapter. We covered the complete browser notifications process from web client permission and subscriptions through notifications and the server process that sends the notification through the browser's push service.

The next chapter is the book's final chapter about service workers. In it, I'll show how to send data between a service worker and the web app it services.

---

12. https://www.npmjs.com/package/node-persist

# 7

# Passing Data between Service Workers and Web Applications

Service workers and web apps have a symbiotic relationship on modern browsers that support service workers; the two work closely together to deliver an improved experience for users. So far, the only interactions I showed between web apps and service workers are situations in which the service worker helps the web app, such as by managing resource fetching and processing push notifications as they arrive. In this chapter, I show how to pass data between a service worker and a web app running in a browser (desktop or mobile). This data communication goes both ways: from a service worker to the web app, from a web app to the service worker, or even from the service worker to all browser tabs running the web app (I show examples of each in this chapter).

As I've described throughout this book, the service worker isn't running all the time: the browser awakens it only when there's work for the service worker to do. Therefore, you cannot implement a full data synchronization solution in a web app using a service worker, as described in Chapter 5, "Going the Rest of the Way Offline with Background Sync." We can, however, use event-triggered actions in a service worker or web app to split processing between the service worker and the app. A web app, for example, could

- Pass data calculation activities off to the service worker to complete.

- Let the service worker know when page data changed so it can let other app instances running in other browser tabs know they need to refresh page content.

- Share application state, such as logged-in user or shopping cart data, across browser tabs through the service worker.

Web developers can already use the `window.postMessage` method to send messages between window objects (between a window and a pop-up it created or between different page components like the page and an iframe embedded in the page). In this chapter, we cover the `serviceWorker.postMessage` method that enables similar communication between a service worker and the web app it serves. We also cover how the `MessageChannel` object creates a two-way communication channel that apps can use to streamline communication between a service worker and the web app it serves.

We build upon the simple push client app we used in Chapter 6, "Push Notifications." Our task in this chapter doesn't relate to push, but the app exhibits certain behavior that lends itself well to the topics in this chapter. For this topic, I deliberately didn't try to manufacture contrived app scenarios because I didn't want to detract from the core capabilities provided by the browser for interprocess communication. I leave it up to you to figure out how to apply these capabilities in your own apps.

# Preparing to Code

The work we do in this chapter revolves around adding some enhancements to the app used in the previous chapter. The code for the server app is available in the book's GitHub repository at https://github.com/johnwargo/learning-pwa-code. I provided complete instructions for how to download the code and configure your development environment in the section "Preparing to Code" in Chapter 3, "Service Workers." If you haven't already completed those steps, go there and complete them first before picking up here again.

Open a terminal window and navigate the terminal into the cloned project's \learning-pwa-code\chapter-07\ folder. This folder contains the completed version of the app as of the end of the previous chapter. Install the app's dependencies by executing the following command:

```
npm install
```

Next, execute the following command:

```
node generate-keys.js
```

This executes a little node.js utility I wrote to generate a set of Voluntary Application Server Iden-tification (VAPID) keys and write them to the configuration files used by the web app. The utility calls the web-push module's webpush.generateVAPIDKeys() method, which handles the whole process[1] for us.

As in previous chapters, I coded the server app in TypeScript, so before you can use the new configuration files just created, you must execute the following command to compile the code into JavaScript:

```
tsc
```

With all the parts in place, it's time to start the server; in the terminal window, execute the following command:

```
npm start
```

If everything's set up properly in the code, the server will respond with the following text in the terminal:

```
learning-pwa-push@0.0.1 start D:\dev\learning-pwa-code\chapter-07
node ./bin/www
```

---

1. You can read about the process at https://www.npmjs.com/package/web-push#usage.

At this point, you're all set—the server is up and running and ready to serve content. If you see an error message, you must dig through any reported errors and resolve them before continuing.

To see the web app in its current state, open Google Chrome or a browser that supports service workers and navigate to

```
http://localhost:3001
```

After a short delay, the server should render the simple web page shown in Figure 6.6. We'll add some extra stuff to the page as we work through this chapter.

# Send Data from a Web App to a Service Worker

We kick off the coding sections of this chapter highlighting how to send data between a web app and a service worker. In the sample app from Chapter 6, the state of the browser changes when the user clicks or taps the Subscribe and Unsubscribe buttons. When that happens, what if the service worker needed to know this and act in some way with that information? The service worker's `postMessage` method enables an app to do this.

When an app needs to send data to a service worker, it can send the data using the following:

```
navigator.serviceWorker.controller.postMessage(DATA_OBJECT);
```

In this example, the `DATA_OBJECT` object is simply a JavaScript object containing whatever data the app wants delivered to the service worker.

To see this in action, open the project's `chapter-07\public\js\index.js` file, and in the file's `doSubscribe` function, look for the block of code that executes after the browser successfully subscribes for notifications. There you'll find the following code:

```
console.log('doSubscribe: Browser subscribed');
```

Immediately following that line of code, add the following:

```
// send a message to the service worker letting it know
navigator.serviceWorker.controller.postMessage({ subscription: true });
```

This code sends a message to the service worker with a data object consisting of the `subscription` property with a value of true. This data tells the service worker the notification subscription state for this browser (true) immediately after the browser subscribes. I show you soon how the service worker uses this information.

Next, in the file's `doUnsubscribe` function, look for the following:

```
if (status) {
```

Immediately following that line of code, add

```
// tell the service worker we unsubscribed
navigator.serviceWorker.controller.postMessage({ subscription: false });
```

This sends the same data object to the service worker with a different `subscription` property value (`false`). This tells the service worker that the browser is no longer subscribed for notifications immediately after the unsubscribe completes.

> **Note**
>
> At this point, you may be asking, Why am I going through all of this when the service worker can check for a subscribed browser using code from Chapter 6? That's true, but the service worker doesn't have a trigger it can use to react to the event. It must rely on the app code completing the subscribe or unsubscribe process to notify it of the event.

Now that our app informs the service worker when subscription status changes, let's look at how the service worker responds to the message. As you probably expect, the arrival of the message from the web app triggers an event in the service worker. To process the message, the service worker must register the `message` event.

Open the project's `chapter-07\public\sw.js` file and add the following code to the end of the file:

```
self.addEventListener('message', event => {
  console.log('SW: Message event fired');
  console.dir(event);
  console.log(`SW: Subscription status: ${event.data.subscription}`);
  // do something interesting with the subscription status

});
```

If you save your changes, open the web app in the browser (http://localhost:3001), and click the Subscribe and Unsubscribe button on the page, you should see output from both the web app and the service worker in the console as shown in Figure 7.1. The "Browser Subscribed" text is from the web app's `index.js` file, and the items prefaced with SW: come from the service worker.

```
Browser subscribed
SW: Message event fired
▸ ExtendableMessageEvent
SW: Subscription status: true
```

Figure 7.1   Web App Output from PostMessage

The service worker accesses the content of the data object passed with the message through the `event.data.subscription` object. I had you write the event's `event` object to the console so you can inspect it and see what other data elements it exposes for the service worker to use.

Now, I agree that the example provided here isn't very exciting, but all I'm trying to do is show the moving parts—how you'll use this in your app will vary. What I've shown is getting data from the web app to the service worker and the distinct place where that data goes into the service worker. In the next section, we do something interesting with the data.

# Send Data from a Service Worker to a Web App

To send data from a service worker to a web app window, the process is a little more complicated. Notice that I said *web app window* instead of *web app*. That's because it's easy for a web app to send data to a service worker, since there's only one service worker. On the service worker side, it can send data to any browser window or browser tab running the web app serviced by the service worker. Because of that, the service worker must do extra work to figure out which window should get the message.

> **Note**
>
> This is probably a good time to remind you that the browser wakes the service worker to process the message sent from the web app window. The service worker therefore has a limited window where it knows about the sender of the message. Once the service worker finishes processing the message, the browser shuts the service worker down and it forgets everything it knew about the sender and the message it sent.

The browser maintains a list of the client windows served by the service worker in the service worker's `clients` object. The service worker needs the ID for the sending window to send a message back to the window. Fortunately, the sending window includes that value in the message event's `event.source.id` property. In its simplest form, the service worker can send a message back to the sending window using the following code:

```
self.clients.get(event.source.id).then(client => {
  client.postMessage(DATA_OBJECT);
});
```

Knowing the service worker has access to an object storing an array of all the client windows served by the service worker, a service worker can send a message to every associated browser window using the following code:

```
self.clients.matchAll().then(clients => {
  clients.forEach(client => {
    client.postMessage(DATA_OBJECT);
  })
});
```

If the browser has copies of the web app open in other windows or tabs, we can use this approach to reset each window to the correct state when one window subscribes or unsubscribes to notifications. Open the project's `chapter-07/public/sw.js` file, and update the service worker `message` event listener from the earlier example to the following code:

```
self.addEventListener('message', function (event) {
  console.log('SW: Message event fired');
  console.dir(event);
  console.log(`Subscription status: ${event.data.subscription}`);
  // get all the client windows
  self.clients.matchAll().then(clients => {
    // loop though each window
    clients.forEach(client => {
```

```
      // send a message to the window
      client.postMessage({ subscription: event.data.subscription });
    })
  });
});
```

In this example, the listener uses `self.clients.matchAll` to build an array of all the client windows. It returns a `clients` object, which we can iterate over using JavaScript's `forEach` iterator. The code sends, to each client window, a simple data object containing the current subscription status for the app:

```
{ subscription: event.data.subscription }
```

You could also accomplish the same result using

```
client.postMessage(event.data});
```

For the web app to process the message, we must add a message event listener there. Open the project's `chapter-07\public\js\index.js` file and add the following event listener to the bottom of the file:

```
navigator.serviceWorker.addEventListener('message', event => {
  console.log('Message listener fired');
  console.dir(event);
  // do we have a subscription object?
  if (typeof event.data.subscription !== 'undefined') {
    console.log(`Subscription event: ${event.data.subscription}`);
    updateUI();
  }
}, false);
```

This code checks to see if the message event includes the `subscription` property. If it does, it logs the subscription status to the console and then calls the app's `updateUI` function to refresh the page. It's in this function that the app decides whether to enable the Subscribe and Unsubscribe buttons depending on subscription status. The result of this is that the subscription state reflected in the button shown by the app synchronizes across all browser windows.

The web app doesn't use the data passed to it from the service worker because the `updateUI` function checks subscription status anyway. But there's no reason the app couldn't use the data—we just don't need it to in this case.

> **Tip**
>
> Remember, the data passing affects only windows that are running the service worker in the current browser (e.g., Chrome). Any browser windows running the app in other browsers at the same time (e.g., Firefox) won't be affected.

Looking at that code, it's clear that there's one flaw with it. The preceding example sends the message to all browser windows, but if you think about it, there's no need to send the message to the window that triggered the original message to the service worker. Let's update the code a bit by adding a check to see if the window we're sending to is the same one that sent the original message. If it is, we skip it and move on to the next one.

```
self.addEventListener('message', function (event) {
  console.log('SW: Message event fired');
  console.dir(event);
  console.log(`SW: Subscription status: ${event.data.subscription}`);
  // get all the client windows
  self.clients.matchAll().then(clients => {
    // loop though each window
    clients.forEach(client => {
      if (client.id === event.source.id) {
        // is the window the same one that told us about
        // the subscription event?
        console.log(`SW: Skipping affected window (${client.id})`);
      } else {
        // send a message to the window
        console.log(`SW: Notifying ${client.id}`);
        client.postMessage({ subscription: event.data.subscription });
      }
    })
  });
});
```

Save all the changes and refresh the app in the browser, then open additional browser windows or tabs pointing to the web app. When you're all set, subscribe or unsubscribe one of the windows and watch what happens in the others.

Pretty cool, right? I know I often have multiple Amazon windows open as I decide what to purchase; this approach could easily enable Amazon's web app to synchronize shopping cart item count across all browser windows, saving me a refresh to see what the current count is as I switch windows.

The complete code for these modifications is in the project's index-71.js and service worker-71.js files in the project's chapter-07\public\chapter-code\ folder.

## Two-Way Communication Using `MessageChannel`

The browser and service worker also support a two-way communication channel using postMessage; this approach uses the browser's MessageChannel[2] interface. When you create a message channel, you essentially create two communications ports: port1 and port2; and each participant uses one of the ports exclusively to send messages and data to the other.

A message channel was essentially designed to let two parts of a web app (for example, the app's main page and an iFrame embedded in it) to create a channel and communicate across it. When used with service workers, things get a little weird because service workers don't run all the time—they're awakened when the browser needs them. Service workers don't maintain state, so a message channel is active only until the service worker is shut down by the browser.

---

2. https://developer.mozilla.org/en-US/docs/Web/API/MessageChannel

Using a message channel in a web app looks like this:

```
const messageChannel = new MessageChannel();
messageChannel.port1.onmessage = function (event) {
  console.log('Message received on channel');
  // do something with the message
};

// send the message to the service worker
navigator.serviceWorker.controller.postMessage(DATA_OBJECT,
  [messageChannel.port2]);
```

Start by creating the message channel, then define an event listener for the messages sent to this side of the channel using port 1. Finally, send a message to the other participant, passing in port 2 as the second parameter to postMessage. It doesn't matter which side uses which port: all that matters is that the app uses one for each end of the communication channel and uses that port exclusively on that end of the conversation.

In the service worker, the message event handler uses the value in event.ports[0] to send a response back to the web app. The value in event.ports[0] contains the value the web app passed in the second parameter to the call to postMessage.

```
self.addEventListener('message', function (event) {
  console.log('SW: Message event fired');
  let responsePort = event.ports[0];
  // send a message back to the web app using
  reponsePort.postMessage("Some message");
});
```

Let me show you the whole process in an example. Open the project's chapter-07/public/ index.html file. Add the following HTML to the bottom of the existing page's content, before the script tags:

```
<div id='actionsContainer'>
  <div id='playback'>
    <div>
      <label for="playbackText">Playback Text</label>
      <input id="playbackText" placeholder="Enter some text here"><br>
      <button type="button" id="btnPlayback">Playback</button>
    </div>
  </div>
</div>
```

This adds an input field and a button to the page.

Open the project's chapter-07\public\js\index.js file then add the following code to the bottom of the file:

```
document.getElementById("btnPlayback")
  .addEventListener("click", doPlayback);
```

This creates a click event listener for the Playback button on the page.

Finally, add the `doPlayback` function above the event listener you just added:

```
function doPlayback() {
  console.log('doPlayback()');
  // create the new message channel
  const messageChannel = new MessageChannel();
  messageChannel.port1.onmessage = function (event) {
    console.log('Message received on channel');
    Swal.fire({
      type: 'info',
      title: 'Message Channel',
      text: JSON.stringify(event.data)
    });
  };
  // send the message to the service worker
  navigator.serviceWorker.controller.postMessage({
    action: 'playback',
    content: $('#playbackText').val()
  }, [messageChannel.port2]);
}
```

This function creates the message channel, defines the `message` event handler for messages returned across the channel, and sends a message with some data (including the channel's port 2—which the service worker will use to send data back to it) to the service worker for processing. The message sent to the service worker includes the content entered in the input field we just added.

What we're going to do next is update the service worker code to process the message when it arrives, then parrot back the text it received from the web app. It will convert the provided text into upper case then send it back to the web app across the message channel's port 2. Back in the web app, the message event handler grabs the result and displays it in a fancy dialog.

Open the project's service worker file located in `chapter-07\public\sw.js`. Refactor the message event listener so it looks like the following:

```
self.addEventListener('message', event => {
  console.log('SW: Message event fired');
  console.dir(event);
  // do we have an 'action' message?
  if (typeof event.data.action !== 'undefined') {
    console.log('SW: Action message received');

  } else {
    console.log(`SW: Subscription status: ${event.data.subscription}`);
    // get all the client windows
    self.clients.matchAll().then(clients => {
      // loop though each window
      clients.forEach(client => {
        if (client.id === event.source.id) {
          // is the window the same one that told us about
```

```
          // the subscription event?
          console.log(`SW: Skipping affected window (${client.id})`);
        } else {
          // send a message to the window
          console.log(`SW: Notifying ${client.id}`);
          client.postMessage({ subscription: event.data.subscription });
        }
      })
    });
  }
});
```

What you're doing here is making room for a couple of actions sent through message channels. In this case, we relegated the existing subscription processing message to the else clause and added a new check for an action object to the message event handler.

With that in place, we need something to process the actions as they come in. Here's what we use to do that:

```
let theAction = event.data.action;
switch (theAction) {
  case 'playback':
    console.log('SW: Processing Playback message');
    event.ports[0].postMessage(event.data.content.toUpperCase());
    break;
  default:
    console.log('SW: Unrecognized action (ignored)');
}
```

The code pulls the value for the action object from the received message and uses it in a case statement we'll add to later. In the solo playback case, it takes the content passed in the message, converts it to uppercase, and sends it back to the web app. Add that code to the message event listener inside the if portion of the if/then statement, as highlighted in the following code.

Here's the complete code for the event listener:

```
self.addEventListener('message', function (event) {
  console.log('SW: Message event fired');
  console.dir(event);
  // do we have an 'action' message?
  if (typeof event.data.action !== 'undefined') {
    console.log('SW: Action message received');
    let theAction = event.data.action;
    switch (theAction) {
      case 'playback':
        console.log('SW: Processing Playback message');
        event.ports[0].postMessage(event.data.content.toUpperCase());
        break;
      default:
        console.log('SW: Unrecognized action (ignored)');
    }
```

```
  } else {
    console.log(`SW: Subscription status: ${event.data.subscription}`);
    // get all the client windows
    self.clients.matchAll().then(clients => {
      // loop though each window
      clients.forEach(client => {
        if (client.id === event.source.id) {
          // is the window the same one that told us about
          // the subscription event?
          console.log(`SW: Skipping affected window (${client.id})`);
        } else {
          // send a message to the window
          console.log(`SW: Notifying ${client.id}`);
          client.postMessage({ subscription: event.data.subscription });
        }
      })
    });
  }
});
```

Save your changes to both files, refresh the web app in the browser, enter some text in the input field, and click the Playback button. You'll see the inputted text returned in uppercase letters, as shown in Figure 7.2.

Figure 7.2   Playing Text Back through a Service Worker

I agree that this example is a little silly, but I merely wanted to show how to define a communications channel between the two entities. You can use this capability to pass calculations on to the service worker to perform, or you can even ask the service worker to fetch and process data (from a local database or server) using this approach.

If your service-worker-side processing will take a little while to complete, remember that you must wrap it in a `waitUntil` to keep the browser from shutting down the service worker until the job's complete. Let me show you an example of this in action.

In the project's `index.html` file, add the following `div` to the bottom of the `actionsContainer` div:

```
<div id="longAction">
  <button type="button" id="btnLongAction">Long Action</button>
  <div id="longActionOutput"></div>
</div>
```

When you're done, the `actionsContainer` div will look like this:

```
<div id='actionsContainer'>
  <div id='playback'>
    <div>
      <label for="playbackText">Playback Text</label>
      <input id="playbackText" placeholder="Enter some text here"><br>
      <button type="button" id="btnPlayback">Playback</button>
    </div>
  </div>

  <div id="longAction">
    <button type="button" id="btnLongAction">Long Action</button>
    <div id="longActionOutput"></div>
  </div>
</div>
```

Next, in the project's `index.js` file, add the following code to the bottom of the file (near the other `click` event listeners):

```
document.getElementById("btnLongAction")
.addEventListener("click", doLongAction);
```

Finally, add the `doLongAction` function to the file, somewhere above the event listener you just added:

```
function doLongAction() {
  console.log('doLongAction()');
  // clear any previous content if we have it
  $("#longActionOutput").empty();
  // create a message channel
  const messageChannel = new MessageChannel();
  // set up the message listener for the message channel
  messageChannel.port1.onmessage = function (event) {
    console.log('Message received on channel');
```

```
    // append content to the page element
    $("#longActionOutput").append(`<p>${event.data}</p>`);
  };
  // send the message to the service worker
  navigator.serviceWorker.controller.postMessage(
    { action: 'longaction' }, [messageChannel.port2]);
}
```

In the service worker (`sw.js`), add the following new case to the existing `message` listener:

```
case 'longaction':
  let limerick = [
    'There once was a farmer from Leeds',
    'Who swallowed a packet of seeds.',
    'It soon came to pass',
    'He was covered with grass',
    'But has all the tomatoes he needs.'
  ]
  console.log('SW: Processing longAction message');
  // do something interesting here
  event.waitUntil(
    new Promise(resolve => {
      // loop around for 5 seconds
      let i = 0;
      let wait = setInterval(() => {
        // increment the counter
        let msg = `${limerick[i]}`
        ++i;
        event.ports[0].postMessage(msg);
        // are we done?
        if (i > 4) {
          // shut down the timer
          clearInterval(wait);
          // resolve the promise
          resolve();
        }
      }, 1000);
    })
  )
  break;
```

For the new long action, the event listener wraps a `waitUntil` around a promise. Inside the promise, the code sends a limerick back to the page one line at a time, one second apart, until all five lines have been transmitted and displayed. This is another silly example, but at least you can see clearly how to create a promise in a `waitUntil`.

Here's the complete listing for the service worker's `message` listener:

```
self.addEventListener('message', function (event) {
```

```
  console.log('SW: Message event fired');
  console.dir(event);
  // do we have an 'action' message?
  if (typeof event.data.action !== 'undefined') {
    console.log('SW: Action message received');
    let theAction = event.data.action;
    switch (theAction) {
      case 'playback':
        console.log('SW: Processing Playback message');
        event.ports[0].postMessage(event.data.content.toUpperCase());
        break;
      case 'longaction':
        console.log('SW: Processing longAction message');
        // do something interesting here
        event.waitUntil(
          new Promise(resolve => {
            // loop around for 5 seconds
            let i = 0;
            let wait = setInterval(() => {
              // increment the counter
              ++i;
              console.log(`Loop #${i}`);
              event.ports[0].postMessage(i);
              // are we done?
              if (i > 4) {
                // shut down the timer
                clearInterval(wait);
                // resolve the promise
                resolve();
              }
            }, 1000);
          })
        )
        break;
      default:
        console.log('SW: Unrecognized action (ignored)');
    }
  } else {
    console.log(`SW: Subscription status: ${event.data.subscription}`);
    // get all the client windows
    self.clients.matchAll().then(clients => {
      // loop though each window
      clients.forEach(client => {
        if (client.id === event.source.id) {
          // is the window the same one that told us about
          // the subscription event?
          console.log(`SW: Skipping affected window (${client.id})`);
        } else {
          // send a message to the window
```

```
            console.log(`SW: Notifying ${client.id}`);
            client.postMessage({ subscription: event.data.subscription });
          }
        })
      });
    }
});
```

Save your changes, refresh the page in the browser, then click the Long Action button. The browser should respond with the limerick, one line every second, as shown in Figure 7.3.

Figure 7.3   Long Action Results

The complete code for these modifications is in the project's index-72.js and sw-72.js files in the project's chapter-07\public\chapter-code\ folder.

## Wrap-Up

In this chapter, I showed several ways to pass data between a web app and the service worker that services it. With this skill, you have a simple way to manage content across multiple browser windows through a service worker.

This is the last service worker chapter in the book. The remaining chapters deal with the tools available to PWA developers to make their lives easier.

# 8

# Assessment, Automation, and Deployment

Throughout this book, we focused on the core capabilities of the browser, and we handcrafted the manifest files and code that make a PWA a PWA. Now that we're past all that, it's time to talk about available tools to help you build and deploy PWAs.

In this chapter, I show tools from Google that developers use to validate the quality of a PWA, identifying where an app fulfills PWA requirements and what must be done to make the app a full-featured PWA. Next, I show some tools from Microsoft that developers can use to convert a web app into a PWA. The first tool shows you how well you've done at delivering your PWA, and the second tool automates much of the stuff you need to do to create a PWA.

## Assessing PWA Quality Using Lighthouse

As I described at the beginning of the book, there are different views of what makes a PWA a PWA. Google tells the story that PWAs are

- Reliable

- Fast

- Engaging

But I argued that there are specific capabilities that define a PWA:

- PWAs are installable: mobile and desktop users can install them on their phone's home screen or desktop using an installation UI provided in the app.

- PWAs cache the app's core UI on the local device, so when the user opens the app, the UI loads quickly before the app goes out to get updated data from the network.

- PWAs run background tasks, enabling background processing and offline resource caching.

- PWAs can receive push notifications from a backend server regardless of whether the app is running.

To make it easier for developers to deliver PWAs that meet either criteria, Google created Light-house.[1] Lighthouse is an open source tool that assesses web apps against Google's criteria for PWAs; the good news is that Google's criteria encompass mine. The tool tests your app, then delivers a report highlighting what must be fixed to create a complete PWA.

There are three ways to run Lighthouse:

- Google Chrome extension
- Google Chrome DevTools
- Node Module

In the sections that follow, I show you how each approach works plus show some sample reports from running Lighthouse against two different versions of the Tip Calculator app from Chapter 2, "Web App Manifest Files."

# Preparing to Code

In this chapter, we work with a stripped-down version of the Tip Calculator app, which doesn't require a lot of coding for our purposes.

The app in Chapter 2 had a rudimentary service worker but no manifest file, so we built out the manifest and associated code to make the app installable. In this chapter, there's no manifest file or service worker; it's just a bare bones web app. You can find the app in the cloned project's `\learning-pwa-code\chapter-08\tip-calc` folder.

Assuming you've worked along with all the code in the book so far and have all the prerequisites installed, you're good to go. If not, please hop over to the Preparing to Code section of Chapter 2 and complete the steps outlined therein before picking back up here.

To use this chapter's version of the app, open a terminal window or command prompt, navigate to the project folder, and execute the following command:

```
http-server
```

You should then be able to open a web browser, navigate to http://localhost:8080/index.html, and see the Tip Calculator we're so familiar with.

We're going to use the Chrome browser next, so if you don't already have it installed, please open a browser, navigate to https://www.google.com/chrome/, and install the latest Chrome version.

## Using the Lighthouse Plugin

The easiest way to use Lighthouse is through the Lighthouse extension[2] Google publishes. To install the extension,

---

1. https://developers.google.com/web/tools/lighthouse/

2. https://chrome.google.com/webstore/detail/lighthouse/blipmdconlkpinefehnmjammfjpmpbjk

- Open Chrome or one of the browsers built using Chromium (like Microsoft Edge), and open the Chrome Web Store (by either opening the Extensions page or searching for it).
- Search for the Lighthouse extension in the store.
- Click the Add to Chrome button to install the extension in the browser.

With the extension installed, Chrome adds a lighthouse icon to the toolbar, as shown in Figure 8.1.

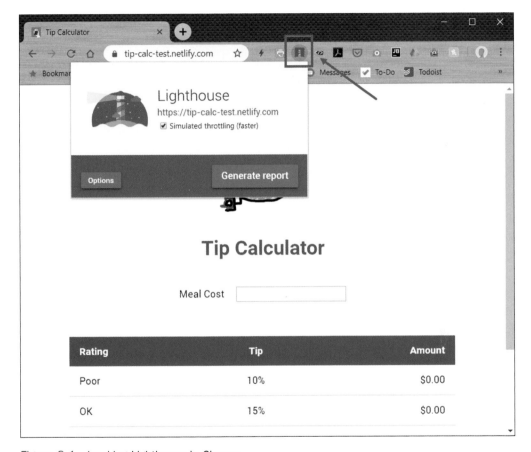

Figure 8.1   Invoking Lighthouse in Chrome

In the browser, navigate to the Tip Calculator app running in the local server process (started in Preparing to Code), then click the Lighthouse button.

### Note

For the screenshot shown in Figure 8.1, I published the app to a GitHub repository, then used Netlify to host the app for free. I did this as an easy way to get an SSL certificate for my app (to increase my Lighthouse scores for this chapter's screenshots).

When you click the Options button, Chrome opens a dialog allowing you to set the scope for the audit performed by the extension, as shown in Figure 8.2. All we care about right now is the PWA report, so enable the Progressive Web App option and disable all others, then click the OK button to return to Lighthouse. You can come back later and try out the other options.

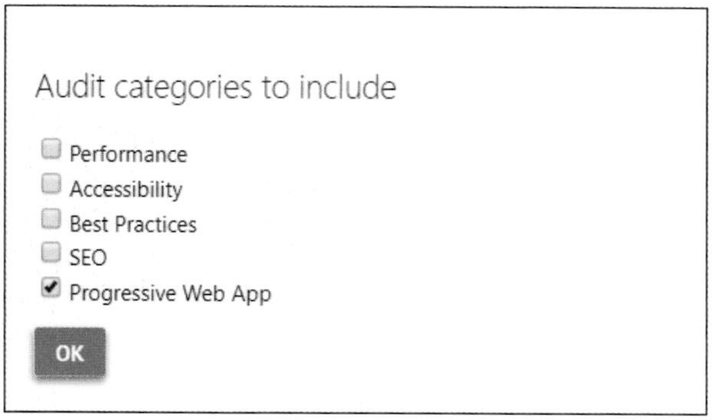

Audit categories to include

☐ Performance
☐ Accessibility
☐ Best Practices
☐ SEO
☑ Progressive Web App

**OK**

Figure 8.2    Lighthouse Options

Click the Generate Report button shown in Figure 8.1, and Chrome opens a new window hosting the selected web app in a simulated mobile device and exercises the app in different conditions. I haven't studied exactly what tests it performs, but you can tell that it's loading the app with and without network connectivity and recording what happens in the app. When it completes its assessment, Chrome opens the page shown in Figure 8.3 listing the results of the audit.

As you can see from the figure, the results are dismal. Remember though, this is the bare bones version of the Tip Calculator app; it doesn't have a manifest file or a service worker, so the results should not be a surprise. Knowing what you know by now about service workers and manifest files, you should be able to see where these files would bolster the results.

Since I'm hosting the app on Netlify, and they automatically provide an SSL certificate, I get a few extra points here. For your locally hosted app, this result should be different, although in my testing, Lighthouse seemed to incorrectly think I was hosting over an HTTPS connection even when I wasn't. This is probably an internal browser hack that enables the browser to run PWAs from localhost.

It's a little hard to see, but at the top of the page is the PWA logo I highlighted in Figure 1.1 so many pages ago. In the report in Figure 8.3, it's greyed out and hard to see because the app is not a PWA, and that's a simple way the extension highlights this fact.

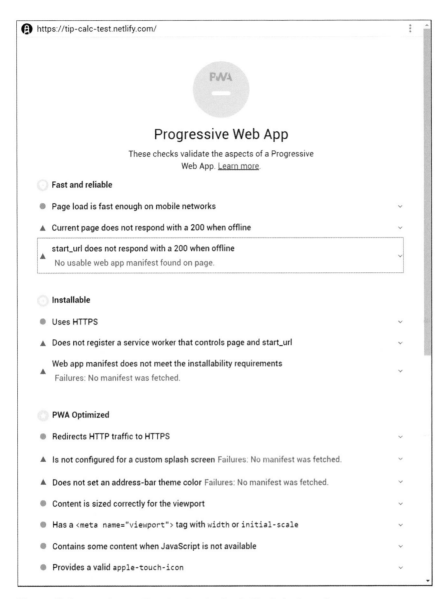

Figure 8.3    Lighthouse Results for the Basic Tip Calculator App

If you rerun the report against the complete PWA from the end of Chapter 2, you get the happier results shown in Figure 8.4. Notice that the PWA logo at the top of the report is complete and colored, plus you have this bold green checkmark proudly proclaiming success.

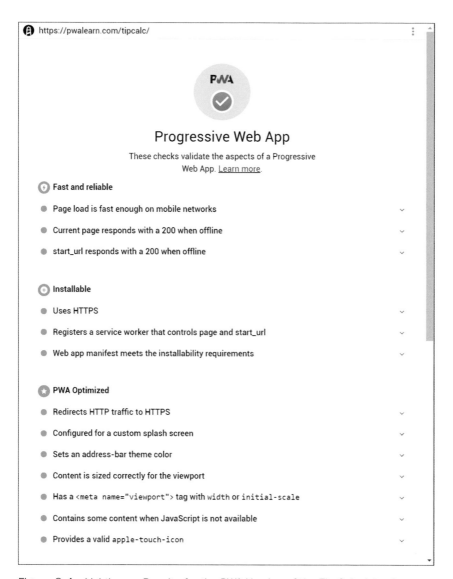

Figure 8.4    Lighthouse Results for the PWA Version of the Tip Calculator App

Lighthouse offers several output options, shown in the upper-right corner of Figure 8.5. You can print short or expanded versions of the report or get the report as HTML or JSON.

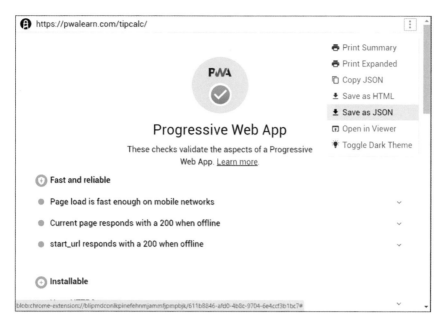

Figure 8.5   Lighthouse Report Output Options

The report lets you know what work you need to do to deliver the full PWA version of the selected app. You may or may not want to do all the work it recommends, but that's up to you. Lighthouse is just a quick and simple litmus test for PWAs.

The browser extension is my preferred approach for running Lighthouse, although I expect that most developers prefer the option outlined in the following section. Generating the report through the extension delivers the report in a new browser window, making it easy to review and print for later reference.

## Using the Lighthouse Tools in the Browser

To make it easier for developers to run Lighthouse during the development process, Google provides a Lighthouse audit right inside the Chrome DevTools. There's no extension to install or any extra setup—it's just there, ready to go to work.

To access Lighthouse through Chrome DevTools, open a web app in the browser, then open DevTools and look for the Audits tab, shown in Figure 8.6.

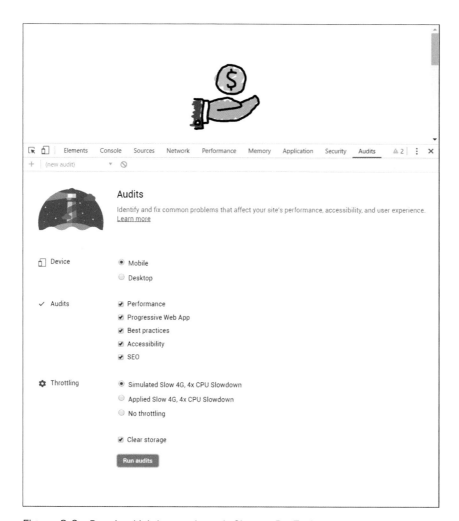

Figure 8.6    Running Lighthouse through Chrome DevTools

Here you have a few more options than what's available through the extension; you can specify to test the mobile or desktop version of the app and control how the tools throttle the network connection during the audit. Select the options that work for your app, then click the Run Audits button to start the test. When Lighthouse finishes its test, it displays the results in the audit window shown in Figure 8.7.

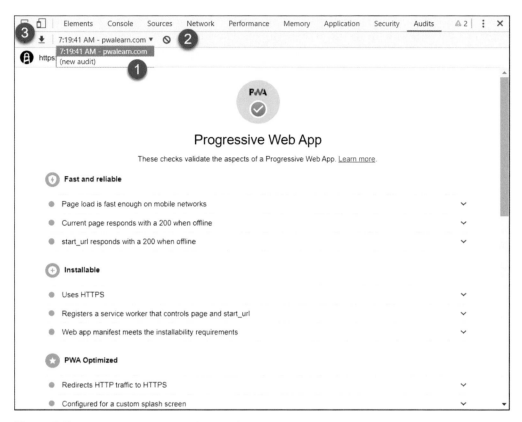

Figure 8.7    Lighthouse Results in Chrome DevTools

From the report page, you have limited options: you can (1) create a new audit, clear (2) the report, or (3) download the report in JSON format.

## Using the Lighthouse Node Module

You can also install Lighthouse as a node module and run it from a command-line or in a node app. To install the module, open a terminal window or command prompt, then execute the following command:

```
npm install -g lighthouse
```

With the module installed, you can run the report against a site using the following command:

```
lighthouse <url>
```

In this example, `<url>` is the site URL you want to audit. For the book's public Tip Calculator app, you would use the following:

```
lighthouse https://learningpwa.com/tipcalc/
```

The module launches Chrome and performs the same tests you've seen before. The only difference is what it does with the results, as shown in the following output:

```
status Generating results... +1ms
Printer html output written to /Users/johnwargo/learningpwa.com_2019-09-05_07-28-40.
  report.html +79ms
CLI Protip: Run lighthouse with `--view` to immediately open the HTML report in your
  browser +2ms
ChromeLauncher Killing Chrome instance 54056 +1ms
```

The Lighthouse module generates its output directly to an .html file in the current folder. If you want the module to launch the report in the browser immediately after generating it, you must add the --view parameter to the command line, as shown in the following example:

```
lighthouse https://learningpwa.com/tipcalc/ --view
```

Since the module writes its results to the current folder, you must make sure you have write rights to the folder before running the test. As I tested this for this chapter's content, I opened a command prompt in Windows, switched to the root of my system's C drive, and executed the command. When the report completed, I received the following error:

```
ChromeLauncher Killing Chrome instance 52092 +80ms
Runtime error encountered: EPERM: operation not permitted, open
  'C:\tip-calc-test.netlify.com_2019-08-31_15-43-46.report.html'
Error: EPERM: operation not permitted, open
  'C:\tip-calc-test.netlify.com_2019-08-31_15-43-46.report.html'
```

This happened because Windows users don't have access to the root of drive C by default. When I switched to a folder where I had write permissions, the module worked as expected.

You can also use the module in a node app, and Google provides complete instructions.[3] I must admit that I struggle to find a use case for this; the results you get from running Lighthouse is a lot of data, and I can't see the need to write an app that parses and understands the results.

# PWABuilder

When you're just getting started building PWAs, Google's Lighthouse is a great tool to help you understand what you must do to your app to make it a PWA and validate your work as you do it. What beginning PWA developers really need is something that helps them do the work to convert an app into a PWA. To address that need, Microsoft created the open source PWABuilder[4] project.

As with Lighthouse, you can use PWABuilder to scan your web site to determine what must be done to it to make it into a PWA, but PWABuilder takes it a step further and actually gives you the code you need to convert the web app to a PWA. You can even use PWABuilder to use your PWA to generate native apps for deployment to Android, iOS, macOS, and Windows devices.

Microsoft also offers a command-line version of PWABuilder that you can use to validate web app manifest settings and generate apps for deployment to Android, iOS, macOS, and Windows

---

3. https://github.com/GoogleChrome/lighthouse/blob/master/docs/readme.md#using-programmatically

4. https://www.pwabuilder.com/

devices. By the time you read this, Microsoft should have released the PWABuilder extension for Visual Studio Code.

> **Note**
>
> PWABuilder started as a Microsoft open source project called ManifoldJS, a framework that enabled developers to create a manifest file and web app, then use a command-line tool to generate apps for multiple target platforms. The framework basically took a web app and generated Apache Cordova apps for several target platforms. It created native apps for each target platform, but the app consisted mainly of the web app running in a native app container.

## Using the PWABuilder UI

To use PWABuilder, fire up your browser of choice and navigate to https://pwabuilder.com; the browser will open the page shown in Figure 8.8. Enter the URL for a publicly available web app in the input field, then click the Start button to continue. You can use my https://tip-calc-test.netlify.com/ app if you'd like.

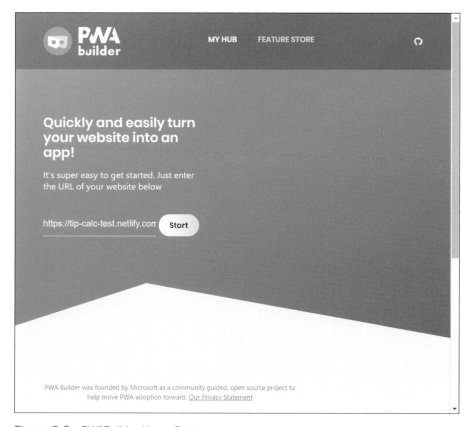

Figure 8.8    PWABuilder Home Page

> **Note**
>
> The site scanned by PWABuilder must be hosted on a publicly available server, since the scanner employed by the PWABuilder server must be able to access the site remotely to do its scan. This is another reason why I hosted this chapter's Tip Calculator app on Netlify.

The app churns for a little while, then delivers the report shown in Figure 8.9. Here, PWABuilder highlights the PWA deficiencies for the provided web app. Reading through this report, you should see that it lists a lot of the same information provided by Lighthouse. What happens next is what differentiates PWABuilder from Lighthouse.

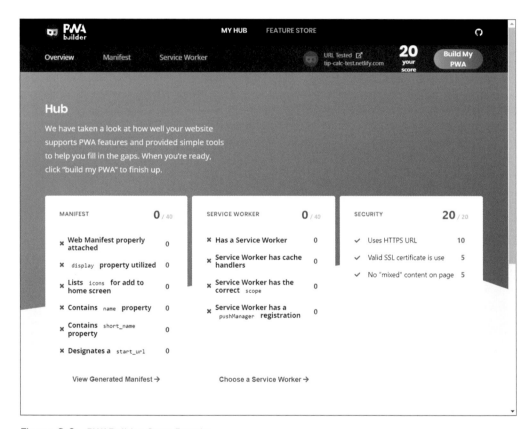

Figure 8.9   PWABuilder Scan Results

Notice the options on the report page to View Generated Manifest and Choose a Service Worker. As part of the work it did scanning the app, it built a manifest file using information it gleaned from the app. PWABuilder also offers a catalog of service workers you can use in your app. I'll cover both options in a minute.

If you scroll down the report page, you'll see a list of options for adding additional features to an app, shown in Figure 8.10. This links you to a catalog of free code snippets you can use. The snippet catalog lists some standard browser capabilities, such as geolocation, copy to clipboard, and the ability to install a PWA (a topic covered in Chapter 2), plus some code to interact with several Microsoft services from Microsoft Graph.

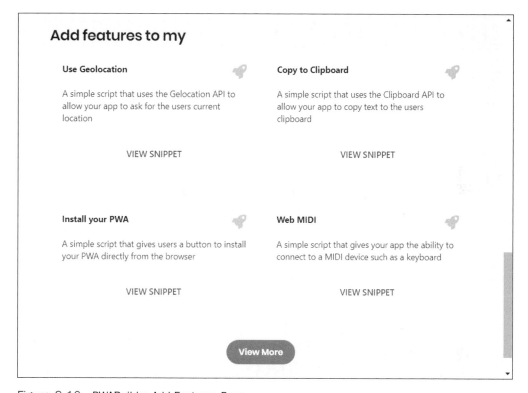

**Figure 8.10**   PWABuilder Add Features Pane

This version of the Tip Calculator app doesn't have a manifest file, so PWABuilder generates one for the app automatically and gives you the ability to tweak it through the web UI. If the app had a manifest file configured, PWABuilder would let you edit it.

At the top of Figure 8.9 is a Manifest tab; click it and you'll see the page shown in Figure 8.11. PWABuilder builds this manifest file using information it's able to learn about the app by scanning its contents. For example, it pulls the values for the manifest file's name and short_name properties from the index.html file's title attribute. For app icons, it pulls in all of the icons referenced in the index.html file's icon link elements.

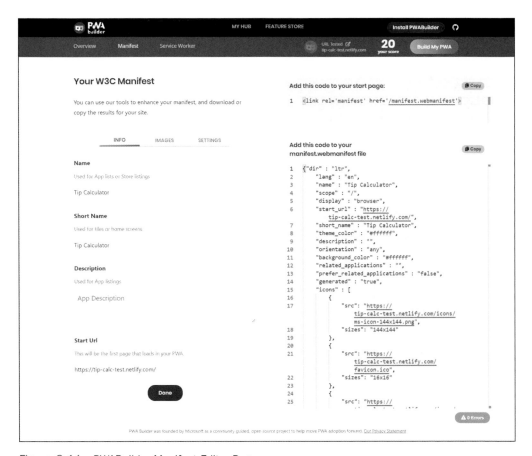

Figure 8.11    PWABuilder Manifest Editor Page

Use the edit fields, shown on the left side of the figure, to change the properties in the manifest file. You can use the Images and Settings tabs in the editor to tweak other aspects of the manifest, adding or removing image files, setting the scope for the app, and more.

With all manifest settings in place, use the code areas on the right side of the page to copy the manifest file and the link to load it over to your web app. The code box in the top-right corner contains the code you must add to your index.html file's head section to load the manifest. The code box in the lower-right corner of the editor contains the actual manifest file content. You should copy the content, then make a new file in the web app project's root folder called manifest.webmanifest and place the copied code there.

This process adds the manifest to the project. To make the app installable, use the code snippet available by clicking View Snippet, as shown in the lower-left corner of Figure 8.10. What you'll find there is pretty much the same code you'll find in early code examples in Chapter 2.

Next, click on the Service Worker tab, and you'll see the page shown in Figure 8.12. Here you'll find sample code and implementation instructions for many of the caching strategies discussed in

Chapter 4, "Resource Caching." PWABuilder doesn't generate anything here specific to your web app. It just offers some standard options you can copy over into your web app and configure for your app's needs.

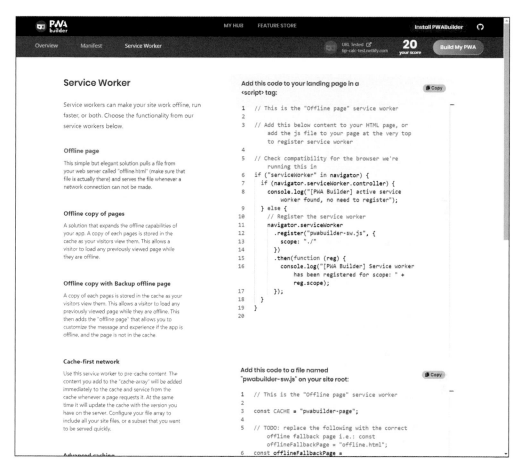

Figure 8.12    PWABuilder Service Worker Page

When you add the manifest file to the project and implement a service worker, then run the scan again; you should see different, and hopefully better, results than the ones shown in Figure 8.9. As you can see, letting PWABuilder help you through the process is much easier than all that coding we did in earlier chapters of this book.

## Creating Deployable Apps

Another feature of PWABuilder is its ability to generate starter projects for deployable apps for Android, iOS, macOS, and Windows, as shown in Figure 8.13. The technologies used to build or package these apps vary depending on the selected target platform.

For Android, PWABuilder generates a Trusted Web Activities (TWA)[5] app, a type of Android app that enables PWAs to run in a simple app shell on Android devices. For iOS, PWABuilder generates an Apache Cordova app you can build and deploy to iOS devices. I cover the options for Windows in PWAs and the Microsoft Store later in the chapter. In my testing, I found that some of the projects were half-baked and missing complete instructions. My suggestion is that you download the packages from this page and look at them; perhaps by the time you read this, what's available will be more useful.

Figure 8.13    PWABuilder Packaged App Options

5.  https://developers.google.com/web/updates/2019/02/using-twa

## Using the PWABuilder CLI

PWABuilder supports a command-line option as well, and what you get is essentially an updated version of what was available with the ManifoldJS project many years ago: the ability to generate deployable apps for multiple target platforms based on a single manifest file.

To install the PWABuilder command-line interface (CLI), open a terminal window or command prompt and execute the following command:

```
npm install -g pwabuilder
```

Next, to generate apps based on the web app at a specific URL, execute the following command:

```
pwabuilder <url>
```

Replace <url> with the full URL pointing to the source web app. For example, to generate apps for the public Tip Calculator app, you would execute the following command:

```
pwabuilder https://learningpwa.com/tipcalc/
```

For a locally hosted web app like the ones we created in this book, use the following command:

```
pwabuilder http://localhost:3001
```

The PWABuilder CLI will scan the file and warn you if it finds any issues with the app, as shown in the top of Figure 8.14. Since it's generating apps for each target platform, you should fix these errors before continuing. Next, the tool creates app for multiple target platforms in a folder named with the short name of the scanned app.

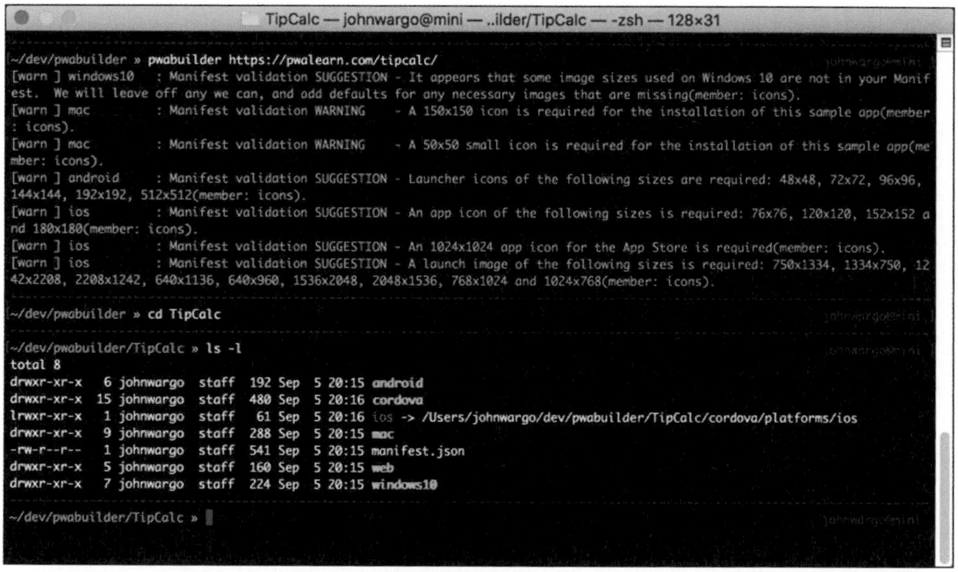

Figure 8.14   PWABuilder CLI Output and Results

You can open the newly created folder and read through the instructions provided with each target platform to build and deploy apps for each.

## PWABuilder and Visual Studio

Right after I finished this chapter, Microsoft released a preview version of the PWABuilder extension for Visual Studio Code. It's still in preview, so I don't know exactly how this will work when it's released, but I can at least show you how it works today and hope it's not too much different in its final form.

To get the extension, open Visual Studio Code and then open the extensions pane, as shown in Figure 8.15. Type pwabuilder in the search field, as shown in the figure, and you should see the extension appear. Click the Install button to add the extension to your Visual Studio Code installation.

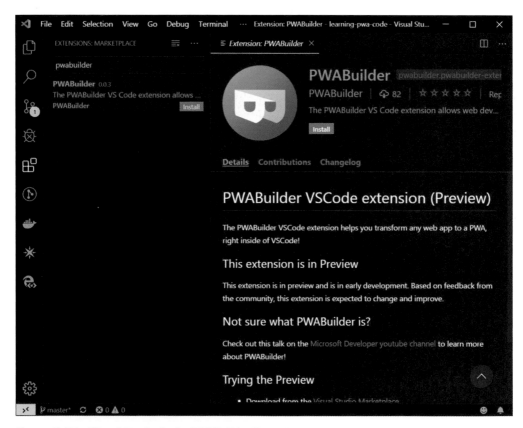

Figure 8.15    Visual Studio Code: PWABuilder Extension

With the extension in place, open a web app project in Visual Studio Code, then open the command palette, as shown in Figure 8.16. Type pwa, and the command dropdown should show the available options for PWABuilder, as shown in the figure.

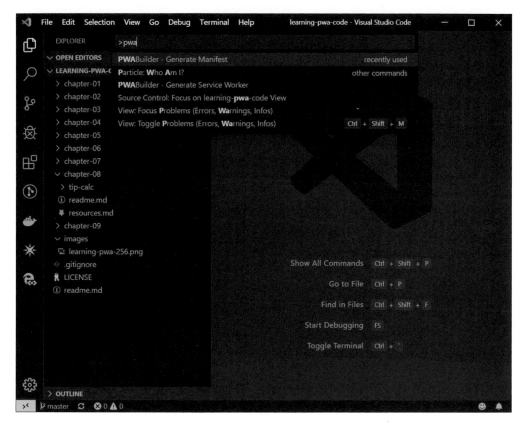

Figure 8.16    Visual Studio Code Command Palette

Right now, the only available options are to generate a manifest file or generate a service worker for the selected app project. Since it's PWABuilder under the covers, what happens next shouldn't be a surprise. If you select Generate Manifest, Visual Studio Code opens the Manifest Generator page, shown in Figure 8.17.

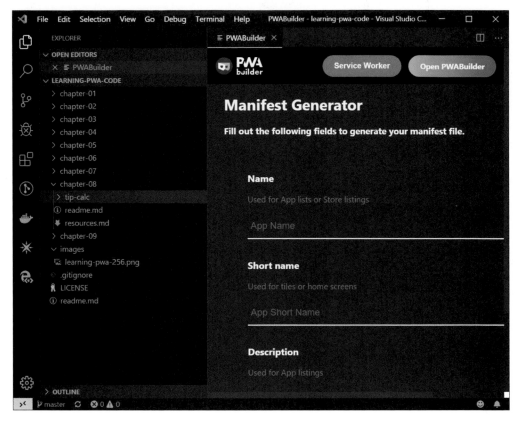

Figure 8.17    Visual Studio Code: PWABuilder Manifest Generator

Populate the form with the same options discussed earlier in the chapter, selecting an icon for the app as well as providing additional settings for the manifest file. When you're done, click the Generate button on the bottom of the form. At this point, Visual Studio Code prompts you to select the target folder for the manifest, which should be the root folder of the app. When you make your selection, the extension saves the manifest file in a file called `manifest.json`, then opens the file for editing, as shown in Figure 8.18.

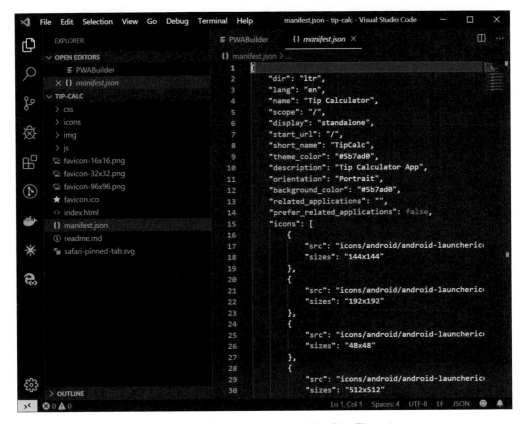

Figure 8.18    Visual Studio Code: PWABuilder Generated Manifest File

The extension doesn't update your project's index.html file to use the manifest, so at this point, you should open that file and add the following line to the <head> section of the file:

```
<link rel="manifest" href="manifest.json">
```

Save your changes to the file, and your app has the first requirement of an installable PWA: a manifest file.

Adding a service worker to your project follows the same process: open the command palette, type pwa, then select Generate Service Worker. When you select this option, you'll see the screen shown in Figure 8.19. In this case, the extension isn't generating a service worker for your project, it's merely displaying the same service worker options you saw in Figure 8.12.

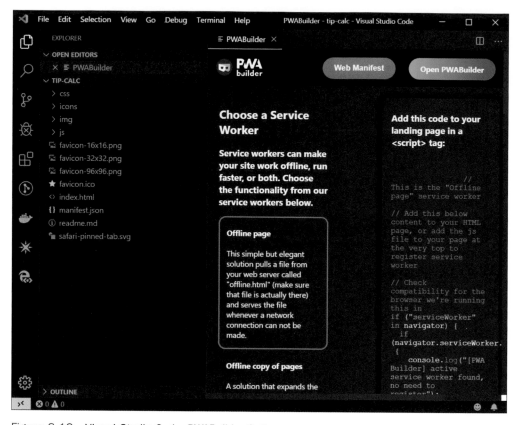

Figure 8.19   Visual Studio Code: PWABuilder Options

Follow the instructions on the page to update your project's landing page (typically the project's `index.html` file) with the code necessary to load a service worker, then select the service worker you want to use and add it to the project as well.

## PWAs and the Microsoft Store

On the Microsoft Windows platform, Microsoft took a unique approach and announced that it would scan the Internet for PWAs and automatically add them to the Microsoft Store. What this means is that Microsoft Windows customers now have a searchable database of PWAs they can install.

The process is automatic, but you can opt out if you don't want your app in the store. To do so, add a `robots.txt` file to the root folder of the app (if one doesn't already exist) and add the following to the file:

```
User-agent: bingbot
Disallow: /manifest.json
```

This tells Bing to ignore the app's manifest for PWA indexing purposes.

You can also package your PWA and deploy it to the Microsoft Store in several ways. One way is through the Windows option shown in Figure 8.12. When you click the Download icon on the Windows section in that figure, PWABuilder displays the dialog shown in Figure 8.20. When you click the Download button, you get a zip file you can use to create a package you can submit to the Microsoft Store. Just download the file, extract the contents to a folder, and follow the instructions in the extracted file's `projects\windows10\Windows10-next-steps.md` file.

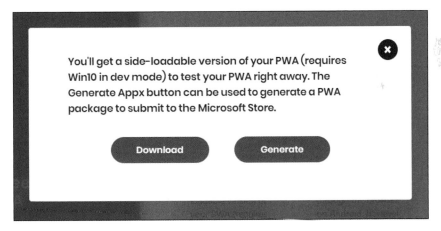

Figure 8.20    PWABuilder Windows App Options

When you click the Generate button, PWABuilder opens the dialog shown in Figure 8.21. Populate the form with the appropriate values from your Microsoft Dev Center account, and PWABuilder will generate the package you need to deploy this app through the Microsoft Store.

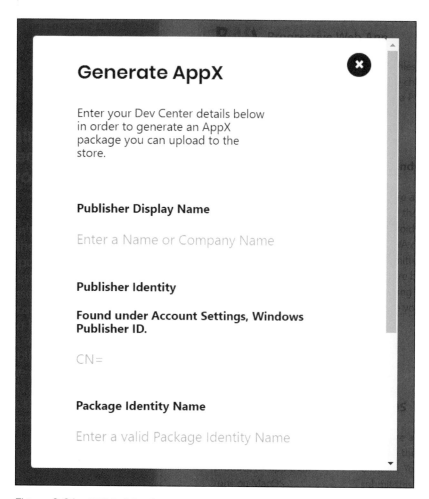

Figure 8.21    PWABuilder Generate Windows Store AppX Package

A third option involves using Visual Studio to package the app for deployment manually. Visual Studio 2017 included a special project type for Progressive Web Apps, as shown in Figure 8.22. When you create a project using this project type, you can add your PWA files to the project and package it for deployment using the instructions in Progressive Web Apps in the Microsoft Store.[6]

---

6. https://docs.microsoft.com/en-us/microsoft-edge/progressive-web-apps/microsoft-store

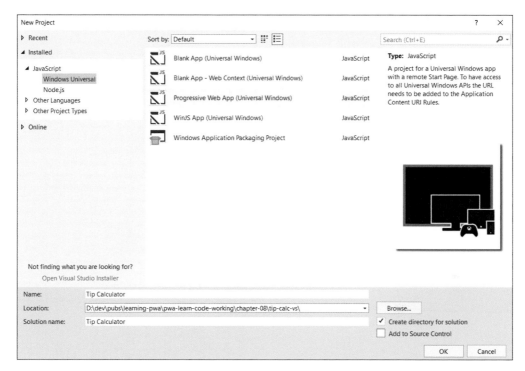

Figure 8.22   Visual Studio PWA Project

> **Warning**
>
> This capability is available only in Visual Studio 2017; Microsoft dropped the Windows JavaScript project type in Visual Studio 2019.

# Wrap-Up

In this chapter, I showed you some of the tools available to web developers to help them deliver better PWAs. When you're just starting out, these tools help kickstart your efforts and help you get the job done. I also showed how to use PWABuilder to help you build deployable versions of your PWAs.

In the next, and final, chapter, I'll show you another tool from Google called Workbox[7] that automates adding offline support to web apps.

---

7.  https://developers.google.com/web/tools/workbox/

# 9

# Automating Service Workers with Google Workbox

In Chapter 4, "Resource Caching," we wrote a lot of code to implement different caching strategies for the PWA News app. You probably completed that chapter and said something along the lines of "there's got to be a better way." Well, there is. With Google Workbox,[1] Google, along with the PWA developer community, provides a toolkit developers can use to more easily deliver robust and capable service workers. I'd like to say that you're writing less code with Workbox, but that's not the case. You're still writing code, but you're writing code that describes how you want your service worker to work rather than the code to actually make it work.

In this chapter, I introduce you to Workbox and show you how you can use it to implement caching strategies for your web apps. I don't cover every capability of Workbox; the library documentation is good, thorough, and full of examples. What I'll show here is how to apply Workbox to an app, using the Tip Calculator app from the beginning of the book.

In the source code for this chapter, I included a slightly modified version of the Tip Calculator used in Chapter 2, "Web App Manifest Files." Rather than start with a clean project and enhance it as you work through the chapter, in this chapter, you'll copy the clean version and work in a copy as you proceed through the different sections.

## Introducing Workbox

Workbox is a service worker toolbox consisting of JavaScript libraries, a Node command-line interface (CLI), and Node modules developers use to create service workers and manage how they work. The JavaScript libraries deliver the service worker–side capabilities of the toolbox, something Google describes as "adding offline support to web apps." The CLI and Node modules automate app resource precaching during the coding and build process.

With Workbox, you can build a service worker that

- Precaches the resources used by a web app and serves them from the cache.
- Implements multiple caching strategies for your web app's resources.

---

1. https://developers.google.com/web/tools/workbox/

- Implements offline capabilities for Google Analytics.

- Queues network requests for later processing using background sync (similar to what you learned in Chapter 5, "Going the Rest of the Way Offline with Background Sync").

- Programmatically sets expiration for cached resources.

- Does all sorts of other stuff.

Workbox abstracts away the complexity of the work that service workers do, letting you describe how you want things to work, and the toolbox handles everything else for you.

In this chapter's examples, I show you how to use the CLI and the JavaScript framework in your PWAs. I leave working with the Node module and build tools for you to research later. Everything you learn in this chapter easily applies to those other topics as well.

## Generating a Precaching Service Worker

With precaching and service workers, you build a list of all the local file resources used by your app, then use code to preload those resources into a device's local cache the first time the app runs on the device; we implemented an example of this in Listing 4.1. In Workbox, Google delivers tools that automate generating that file list plus generating the service worker that caches the files and serves them from the cache.

Start by making a copy of the project's `chapter-09/tip-calc` folder. Copy the folder, then paste it back to the same location, renaming the folder copy to `tc1` during the process. When you're done, you'll have two folders in the `chapter-09` folder: `tip-calc` and `tc1`.

Next, open a terminal window or command prompt, navigate into the `tc1` folder, and execute the following command:

```
npm install –g workbox-cli
```

This command installs the Workbox CLI for us to use. After the installation completes, execute the following command:

```
workbox wizard
```

This starts the process Workbox uses to generate the resource list and service worker for your PWA. The wizard will ask you a few questions, then create the configuration file that drives the precaching and service worker generation process. Figure 9.1 shows the first step in the process.

The wizard assumes you have a folder structure with a source and distribution folder (or some variant), so the first thing it does is ask for the location of the app's source files. For this simple project, everything is in the `tc1` folder, so select Manually enter the path, as highlighted in the figure, then press Enter.

The wizard then requests the following:

```
? Please enter the path to the root of your web app:
```

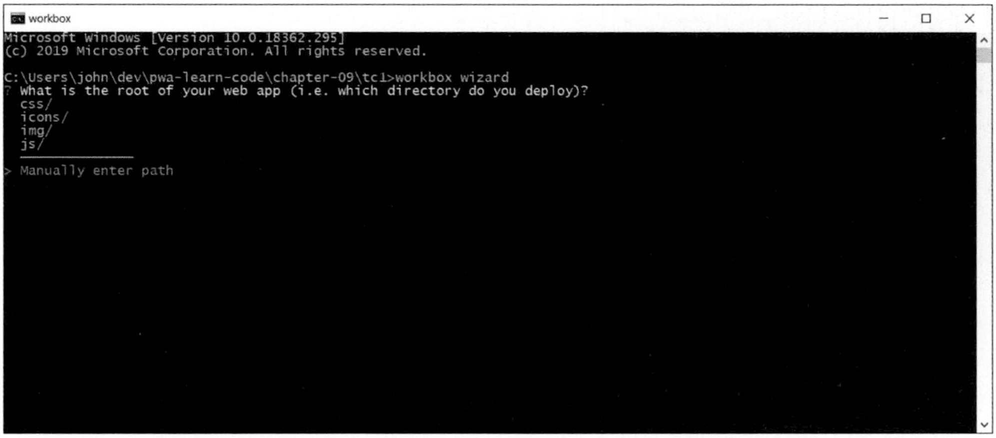

Figure 9.1   Workbox Wizard Starting Up

Enter a single period (.), then press Enter. The period indicates the current folder (make sure you're in the tc1 folder when you start the wizard).

Next, the wizard asks you to select the subfolders containing resources that require precaching:

```
? Which file types would you like to precache? (Press <space> to select, <a> to
  toggle all, <i> to invert selection)
>(*) css
 (*) png
 (*) ico
 (*) html
 (*) js
 (*) md
 (*) svg
```

The wizard selects all folders by default, so for this project just press Enter to accept the defaults. If you want to omit a folder, use the arrow keys to move up or down the list, then press the *a* key to toggle the selected folder or *i* to invert the current selections.

Next, the wizard asks for the file name for the generated service worker file. In this project, I've already configured the code that registers the service worker (in /js/sw-reg.js) to look for the service worker in a file called sw.js, so you can just press Enter to accept the default value provided.

```
? Where would you like your service worker file to be saved? (sw.js)
```

> **Note**
>
> If you change this value to a different file name, be sure to update the sw-reg.js file to use the new service worker file name.

Finally, the wizard asks for the file name for the configuration file used by Workbox to store the settings you just provided. Press Enter to accept the default (`workbox-config.js`).

```
? Where would you like to save these configuration options? (workbox-config.js)
```

> **Note**
>
> The Workbox CLI assumes this file name for related CLI commands, so if you change this value from the default, you must provide the file name in every CLI command that uses this file. For that reason, it's probably best to just leave it at the default value.

When you press Enter, the Workbox CLI writes the configuration values you provided to the configuration file you specified in the last step. At the conclusion of the process, the CLI outputs the following message:

```
To build your service worker, run

  workbox generateSW workbox-config.js

as part of a build process. See https://goo.gl/fdTQBf for details.
You can further customize your service worker by making changes to workbox-config.js.
  See https://goo.gl/8bs14N for details.
```

At this point, all you have is the Workbox configuration file shown in Listing 9.1. Nothing's been done to generate the service worker file we need for this app; we'll do that next.

**Listing 9.1    Workbox Configuration File: `workbox-config.js`**

```
module.exports = {
  "globDirectory": ".",
  "globPatterns": [
    "**/*.{css,png,ico,html,js,svg}"
  ],
  "swDest": "sw.js"
};
```

In the terminal window, execute the following command:

```
workbox generateSW workbox-config.js
```

This launches the Workbox process that generates the service worker file specified in the configuration file. Since we used the default configuration file name, you can simplify things and execute the following instead:

```
workbox generateSW
```

At this point, Workbox scans the selected source code folders, then generates the service worker shown in Listing 9.2 (redacted to show only the first and last resources in the precache manifest array).

Listing 9.2   **Workbox Generated `sw.js` File in `tc1`**

```
/**
 * Welcome to your Workbox-powered service worker!
 *
 * you'll need to register this file in your web app, and you should
 * disable HTTP caching for this file too.
 * see https://goo.gl/nhQhGp
 *
 * the rest of the code is auto-generated. Please don't update this
 * file directly; instead, make changes to your Workbox build
 * configuration and rerun your build process.
 * see https://goo.gl/2aRDsh
 */

importScripts("https://storage.googleapis.com/workbox-cdn/releases/4.3.1/
  workbox-sw.js");

self.addEventListener('message', (event) => {
  if (event.data && event.data.type === 'SKIP_WAITING') {
    self.skipWaiting();
  }
});

/**
 * the workboxSW.precacheAndRoute() method efficiently caches and
 * responds to requests for URLs in the manifest.
 * see https://goo.gl/S9QRab
 */
self.__precacheManifest = [
  {
    "url": "css/main.css",
    "revision": "50c72ce0e72508baa767491be65455cd"
  },

  // redacted: MORE RESOURCE FILES HERE

  {
    "url": "workbox-config.js",
    "revision": "ffc90338931ec8f867b11b3c6da129fd"
  }
].concat(self.__precacheManifest || []);
workbox.precaching.precacheAndRoute(self.__precacheManifest, {});
```

If you look at the file, you'll see that it starts with the following import:

```
importScripts("https://storage.googleapis.com/workbox-cdn/releases/4.3.1/
  workbox-sw.js");
```

This loads the Workbox JavaScript library used by everything in the file.

What follows is a complete service worker for the app. The most important part is the precacheManifest, an array of objects representing every file resource in the app. Each object consists of a url property containing a relative path pointing to the resource file, and the revision property, which is a hash of the file. Workbox uses this hash to determine when the file changes so it can update the cache.

At the end of the generated file is the following code:

```
workbox.precaching.precacheAndRoute(self.__precacheManifest, {});
```

This code initiates resource precaching and instructs the Workbox JavaScript library to serve resources from the cache. That's it; that's a complete precaching service worker using Workbox.

Switch back to the terminal window and start the local web server we used in Chapter 2 by executing the following command:

```
http-server
```

Open a browser and point it to http://localhost:8080/index.html; the browser will show the page you've already seen from Figure 2.1. Nothing has changed in the UI; what's different is under the covers. Open the browser's developer tools panel and look at the console. You should see the output shown in Figure 9.2.

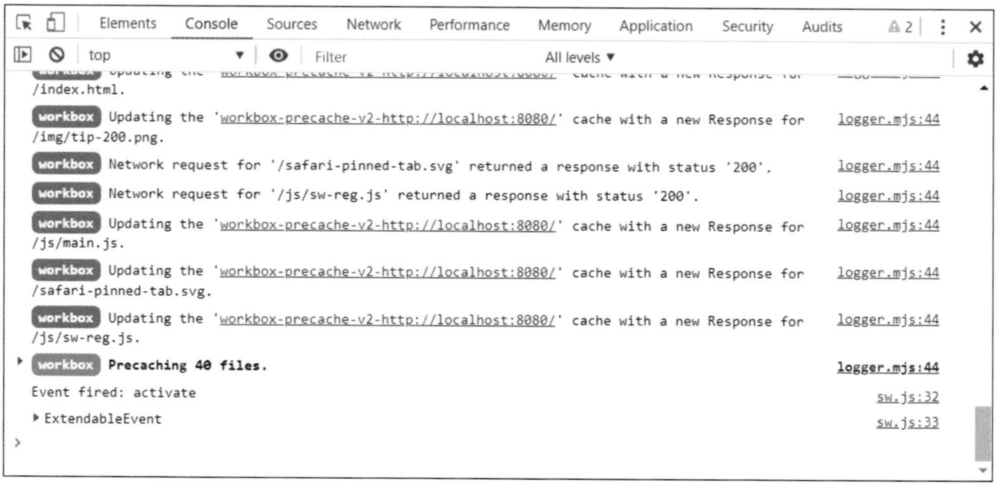

Figure 9.2    Workbox Precaching Tip Calculator Files

Our generated service worker cached 40 files, and those resources are cached and ready to enable the browser to run the app offline. To test it, turn off the network, reload the app, and look at the console output. You'll see output indicating the service worker serving resource files from cache, as shown in Figure 9.3.

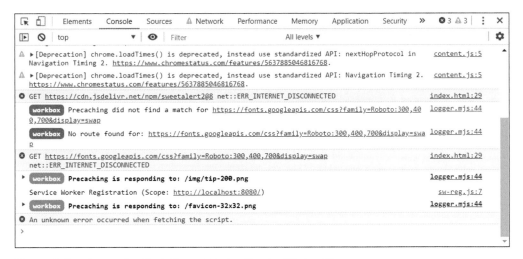

Figure 9.3    Chrome DevTools Error: Missing Service Worker File

When you look at the local cache, there are some extra files in the cached file list that we know we'll never need, such as the sw-start.js and workbox-config.js files. Fortunately for us, there's a solution. The workbox-config.js file supports a globIgnores property you can use to list the files or file specifications for files you want ignored during the cache manifest generation process. To omit those two files, add the following property to the workbox-config.js file:

```
"globIgnores": [
  '**/sw-start.js',
  '**/workbox-config.js'
],
```

You'll find the complete contents for the file in Listing 9.3.

Listing 9.3    **Workbox Configuration File: workbox-config.js in tc1**

```
module.exports = {
  "globDirectory": ".",
  "globPatterns": [
    "**/*.{css,png,ico,html,js,svg}"
  ],
  "globIgnores": [
    '**/sw-start.js',
    '**/workbox-config.js'
  ],
  "swDest": "sw.js"
};
```

Figure 9.3 shows a few errors as well, so apparently not everything the app needs is cached correctly.

The last error in the list doesn't tell you much about its cause; the browser generates that error when it attempts to load the service worker file as it loads the page. If you look at the precache array, you'll see that the service worker isn't listed. As you probably remember from Chapter 3, "Service Workers," the browser loads the service worker with every page load to check whether there's a new version to install. Since Workbox omits the service worker, you get this error.

I got around this error in Chapter 3 when I included the service worker in the list of cached files. You don't need to include your service worker in the cache. If it's not there, the browser generates an error and continues. To help me learn more about how Workbox works, and to avoid the error, I set about trying to figure out how to include the service worker in the cache (just for fun).

Since we're using Workbox to generate the service worker, I don't want to manually add the file to the precache array because Workbox will overwrite it whenever I generate the file.

I thought a possible solution existed in the `workbox-config.js` file. Open the file and look for the following:

```
"globPatterns": [
  "**/*.{css,png,ico,html,js,svg}"
],
```

This is the file specification that tells Workbox how to identify files we want precached. I tried adding the service worker to the list of precached files by adding the following entry to the `globPatterns` array:

```
"./sw.js"
```

Here's the complete array definition:

```
"globPatterns": [
  "**/*.{css,png,ico,html,js,svg}",
  "./sw.js"
],
```

When I regenerated the service worker and tested it in the browser, Workbox dutifully added the service worker to the cache as instructed, but the browser still reported the same error. Apparently, Workbox can't handle caching its own service worker. Sorry.

I'm going to ask you to ignore the other errors for now; I'll cover them in "Controlling Caching" Strategies later in the chapter.

As you can see, for simple static sites, this approach generates a service worker in no time and immediately improves the offline performance of the site. Unfortunately, it caches everything for the site, even if it's not used (like many of the icon files I have in the app).

You can also use the Workbox NodeJS module and Webpack plugin to generate or update the service worker in your project at build time. Since the focus of this book is service workers and PWAs, I'm going leave the details of that for your future research.[2]

---

2. You can learn more about this topic at https://developers.google.com/web/tools/workbox/modules/workbox-build.

# Add Precaching to an Existing Service Worker

Many developers want more control over their app's service worker, so Workbox supports a workflow for that use case as well. With this approach, you make some simple changes to a service worker, then use the Workbox CLI to populate the resource array you saw in the previous section. With the resource list in place, you add code to the service worker to enable the appropriate caching strategies for your app's resource types.

To get started, make another copy (our second) of the project's chapter-09/tip-calc folder, and call this version tc2. If, for some reason, you didn't complete the Node module installation in the previous section, open a terminal window, navigate to the new tc2 folder, then execute the following command:

```
npm install -g workbox-cli
```

The chapter's sample project includes a simple service worker in a file called sw-start.js. Open that file now in the tc2 folder and add the following lines of code to the top of the file:

```
importScripts('https://storage.googleapis.com/workbox-cdn/releases/4.3.1/
  workbox-sw.js');

workbox.precaching.precacheAndRoute([]);
```

This adds the Workbox library to the service worker and a placeholder for the resource array you saw in the previous section.

In the same terminal window, execute the following command:

```
workbox wizard -injectManifest
```

This runs the Workbox Wizard, as we did in the previous section, enabling a mode that instructs the CLI that it must prepare its configuration file to update an existing service worker rather than generate a new one. The wizard works the same way we saw in the previous section with only one additional change.

The wizard starts by asking for the app's source code folder:

```
? Please enter the path to the root of your web app:
```

Enter a single period (.), then press Enter. The period indicates the current folder (make sure you're in the tc2 folder).

Next, the wizard asks you to select the subfolders containing resources that require precaching:

```
? Which file types would you like to precache? (Press <space> to select, <a> to
  toggle all, <i> to invert selection)
>(*) css
 (*) png
 (*) ico
 (*) html
 (*) js
 (*) md
 (*) svg
```

At this point, the wizard asks for the existing service worker file you want updated with the resource array:

```
? Where's your existing service worker file? To be used with injectManifest, it
  should include a call to 'workbox.precaching.precacheAndRoute([])'
```

Enter `sw-start.js` and press Enter.

Next, the wizard asks for the file name for the generated service worker file. In this project, I've already configured the software that registers the service worker (`/js/sw-reg.js`) to look for the service worker in a file called `sw.js`, so you can just press Enter to accept the default value.

```
? Where would you like your service worker file to be saved? (sw.js)
```

> **Note**
>
> If you change this value to a different file name, be sure to update the `sw-reg.js` file to use the new service worker file name.

Finally, the wizard asks for the file name for the configuration file used by Workbox to store the settings you just entered or selected. Press Enter to accept the default (`workbox-config.js`).

```
? Where would you like to save these configuration options? (workbox-config.js)
```

> **Note**
>
> The Workbox CLI assumes this file name for related CLI commands, so if you change this value from the default, you must provide the file name in every CLI command that uses this file. For that reason, it's probably best to just leave it at the default value.

When you press Enter, the Workbox CLI writes the configuration values you provided to the configuration file you specified in the last step. At the conclusion of the process, the CLI outputs the following message:

```
To build your service worker, run

  workbox injectManifest workbox-config.js

as part of a build process. See https://goo.gl/fdTQBf for details.
You can further customize your service worker by making changes to
  workbox-config.js. See https://goo.gl/8bs14N for details.
```

At this point, all you did is create the Workbox configuration file shown in Listing 9.4.

**Listing 9.4  Workbox Configuration File: `workbox-config.js` in `tc2`**

```
module.exports = {
  "globDirectory": ".",
  "globPatterns": [
    "**/*.{css,png,ico,html,js,svg}"
  ],
```

```
    "swDest": "sw.js",
    "swSrc": "sw-start.js"
};
```

For the most part, the configuration file has a lot of the same settings from the previous section. What's new is the `swSrc` property, which tells Workbox what file to use as the base for the updated service worker.

In the terminal window, execute the following command:

```
workbox injectManifest
```

This command kicks off the resource manifest generation we saw in the previous section. Remember, we selected the default configuration file name, so we don't have to pass its file name on the command line here.

In this case, it updates the existing service worker shown in Listing 9.5 (redacted to show only the first and last resources in the precache manifest array).

Listing 9.5  **Workbox Generated `sw.js` File in `tc2`**

```
self.addEventListener('install', event => {
  // fires when the browser installs the app
  // here we're just logging the event and the contents
  // of the object passed to the event. the purpose of this event
  // is to give the service worker a place to setup the local
  // environment after the installation completes.
  console.log(`Event fired: ${event.type}`);
  console.dir(event);
});

self.addEventListener('activate', event => {
  // fires after the service worker completes its installation.
  // it's a place for the service worker to clean up from previous
  // service worker versions
  console.log(`Event fired: ${event.type}`);
  console.dir(event);
});

importScripts('https://storage.googleapis.com/workbox-cdn/releases/4.3.1/
  workbox-sw.js');

workbox.precaching.precacheAndRoute([
  {
    "url": "css/main.css",
    "revision": "50c72ce0e72508baa767491be65455cd"
  },
```

```
// redacted: MORE RESOURCE FILES HERE

  {
    "url": "safari-pinned-tab.svg",
    "revision": "7a812aea31a92da37ba82be39fa3084a"
  }
]);
```

When you load this version of the Tip Calculator app in the browser, you should see the same results from the previous section. The only difference between the two is that we provided the starter service worker file for this version.

You can also use the Workbox Node module and Webpack plugin to generate or update the service worker in your project at build time. Since the focus of this book is service workers and PWAs, I'm going to leave the details of that for your future research.[3]

## Controlling Cache Strategies

Many developers want more control over what's cached by the service worker and how the service worker caches the resources. If you look at the cache from one of the examples from the previous sections, shown in Figure 9.4, you'll see that the app cached all application icons even though the app doesn't need all of them on this browser.

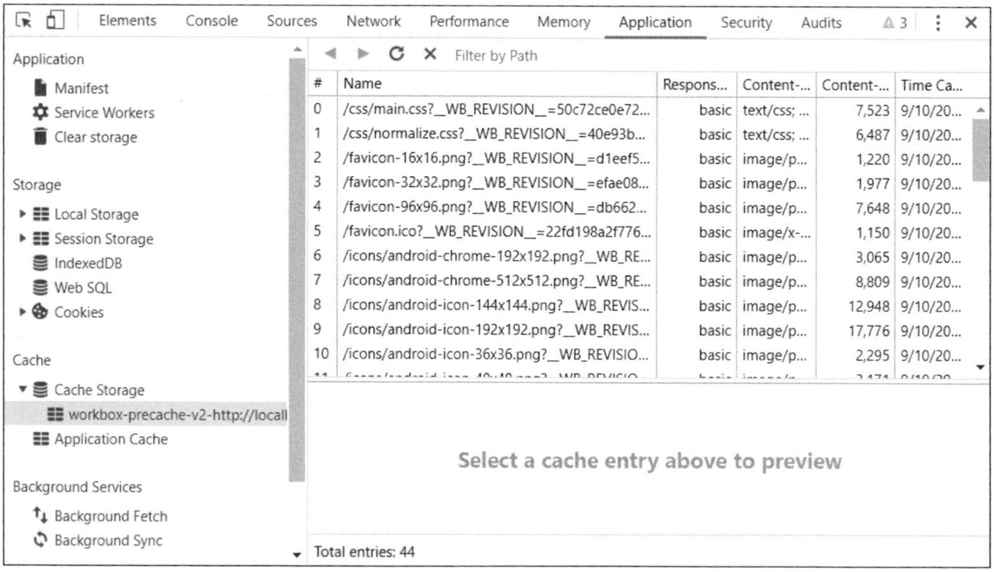

Figure 9.4   Tip Calculator Precached Files

3. You can learn more about this topic at https://developers.google.com/web/tools/workbox/modules/workbox-build.

When we skip the whole precaching process, we can build a service worker that uses Workbox to implement caching strategies for only the app resources needed by the app. Before I show you how to do that, I must first cover the different caching strategies available through Workbox. Here we go!

Workbox provides support for the following caching strategies:

- `CacheFirst`: Return the cached version of a resource, retrieving the resource from the network (and adding it to the cache) if it's not already in the cache.

- `CacheOnly`: Return the resource from the cache. If the resource is not in the cache, the fetch will fail. Your service worker must populate the cache during service worker installation to enable this option.

- `NetworkFirst`: Return the network version of the resource, retrieving the resource from the cache if the network is not available. The fetch fails when the network version is not available and the resource is not in the cache.

- `NetworkOnly`: Return the network version of the resource, failing if it's not available.

- `StaleWhileRevalidate`: Return the cached version of a resource, then update the cached version from the network so it's there the next time the app requests the resource. This gets resources to an app quickly, but it may not always be the most recent version.

To use a caching strategy when a web app requests resources, register a route to the resource using the following code:

```
workbox.routing.registerRoute( match, handler );
```

In this example, the `match` parameter refers to one of the following options used to match the requested resource with this route:

- Callback function

- Regular expression

- String

The `handler` parameter refers to one of the caching strategies listed earlier in this section.

Let's see all of this in action.

For the callback option, you provide a function Workbox executes to determine whether the requested resource matches the selection criteria for this route. Here's an example:

```
const matchX = ({ url, event }) => {
  return url.href.includes('x');
};

workbox.routing.registerRoute(
  matchX,
  new workbox.strategies.StaleWhileRevalidate()
);
```

In this example, the route matches the request URL if the full URL to the requested resource contains an x. If it does, the service worker uses the `StaleWhileRevalidate` strategy for the resource. If not, this resource is ignored and hopefully picked up by some other route.

You can match resources using a regular expression, as shown in the following example:

```
workbox.routing.registerRoute(
  /\.(?:html)$/,
  new workbox.strategies.NetworkFirst(),
);
```

In this example, the regular expression in the first parameter matches any file that has `.html` in the resource path. When the app requests an HTML file, the service worker will return the resource using the `NetworkFirst` strategy.

You can also use different caching strategies for different types of files. For example, the following code uses the `StaleWhileRevalidate` strategy for `.js` and `.css` files, but `NetworkFirst` for `.html` files:

```
workbox.routing.registerRoute(
  /\.(?:js|css)$/,
  new workbox.strategies.StaleWhileRevalidate(),
);

workbox.routing.registerRoute(
  /\.(?:html)$/,
  new workbox.strategies.NetworkFirst(),
);
```

Finally, you can match resources using a string value, as shown in the following example:

```
workbox.routing.registerRoute(
  '/img/my-logo.png',
  new workbox.strategies.CacheFirst(),
);
```

In this example, the route matches if the requested resource is the app's `/img/my-logo.png` file. When the app requests the logo file, the service worker will return the resource using the `CacheFirst` strategy.

Let's add some caching to the Tip Calculator app. Make another copy of the project's `chapter-09/tip-calc` folder, and call this version `tc3`. Next, rename the copied project's `sw-start.js` file to `sw.js` and open the renamed file in your code editor.

At the top of the file, add the following import:

```
importScripts('https://storage.googleapis.com/workbox-cdn/releases/4.3.1/
  workbox-sw.js');
```

This adds the Workbox library to the app.

Next, at the bottom of the file, add the following code:

```
workbox.routing.registerRoute(
  /\.(?:png|svg|js|css|html)$/,
  new workbox.strategies.StaleWhileRevalidate()
);
```

This uses a regular expression to apply the `StaleWhileRevalidate` caching strategy to all .png, .svg, .js, .css, and .html files for the app. This is a simple but effective approach to caching app resources and should cover most web app resource types.

If you have other file types in your web app, you can add the resource's file extension to the regular expression.

When you load the app in the browser and look at its cache storage, as shown in Figure 9.5, you'll see that all matching file types are cached.

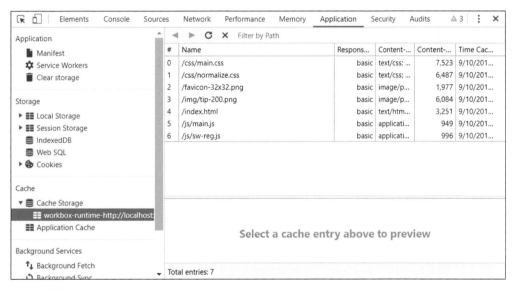

Figure 9.5    Workbox Cache in Action

To see the caching strategy in action, disable the network in the browser developer tools, then look at the results in the Network panel, shown in Figure 9.6. As you can see from the figure, the service worker returns the requested resource if it has it, then the `fetchWrapper.mjs` file tries to retrieve an updated version of the file from the network (and fails).

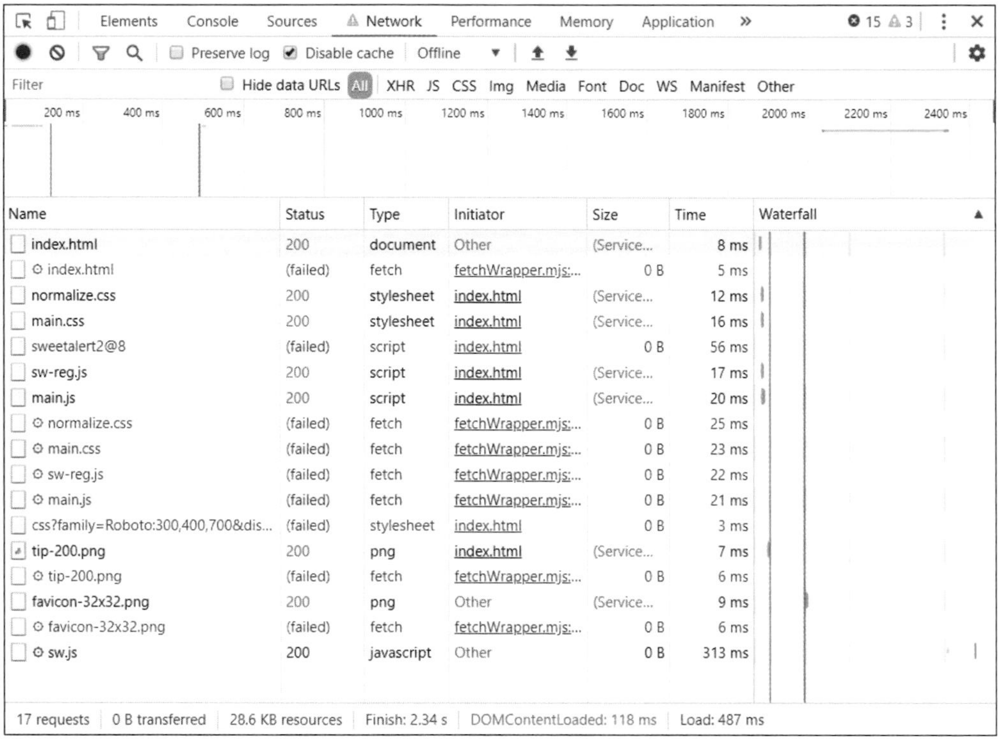

Figure 9.6    Workbox Caching Shown through Developer Tools Network Panel

Workbox supports plugins as well, and there are many available for you to use. For example, there's an expiration plugin you can use to keep resources in a cache for a specific number of seconds:

```
workbox.routing.registerRoute(
  /\.(?:png|jpg|svg)$/,
  new workbox.strategies.CacheFirst({
    cacheName: 'app-images',
    plugins: [
      new workbox.expiration.Plugin({
        maxEntries: 50,
        maxAgeSeconds: 864000
      }),
    ],
  }),
);
```

This example caches a maximum of 50 .png, .jpg, and .svg files for 10 days (864,000 seconds). The example also adds an additional cache called app-images just for those image files.

When you turn off the network connection in the browser developer tools and reload the app, you'll see that this version of the app has some of the same problems highlighted in Figure 9.3. In this case, the issue is that our caching strategy isn't caching several of the external resources used by the app (some fonts and the SweetAlert2 library). There are several approaches to solving this problem.

You can add handlers for specific resources, putting them in a separate cache, as follows:

```
workbox.routing.registerRoute(
  'https://cdn.jsdelivr.net/npm/sweetalert2@8',
  new workbox.strategies.CacheFirst({
    cacheName: 'external-cache',
    plugins: [
      new workbox.cacheableResponse.Plugin({
        statuses: [0, 200],
      })
    ]
  })
);
```

In this example, I use the cacheableResponse plugin to enable caching resources that won't normally be cached by a service worker because of cross-origin resource sharing (CORS) issues. I explained this issue in Chapter 4, "Resource Caching."

You can also implement a route that matches any requests for fonts from https://fonts.googleapis.com and stores them off in a cache:

```
workbox.routing.registerRoute(
  /^https:\/\/fonts\.googleapis\.com/,
  new workbox.strategies.StaleWhileRevalidate({
    cacheName: 'external-cache',
  }),
);
```

Probably the easiest solution in this case is to just set a default handler for any missed resources, catching any resources that aren't matched using any other routes. Add the following code to the bottom of the service worker:

```
workbox.routing.setDefaultHandler(
  new workbox.strategies.NetworkFirst({
    cacheName: 'default-cache'
  })
);
```

In this example, we added a cache called default-cache and told Workbox to put all unmatched resources there. When you reload the app and look at cache storage, you'll see the external resources cached, as shown in Figure 9.7.

Figure 9.7    The Tip Calculator's Default Cache

# Wrap-Up

In this whirlwind chapter, I showed you how to use Google's Workbox toolkit to generate service workers for your app or build service workers using Workbox's modular caching strategies rather than writing and maintaining all the caching code yourself. The material provided in this chapter merely scratches the surface of what you can do with Workbox. You should spend some time with Google's Workbox documentation and samples to learn more about how Workbox can make your life easier.

This chapter wraps up the book as well. I truly hope you enjoyed this journey from manifest files to service workers and all the capabilities they provide. You now have the knowledge you need to supercharge your web apps with PWA capabilities. Enjoy!

# Index

## D

# Credits

Foreword, back cover quote: Reprinted with permission from Simon MacDonald.

Page 1: Figure 1.1, The Community-Driven PWA Logo. By diekus.

Page 2: "apps taking advantage . . . native operating system (OS)." Alex Russell, "Progressive Web Apps: Escaping Tabs Without Losing Our Soul". Retrieved June 15, 2015.

Page 2: "PWAs are . . . Reliable . . . Fast . . . Engaging." Google.

Page 15: Figure 2.6, background photo of dogs. Courtesy of Anna W. Wargo

Page 16: "defines a JSON-based manifest file that provides developers with a centralized place to put metadata associated with a web application." World Wide Web Consortium (W3C).

Page 24: "The scope defines . . . within the scope." Matt Gaunt, The Web App Manifest.

Page 46: Figure 3.2, Chrome Advanced Settings. Screenshot of Google Chrome © Google 2019.

Page 48: Figure 3.3, PWA News Application Source Folder. Screenshot of Microsoft Corporation © Microsoft 2019.

Page 131: Figure 6.4, Twitter Complaint about Push Permission Prompts. Reprinted with permission from Amber Naslund.

Page 147: Figure 6.13, A Notification with a Body, Icon, and Random Image. Photo from Unsplash.

Page 147: Figure 6.14, Barren mountain blanketed in snow. Nitnot Studio/Shutterstock.

Page 158: Figure 6.18, Displaying Browser Subscriptions Using Postman. Screenshot of Browser Subscriptions © 2019 Postman, Inc.

Page 159: Figure 6.19, Sending a Browser Notification Using Postman. Screenshot of Browser Subscriptions © 2019 Postman, Inc.

Page 181: "Reliable . . . Fast . . . Engaging". Google.

Page 183: Figure 8.1, Invoking Lighthouse in Chrome. Screenshot of Lighthouse © Google 2019.

Page 184: Figure 8.2, Lighthouse Options. Screenshot of Lighthouse © Google 2019.

Page 185: Figure 8.3, Lighthouse Results for the Basic Tip Calculator App. Screenshot of Lighthouse © Google 2019.

Page 186: Figure 8.4, Lighthouse Results for the PWA Version of the Tip Calculator Application. Screenshot of Lighthouse © Google 2019.

Page 187: Figure 8.5, Lighthouse Report Output Options. Screenshot of Lighthouse © Google 2019.

Page 188: Figure 8.6, Running Lighthouse through Chrome DevTools. Screenshot of Lighthouse © Google 2019.

Page 189: Figure 8.7, Lighthouse Results in Chrome DevTools. Screenshot of Lighthouse © Google 2019.

Page 191: Figure 8.8, PWABuilder Home Page. Screenshot of PWA builder © Microsoft 2019.

Page 192: Figure 8.9, PWABuilder Scan Results. Screenshot of PWA builder © Microsoft 2019.

Page 193: Figure 8.10, PWABuilder Add Features Pane. Screenshot of PWA builder © Microsoft 2019.

Page 194: Figure 8.11, PWABuilder Manifest Editor Page. Screenshot of PWA builder © Microsoft 2019.

Page 195: Figure 8.12, PWABuilder Service Worker Page. Screenshot of PWA builder © Microsoft 2019.

Page 196: Figure 8.13, PWABuilder Packaged Application Options. Screenshot of PWA builder © Microsoft 2019.

Page 197: Figure 8.14, PWABuilder CLI Output and Results. Screenshot of PWA builder © Microsoft 2019.

Page 198: Figure 8.15, Visual Studio Code: PWABuilder Extension. Screenshot of Visual Studio Code © Microsoft 2019.

Page 199: Figure 8.16, Visual Studio Code Command Palette. Screenshot of Visual Studio Code © Microsoft 2019.

Page 200: Figure 8.17, Visual Studio Code: PWABuilder Manifest Generator. Screenshot of Visual Studio Code © Microsoft 2019.

Page 201: Figure 8.18, Visual Studio Code: PWABuilder Generated Manifest File. Screenshot of Visual Studio Code © Microsoft 2019.